RELIGION, REASON, AND TRUTH

RELIGION, REASON, AND TRUTH

Historical Essays
in the
Philosophy of Religion

STERLING M. McMURRIN

UNIVERSITY OF UTAH PRESS — 1982

Copyright 1982 by Sterling M. McMurrin
ISBN 0-87480-203-2
University of Utah Press, Salt Lake City, Utah 84112
Printed in the United States of America

Library of Congress Cataloguing in Publication Data

McMurrin, Sterling M.
    Religion, reason, and truth.

    Includes index.
    1. Religion — Philosophy.   I. Title
BL51.M478   200'.1   82-4813
ISBN 0-87480-203-2   AACR2

The paper in this book meets the standards
for permanence and durability established by
the Committee on Production Guidelines for Book Longevity
of the Council on Library Resources.

for Natalie
who has a transparent soul

Two things move me to ever greater awe —
The starry heavens above me
And the moral law within me.

— Immanuel Kant

Contents

Preface

The essays in this volume were written independently, to be read as separate pieces. I have, therefore, permitted some repetition to ensure the integrity of their thought and argument.

"The Personal and Impersonal in Metaphysics and Theology" was originally published under the title "Metaphysical Diversity and Cultural Disposition" by *Philosophy East and West*. "Theses on the Idea that God Is a Person" was first published by the University of Utah Press. "Comments on the Meaning of Immortality" was published as a Garvin Lecture on God and Immortality. The publishers of these papers have kindly given permission for their reprinting here with some modification.

For his critical comments, I am indebted to Professor John E. Smith of Yale University, who read the manuscript of this volume for the University of Utah Press. Helen Hyer and Jacqueline Jacobsen prepared the manuscript with uncommon care and skill. From past experience, I know that the published volume will exhibit the exceptional artistry in design and typesetting of Donald M. Henriksen and the truly superb editing of Trudy McMurrin.

Needless to say, in my views on the philosophy of religion I have been greatly influenced by my teachers, associates, friends, and family. In accordance with good preface tradition I fully accept censure for my errors, which must be legion, but in deference to my views on causation and human freedom I must insist that these others hold some causal responsibility for my errors as well as for any statements in these essays that may be true or judgments that may be good. I am not willing to let them completely off the hook. To name a few of them and acknowledge my indebtedness calls for a brief confessional statement.

Zelta Ballinger, my English teacher in the seventh, eighth, and ninth grades, a rigorous disciplinarian in intellectual matters, introduced me to the fascinating world of ancient Greek culture; and

Bertha Rutledge, my main high school Latin teacher, instilled in me a lasting fascination and appreciation for ancient literature and Roman civilization.

I owe to Hugh Miller my introduction to the serious study of Greek philosophy, and to the Swedish-American philosopher John Elof Boodin my first acquaintance with medieval and early modern philosophy. I will always honor the memory of Ephraim E. Ericksen, who convinced me that the unreflective life is not worth living. After Ericksen had worked me over thoroughly, I was almost convinced that anyone who was truly reflective must be a pragmatist; but my subsequent studies with Ralph Tyler Flewelling, Edgar Sheffield Brightman, and others among the idealists shocked me into the realization that idealism was not entirely dead. Indeed, so appealing was their world view, so impressive their logic and strong their conviction, that I was almost converted to personalistic idealism.

I desperately wanted to believe that idealism is basically true, but I was deprived of its comforts and perhaps saved from a vocation in speculative metaphysics by Heinrich Gomperz, whose massive scholarship and cautious skepticism interrupted my career in metaphysics before it got off the ground. And to make matters worse, a dissertation designed to refute the logical positivists came dangerously close to converting me to positivism. A brief association with Carl Hempel, the most brilliant in-house critic of logical positivism, convinced me of both the strengths and weaknesses of the positivistic position. But if the positivists saved me from the seductions of idealism, it was especially the realism of William Pepperell Montague — one of T. V. Smith's creative skeptics, whom he aptly called a "belief-ful" doubter — that rescued me from the reductions of positivism. I well recall a conversation in which Montague, with his penetrating humor, referred to "this negativism called positivism."

There are others among my early teachers in philosophy whom I should name with appreciation: Milton Bennion and Stephen Chak Tornay. Later, Walter G. Muelder, who attempted to discipline my thinking in philosophical theology, and Daniel S. Robinson, Paul R. Helsel, Wilbur Long, and Herbert L. Searles, who both advised and tolerated me as a student and colleague. And Paul Tillich, whose lectures affected my views on religion — not his existentialist theology, which has never appealed to me, but rather his interpretations of the history of Christianity, particularly of Calvinism and Lutheranism. I am greatly indebted to Brand Blanshard, one of this century's foremost philosophers. It was never my privilege to study with Blanshard, but I have had a brief but extremely valuable association with him. It is not his objective idealism that attracts me, nor his technical rationalism, but rather his dedication to reasonableness. Blanshard's devastating attack upon irrationality in contemporary morals and religion, as found in his Gifford Lectures, is a major contribution to the philosophy of religion.

James L. Jarrett, with whom I have collaborated on matters pertaining to contemporary philosophic thought over many years, though difficult at times, has been a proper gad-fly in the classical sense — a persistent irritant.

Among my teaching colleagues in philosophy, there are two with whom I have engaged in countless hours of discussion and argument on matters pertaining to religion and the philosophy of religion and who have profoundly influenced me — Waldemer P. Read and Obert C. Tanner. Read was a confirmed pragmatist of the Dewey strain, who, like others of his species, was suspicious of all forms of philosophic speculation and insisted on grounding philosophy in practical experience and religion in morals. He benefited the thinking of everyone who had the good fortune of his association.

Obert Tanner is a philosopher of broad and varied experience and practical wisdom, who argues with fine humor and has an admirable talent for cutting through verbiage and technical nonsense and getting right to the heart of the matter. His is a world of books and ideas, but also of decision and civic action. He is a prototype of the philosopher–statesman.

A reader of these essays may well ask what is the author's position with respect to the large questions of the philosophy of religion. I have written primarily not to express my own views on religion but rather simply to examine some of the more important ideas in the history of occidental religious thought. Yet it seems to me that here and there something of a position shows through, though perhaps not clearly — certainly not in a way that would satisfy those who are looking for answers. It is the fate of humankind that we can ask more questions than we can answer; and the questions that must remain unanswered, except by those who are blessed with a special knowledge that unfortunately many of us do not possess, are among the most important. They are the most ultimate in meaning, where they have any genuine meaning, and certainly they are the most desperate in importance.

Perhaps I should confess that I am tinged with idealism, singed by positivism, and severely infected with pragmatism; that I am suspicious of existentialism and strongly attracted to realism. I am less a liberal in religion than a renegade, fascinated by theology but distrustful of all theology and theologians, an advocate of rationality who is convinced that reason both purifies and destroys the religious. I am contemptuous of dogmatism and am possessed of an uneasy union of skepticism with what seems to me to be a genuine religious disposition and quite profound religious feeling. In the philosophy of religion I must settle for some kind of naturalistic humanism despite the precious promises and the consolations of the soul that are the gifts of a proper theism. But enough of incriminating self-analysis, which is usually unreliable anyway.

I would like to acknowledge here my gratitude to my parents — my father, Joseph W. McMurrin, Jr., who first cultivated in me a love of books and ideas and who directed me to read Darwin, Plato, and Gibbon as well as to pray and attend church; and my mother, Gertrude McMurrin, whose nobility of character and unerring good sense and humor tempered my tendencies toward intellectual and sentimental excess.

My children live in a world that in many ways is different from mine. They have made me sensitive to values that I had severely neglected and I have learned more from them than they can realize. They have saved me from the foolishness of supposing that anything of ultimate importance will be consummated in my generation — unless it is the annihilation of the human race.

And finally, there is my unbounded gratitude to my wife, Natalie, for her compassion and patience, her understanding, her unfailing cooperation and encouragement, and her devotion to the quest for truth.

RELIGION, REASON, AND TRUTH

1

Religion, Reason, and Truth

I

Because religion is not essentially an intellectual discipline, there is a sense in which the question of its reasonableness is not appropriate. The domain of reason is the realm of ideas or of symbols and their relation to one another. The reasonable person is one who has reasons, that is, the ideas or propositions which he holds are logically entailed by other ideas or propositions which he assumes or to which for one cause or another he has given intellectual assent. But religion is not a set of symbols or propositions, nor is it an idea or a composite of ideas. Rather it is a matter of personal commitment, of sentiment, of practical attitudes of hope and faith, or of ritual or moral action. Religion considered in its common forms is not in its essential character the kind of thing that is basically either reasonable or unreasonable. It is an experience. A sentiment or commitment, a hope or affection may well be related to matters involving knowledge and reason, but in itself it is not justly described simply as rational or irrational.

It is obvious that religion is reasonable in the sense that it can be reasoned about, just as it is possible to reason about love, though in itself love is a quite nonrational matter. And, of course, it is quite possible for a reasonable person to be religious in a traditional sense, unless he insists on being reasonable all the time. If he insists on being reasonable all the time, he not only must forego religion; he must as well give up love, avoid art, and in general become quite a disgusting person. He must give religion up unless reason and rationality in a sense become his religion, as was the case in theory for the Stoics and in fact for Spinoza. But however commendable the life of reason may be, a rigorous adherence to Stoic principles could well destroy much of the richness and value of human experience; and a world full of Spinozas would be a world of rational saints intent on a full control of their emotions and on the intellectual love of God, determined to view the world under the aspect of eternity and Euclid — a world become precise, prosaic, unexciting, and uninteresting.

But, leaving such considerations aside, it seems appropriate to regard a person as rational who not only respects the canons of evidence and logic in cognitive matters but whose affective life and volition are in some way brought under the dominion of knowledge and reason, who is governed in part at least by his intellect. The reasonable person is one whose thought and ideas determine, or at least temper, his attitudes and actions. It is in this sense, of course, that religion may be considered rational or irrational, or perhaps as nonrational. In his religious moments is a person controlled to an effective degree by thought rather than passion? Is his religion grounded in some measure in ideas, or is it generated entirely by habit and emotion? Are his religious beliefs, whatever their source and occasion, justifiable by reasons? More than that, are those reasons good reasons; do they rest ultimately on acceptable premises, and are those premises supported at least by claims of evidence?

It is the religious person that is rational or irrational, not the religion in itself. There is no religion *in itself.* But the established ideologies, ecclesiastical forms, and ritual practices associated with religious belief and worship are strong determinants of the character and quality of the religious experience of an individual or group, and in a manner of speaking they may be regarded as rational or irrational. Even in the more elemental religions, despite the important role of myth and symbolism, ideas, even when inarticulate, have a larger place than we commonly recognize. Religious thought ranges upward from the most abject superstition and nonsense to metaphysical arguments that are a sincere effort to establish the intellectual ground of religion on foundations which are compatible with the whole of human experience, including the best achievements of the sciences. Clearly, some religions are thoroughly irrational while some are indifferent to the claims of rationality, but others achieve varying levels of reasonableness and respect for knowledge.

To establish reasonableness in religion is the task of theology and philosophy — theology where the issue is the internal structuring of ideas in the interest of consistency and general intellectual acceptability, philosophy where the occasion prescribes the analysis or criticism of basic concepts, assumptions, or methods; theology when there is an ordering of accepted beliefs and precepts and their reconciliation to a system of thought is at issue; philosophy of religion when such reconciliation demands a fundamental structuring of method and knowledge that will embrace both sacred dogma and secular science. To put it politely, the function of theology and the philosophy of religion in occidental thought has been to make the divine revelation meaningful and acceptable in terms of the science and philosophy given in the culture. To put it impolitely, their function has been to save religion from superstition, nonsense, and moral barbarism.

It is an error to suppose that theology has suffered from a lack of high-level intellectual talent. St. Augustine, St. Anselm, Calvin, and Jonathan Edwards were men of great intellectual stature. No one has written more brilliantly on the nature of time than St. Augustine, and no writer ever made a greater impact on the world in which he lived. And no one has surpassed Edwards in his analysis of the freedom of the will. It isn't that these men lacked genius as theologians or were irresponsible in their logic. It's simply that all too often they held indefensible ideas. Notwithstanding their analytical powers, the grounds of their premises were defective, their canons of evidence inadequate, or their credulousness too much enslaved to tradition and the authority of the past. At least their ideas were indefensible when judged by today's knowledge and logic and the patterns of thought that are compatible with the intellectual temper and methods that we now regard as acceptable. But, of course, while we may judge their ideas by our criteria, that may not be a fair judgment upon them.

We should remember that theologians, like the rest of us, are victims of countless intellectual and social forces, forces that are both subtle and persuasive, and that they, unlike most of us, are often implicated in the difficult if not impossible task of compounding antique tradition with the latest accepted philosophy and serving it up in a form which renders it at once both intellectually palatable and logically and factually invulnerable. The theologian, it must also be remembered, is not directly a purveyor of religion. For religion we must look to the saints and the prophets and to those persons of authentic piety who are to be found in every society. Theology is a department of metaphysics and theologians are a subspecies of philosopher. We cannot today subscribe to the tradition that theology is a science and theologians scientists. Theologians, like typical metaphysicians, are too much involved in speculative thought. Their task is to treat the philosophic and scientific ideas that in some way relate to religious experience, but real religion is found not in their ideas but in the experience of the religious person or the religious community.

A glance at the internal structure of some of theology's more prominent exhibits reveals at times an admirable and even forbidding rationality. Calvin's *Institutes of the Christian Religion*, perhaps the foremost theological treatise in Protestant theology, has the qualities that both attract and repel in a closely written, cold-blooded legal brief. The *Summa Theologica* of St. Thomas is a remarkable example of the powers of the human mind to bring together in a coherent system a vast assemblage of ideas gathered from sources of radically diverse character. Among the classical theological symbols are some that are quite remarkable for their intellectual appeal. No statement of faith has ever more effectively treated a seemingly insoluble problem than the Nicene Creed, which from the fourth century has been the standard device for settling the intricate issue generated by a religion engaged in the worship of more than one God in a culture committed to monotheism. Whatever its merits or deficiencies, it was produced by a meticulous piece of reasoning involving technical metaphysics and the most subtle kind of grammar. Or in St. Anselm's satisfaction theory of the atonement, which from the eleventh century has been more or less normative for most occidental Christianity, there is an argument quite remarkable for its ingenuity which far surpassed in intellectual and moral refinement everything that Christian thought had been able to produce over a thousand years as a rationalization of the belief in the incarnation of God in Christ. Moreover, despite its founding in feudal juridical concepts, it offered an interpretation of the nature of God that for millions has satisfied the problem of the contradiction between divine justice and mercy that has seriously embarrassed occidental religion at least since the days of Amos and Hosea. Although these examples may appear specious and sophistical to most of us today, they are truly impressive instances of the attempt to make religion reasonable.

In occidental culture much philosophy of religion and theology are typically efforts to reconcile religion with secular thought. They are attempts to make what is taken on revelation or simply by authority or faith intellectually acceptable as meaningful and rational by establishing its compatibility with the general deposit of knowledge in the culture and with the ideal values that have issued from moral insight and common experience. Philo Judaeus, the foremost Jewish philosopher of antiquity, who designed the basic format for much occidental theology, labored with great diligence to effect a reconciliation of hellenistic Platonism with the Torah, convinced that Plato expressed the mind of God as Moses expressed his will. Some of the most crucial problems of early Christian theology were treated by the allegorical method which Philo had used in arguing that the Bible meant what it obviously did *not* mean, but which was nevertheless more acceptable to the believer with a Greek education than was what it obviously *did* mean. Millions of Jews and Christians even today, like Philo and the Alexandrian theologians, are native to two cultural traditions — the biblical and the classical — and they live therefore inevitably under the familiar tensions of faith and knowledge, sentiment and reason. Being born into a world whose intellectual, moral, and spiritual foundations are compounded of conflicting methods, attitudes, and ideas — a world which teaches them that factual knowledge must be achieved by scientific intelligence and yet so often insists that the highest truths are apprehended by acts of faith or are given in sacred writings or by supernatural revelation — it is their common fate to struggle with themselves and their native cultures to become free from bondage to the traditional faith or from reason and scientific intelligence, or to achieve some synthesis that, however precarious and ambiguous, satisfies their demand for both intellectual integrity and religious piety.

Three basic positions on the matter of the reasonableness of religion have been advanced in the interest of defending religion. That reason and faith are in full harmony, for instance, was argued by persons as far apart and unlike as Justin Martyr and Hegel. That faith is compatible with reason yet transcends it was held by persons as unlike as Aquinas and Locke. And that faith and reason are in contradiction but that both have justifiable intellectual claims was held by persons as distant from one another as Tertullian and Luther.

It is in the scholastic philosophy that Christianity made its most impressive attempt to reconcile reason to faith — a philosophy cultivated out of respect for reason and from a firm resolution that faith and reason are not contradictory. The Vatican Council formulated a simple decree that sets forth the familiar principle: "Although faith is above reason, there can never be any real discrepancy between faith and reason, since the same God who reveals mysteries and infuses faith has bestowed the light of reason on the human mind and God cannot deny himself, nor can truth ever contradict truth." [1]

The idea of mysteries — usually defined in theology as truths that by their nature can be neither discovered nor understood by any created or natural intelligence — does not in principle vitiate the traditional Catholic commitment to reason, since such mysteries, though they must be apprehended by faith and are available only through revelation, are nevertheless held to be above reason rather than against it. Moreover, it is held that a partial knowledge of the mysteries is possible through analogy, through an understanding of some of the ideational ingredients of the doctrine, as in the instance of the Aristotelian concept of substance that lies at the foundations of the mysteries of the Trinity and transubstantiation. But even more

---

[1] Dogmatic Decrees, 1870, chap. 4, *On Faith and Reason.*

important here as a protection of Catholic rationality is the widely
accepted principle enunciated by Hugo of St. Victor in the twelfth
century that the limits of reason are to be established by reason itself.
The decision, therefore, as to what is or is not a mystery and what is
or is not capable of being understood is a rational decision. This
principle, under which, for instance, it is held that the existence of
God can be known by the natural, unaided reason while certain facets
of his nature are mysteries and cannot be known by natural reason,
is a basic factor in the general position of Catholicism that is central
to its traditional support of reason and knowledge in matters pertaining to religion.

The victory in Catholicism of the champions of rationality in
religion is quite surely related to the large elements of Platonism
and Aristotelianism in the basic philosophy that lies at the intellectual foundations of the church. That victory is exhibited in the
fact that it was typical of the Dominicans, who have been the chief
guardians of scholastic philosophy, to hold that the will of God is
subservient to his intellect, so that, for instance, God wills an act
because he knows it to be good. Whereas the Franciscans, who
achieved less influence over the intellectual life of the church, held
in the earlier period that God knows an act to be good because he
wills it, since his intellect is under the dominion of his sovereign
will. The difference has been decisive for the church primarily
because the doctrine of God's primary intellectual nature underwrites
the rational structure of the religion in a manner that would have
been impossible on the basis of Franciscan voluntarism.

Voluntaristic theology is not necessarily an anti-intellectualistic
position when it is established and defended on rational grounds, as
in the case of St. Augustine, who since the fifth century has been the
chief fountainhead of voluntarism in philosophy and theology. The
doctrine of the primacy of the will, whether divine or human, was
compatible with Augustine's own moralistic temperament and his
essentially practical orientation to religion.

The Protestant reformers were quite generally under the influence
of Augustine's voluntarism. Moreover, they found in Augustine, as
opposed to the scholastics against whom they were in part contending, a celebration of the biblical and Hebraic elements of religion

which center on the concept of God as moral will and which were probably deeply rooted in primitive Palestinian Christianity and present to the church especially because of its adoption of the Hebrew Bible as sacred scripture. This was true of Augustine notwithstanding that due to his conditioning by Neoplatonism his thought was quite saturated with Greek rationalistic metaphysics, even to the point of his locating the Platonic universals in the mind of God. This Platonism meant in his theology, of course, an ultimate supremacy of the divine intellect over the divine will despite his strong voluntarism.

But the reformers were less inclined toward Platonism than was Augustine, and in Calvin, and in Reform theology to the present day, the central doctrine that relates most importantly to the moral and religious life is the absolute sovereignty of the will of God. Calvin was more a voluntarist than St. Augustine, and his voluntarism was in some respects productive of irrationalism, though not so much in his own theology as in that of some who were under his influence. The point here is that insofar as God is described essentially as sovereign and transcendent will, where will is subject not even to the divine intellect, his nature is unavailable to human understanding. From the human perspective, therefore, God is not only arbitrary but unreasonable. As Sören Kierkegaard held, God is the most ridiculous of all beings, that is, his acts appear totally ridiculous to human reason. There is no justifiable ground, for instance, for the complaint against God of injustice for creating some souls for the ultimate purpose of their damnation in hell while others are created for heaven, for the reason of man is utterly impotent to know or to judge the affairs of God. Indeed, both Luther and Calvin were inclined to regard as sinful any attempt to understand God, a position far removed from the classic *credo ut intelligam* of St. Anselm which has exerted such a powerful influence on the intellectual life of Catholicism: "I believe that I might understand."

It is not irrelevant here that the Genesis assertion that man is created in the image of God is often interpreted by Catholic theologians to mean that man is essentially a rational being — a concept clearly descended from the hellenic rather than the biblical antecedents of Christianity — or that in the accepted Catholic doctrine of original sin, the fall did not deprive man of genuine and meritorious rationality. Moreover, the difference between Protestantism and Catholicism is further evidenced by the fact that existentialism, the most important recent species of irrationalism, was a dominant philosophical factor in the neo-orthodox movement that in this century attended the decline of Protestant liberalism, whereas in Catholicism existential thought was largely accommodated to the more rationally temperate scholasticism to which the church is still quite strongly committed. This difference is clear to those who compare, for instance, the dialectical theology of Emil Brunner, one of Protestantism's most creative contemporary theologians and whose thought is closely tied to existentialism, with the realistic metaphysics of Jacques Maritain, Catholicism's foremost recent philosopher and one who has faced the existential issue.

Or in a larger context the difference can be seen in that while under the impact of the First World War much European Protestantism was seduced by the irrationalism of Karl Barth — who argued not only against rational theology but even against religious philosophy — during the same period the dominant trend in Catholicism was the rise of the neoscholasticism which had earlier been enjoined by Pope Leo XIII explicitly in the interest of overcoming the idealistic and subjectivistic trend in religious thought and of achieving a reasonable accommodation of religion and science. The encyclical *Aeterni Patris* of 1879 had clearly enunciated the determination of the church to revive in principle for the modern era the philosophy that seemed effectively to synthesize natural knowledge and divine revelation in late medieval times and had thereby effected with quite remarkable success a practical reconciliation of reason and faith. In the encyclical *Studiorem Ducem* in 1923 Pope Pius XI reaffirmed the fundamental importance of the theology of Aquinas. Today, of course, the place of Thomistic scholasticism is not infrequently challenged by Catholic thinkers, as by those who are attracted to Whitehead's process philosophy as a philosophical model. But this trend away from neoscholasticism in search of a metaphysic that will more adequately relate God to the temporal world of human experience is not necessarily a movement toward the irrational. It would be a grave error for Catholic philosophers and theologians to assume or argue that a commitment to rationality in religion necessarily entails allegiance to the scholastic principles.

In pointing to the long tradition of Catholic respect for reason, I do not mean to suggest that by contrast Protestantism is an irrational or anti-intellectualistic religion. In this matter numerous currents and crosscurrents have been strong factors in the history of both Catholicism and Protestantism. Catholicism has not been free, for instance, from theologians who have followed the dictum of Tertullian, who in the second and third centuries at times set faith against reason and the church against the secular culture, and for whom the Gospel of Christ meant the paradox of "I believe because it is absurd" or the incarnation of Christ "is certain because it is impossible." And on the other hand, it was largely within the Protestant civilization and culture that the so-called Enlightenment developed with its powerful commitment to reason and reliable knowledge, and it was within the Protestant intellectual tradition that the massive rational structure of idealistic metaphysics and logic appeared. Protestant philosophy attempted in the nineteenth century and even into the twentieth to reconcile Christian theology to science while at the same time accounting for secular civilization within the context of religious history and providing for the critical analysis of sacred literature. But the great impact of Schleiermacher, for instance, Protestantism's most influential theologian of this period, whose subjective treatment of the nature of religion was a central factor in the whole romantic movement, weakened rather than strengthened the claim of reason upon religion.

The idealism that was cultivated especially on Kantian and Hegelian foundations, while sometimes pretending to be orthodox in character, added greatly to the thrust of the Protestant liberalism that had already begun to flourish in the Enlightenment, which had produced almost a deification of reason. Together the Enlightenment and the idealistic movement, which were substantially heretical, contributed importantly to the dissolution of orthodoxy and the shaping of modern secularism, not only by their celebration of reason and the romantic subjectification of religion, but as well through their encouragement of historical and biblical scholarship.

II

The question of the reasonableness of religion becomes a question of the truth of religion, or at least of the possibility or probability of its being true. Most people who ask whether religion is reasonable probably do not mean to inquire into such matters as the logical structuring of theology, or even the rational tempering of the religious emotions, but rather into the justification of the truth claims of religion. Truth and reason, of course, are often related, but they are by no means the same. Rationality pertains to relationships that obtain among ideas or propositions and the ways in which they are derived or their retention justified. Truth, on the other hand, is a property of the ideas themselves or, more technically, of the propositions which articulate and express those ideas. The question of whether a factual proposition is true is the question of whether it represents a fact or facts as it purports to do.[*]

The chief intellectual foundation of the theistic religion of the Occident, Judaic–Christian–Islamic religion, is, of course, the belief in the existence of God. This belief has commonly been grounded in revelation, intuition, or authoritative tradition, but it has also generated centuries of effort to construct arguments or "proofs." Much talent and intellectual energy have been invested in the effort to construct a persuasive proof of the existence of God, but at best the results have been questionable.

The most celebrated attempt to ground theism on a strictly rational foundation was the eleventh-century ontological argument of St. Anselm, who undertook to demonstrate the existence of God by an exercise in pure reason without recourse to experiential data. The very conception of God, Anselm argued, entails his existence. It is, therefore, logically impossible that any conceivable factual evi-

---

[*] To facilitate discussion, I am assuming here the common-sense correspondence or semantic conception of the nature of truth without arguing the case against its competitors, especially the coherence and pragmatic or instrumentalist treatments of truth. The problem of the truth value of the knowledge claims of religion does not, it seems to me, depend in any fundamental way on a decision regarding the conflicting claims of the several conceptions of truth.

dence could count against the claim of God's existence.[3] Although several celebrated thinkers, including Descartes and Hegel, defended the ontological argument, it was rejected by Thomas Aquinas and has no accepted status today in Catholic philosophy. In recent years there has been a strong revival of interest in the ontological argument, perhaps more as a problem in logic and metaphysics than for religious concern, and the position of Anselm, especially his insistence that the idea of God *necessarily* entails existence, has some support from philosophers of high competence; but for the most part it is rejected on the ground that a factual statement asserting the existence of an entity requires empirical support.[4]

Aquinas favored the cosmological and the teleological proofs, both of which are experientially grounded and are inheritances from Greek thought. Even today these arguments are well respected in Catholic philosophy but receive much less approval outside Catholicism. The cosmological argument, which appears in several modes, derives God as first cause from the causal structure of the world or the ontological requirement of the reality of necessary being to account for the world of contingent things and events. The teleological, which also has several forms, is an argument for God as a purposive, creative force evidenced by the alleged design or adaptation to ends observable in the natural world.

Five centuries after St. Thomas, Immanuel Kant, the foremost philosophical influence on Protestant thought, constructed in his *Critique of Pure Reason* a rigorous refutation of all three arguments, concluding on logical and empirical grounds that are widely but not universally accepted today that it is impossible to establish the existence of God by either rational or empirical methods. But Kant's position is essentially agnostic rather than atheistic, and on the grounds of his argument, as he himself held, it is equally impossible

---

[3] The ontological argument or proof is generally regarded as strictly "rationalistic" in the methodological sense as opposed to simply "rational" in the sense of being reasonable. Empirical arguments, if they are logically constructed, are reasonable.

[4] The foremost proponent of the ontological argument at the present time is the American philosopher Charles Hartshorne, whose analysis of Anselm's position has received support from Norman Malcolm and others.

to disprove the existence of God. Having, as he believed, destroyed the rational foundation of theology, removing it from the domain of science and scientific knowledge, Kant proceeded to construct a carefully reasoned non-empirical argument to justify the assertion of God's existence as an a priori postulate necessary to the meaningfulness of morality. This argument, developed in his *Critique of Practical Reason*, became the philosophical foundation for the not uncommon Protestant position that God must be taken as an object of rational faith rather than as an object of metaphysical knowledge. And it provided as well the primary ground for the romantic German theology which received expression in Schleiermacher's subjectivistic definitions of religion and the important tradition of Ritschlian theology which tended to identify religion with ethics. Moreover, it was also a major factor in the eventual production of much of the natural theology of the English-speaking world which a century and more later was frequently concerned with the so-called moral argument for God.

Now if a theology were to be judged by the degree of its rational purity rather than simply by its reasonableness, Anselm's position would be more acceptable than that of Aquinas because it is more strictly rationalistic in the sense of excluding empirical considerations. And Aquinas would have the edge on Kant because he allows a larger place to reason. Aquinas held, quite properly, that Anselm failed to recognize certain limitations of pure reason with reference to the objects of knowledge, and Kant held that Aquinas failed to recognize others. Now the contemporary positivists insist that Kant, even in his agnosticism, was in principle as wrong as both Anselm and Aquinas. But here is a major issue in the question of the reasonableness of religion. Is it more reasonable or less reasonable in a religious discussion to place limits on the capabilities of reason? Obviously, whether Kant or Aquinas is right depends on logic and the facts, and what the facts are is a matter of major dispute. But it cannot be said that a person is less reasonable because he believes that both logic and the nature of the case require a recognition of the limits of reason. Yet where does this sort of thing end? The direction indicated by the subjectivism of Schleiermacher, based on Kantian foundations, led to what it now seems justifiable to call just plain irrationalism, as in the case of the theology of Karl Barth.

No one would argue that Kant was in principle irrational, non-rational, or anti-intellectual in his method. By the most rigorous rational procedures he analyzed the structure of reason in the knowing process and undertook to discern its limitations. He concluded that the reason cannot prove the existence of God, as "God" is customarily defined in cultured religion, because of the absence of relevant empirical data. It was the overwhelming influence of Kant in his critique of reason that laid the foundations not only for the subjectivism and idealism of German thought in the nineteenth century, but also for the pragmatism of America in the twentieth. Pragmatism, to employ the terminology of William James himself, is in its classical form anti-intellectualistic, since it is set against the rationalistic structuring of much traditional philosophy. For pragmatism, religion is not something that has an internal logical structure discernible by reason, and the pragmatists are wary of all types of metaphysics, including theology. Religion for them is essentially a practical affair that is grounded in moral, social, or mystical experience, and whatever justifiable claims it may make are not primarily rational in character. Yet it seems to me that we should not accuse the pragmatists of being unreasonable about religion.

The French philosopher Henri Bergson, who was a kind of pragmatist–mystic, constructed an interesting critique of reason which is relevant to the problem of religion and reasonableness. Reason, insisted Bergson, in the sense in which we ordinarily employ that term in relation to science or discursive thought generally, though useful, is entirely deceptive in its descriptions of reality. For reality is dynamic, temporal process, and the logico-mathematical techniques of reason, despite the usefulness of the calculus in treating motion, describe it as totally motionless, timeless, and lifeless. The method proper even to metaphysics, insisted Bergson, to say nothing of religion, is mystic intuition, for intuition, especially the intuition of the temporal process, establishes an immediate apprehension of reality; at best reason describes reality externally and in doing so completely distorts it by destroying its dynamic character. Bergson's argument on this point does not command general assent, but it deserves the most careful consideration.

A few decades ago there was a strong reaction in Protestant circles in America as well as in England against the subjectivist trend in religious thought that made God an object of faith rather than knowledge. Although some argued that it was better anyway for religion to be grounded in faith rather than knowledge, because this guaranteed to religion much of its most precious quality, there were some who refused to go along with what they considered an unwarranted capitulation to a technical agnosticism. By a thoroughgoing examination of the entire epistemological problem and the methodology of the sciences and a reconstruction of the meaning of religion in objective terms, an effort was made, particularly in the camp of the realists, to show that knowledge of the divine object is possible and that it is verifiable by methods of cognition which are essentially scientific in character. A correlative task was the construction of an experientially grounded proof of the existence of God which would not be vulnerable to the traditional objections that plagued the classical arguments. Today, with the popular renascence of supernaturalism even in the former stronghold of liberal scholarship, such attempts to justify religion by a natural theology that comes to terms with empirical methodology seems to have been largely abandoned as both unnecessary and inconclusive. Nevertheless, the work of such men as Frederick R. Tennant in England is a symbol of the determination of the liberal mind to maintain its fullest respect for critical reason while attempting to make a sound case for theistic religion. Certainly Tennant's monumental *Philosophical Theology* will stand for a long time as a landmark in the history of religious thought, a brilliant attempt to treat religion according to the most rigorous canons of thought in order to find a ground upon which its intellectual foundations can be secured in a world that is committed to scientific intelligence.

Over the past half century philosophy's main gift to theology has been to question its very meaningfulness. Unless a proposition has cognitive meaning, it can be neither true nor false, and the verdict of much analytical philosophy has been that the key propositions of the theology basic to the intellectual foundations of cultured religion are meaningless — meaningless because, while they appear to be genuine assertions, their key terms such as "God" and "soul" are without semantic reference, or because logical and syntactical analysis exposes them as disguised tautologies without factual content. Neither logical nor linguistic analytical philosophy is inclined today to push its criticism as far as the logical positivists did in disposing of all metaphysics, including theology, as cognitive nonsense, or in describing normative sentences as expressions of emotions, or something of the kind; but the message is loud and clear, that metaphysicians and theologians should reexamine critically not only their methods but as well the traditional grounds in which their presumptions of meaningfulness are rooted. I believe that while with care it may well be possible to formulate cognitively meaningful sentences in theological discourse, this is rarely done by theologians, and therefore much of the theology of the past and present is indeed technically meaningless.

Of course, at the opposite end of the spectrum is the view that religion is really a form of poetry and theological statements should make no claim to truth as they have poetic value but no cognitive meaning. The most eloquent advocate of this poetizing of religion was Santayana, who held that

> religious doctrines would do well to withdraw their pretension to be dealing with matters of fact. That pretension is not only the source of the conflicts of religion with science and of the vain and bitter controversies of sects; it is also the cause of the impurity and incoherence of religion in the soul, when it seeks its sanctions in the sphere of reality, and forgets that its proper concern is to express the ideal . . . . The excellence of religion is due to an idealization of experience which, while making religion noble if treated as poetry, makes it necessarily false if treated as science.[5]

But few religionists and fewer theologians would accept this relegation of religion to the realm of poetry. They insist, rather, that the claims of religion and theology are factual, that basic theological statements are true or false. They must face the demand, therefore, of a meticulous attention to criteria of meaningfulness,

[5] George Santayana, *Interpretations of Poetry and Religion* (New York, 1900), pp. v–vi.

both factual and formal, a concern for the intricacies of language and definition, and perhaps a more profound grasp of the nature of religion. If theology is to be cognitively meaningful in its assertion of the existence of God, it must be able to tell us in experiential terms what the world would be like if its propositions were true as distinguished from what it would be like if they were false. The existence of God must make a difference that can be expressed in propositions for which we can at least describe a method of verification or disconfirmation, even though we may not be able to have the requisite experience necessary to such verification. If God is defined as an objective reality, as in traditional theistic religion, to have meaning within the context of knowledge the propositions asserting his existence must be in principle testable as true or false, or, more correctly, as probable or improbable.

I am aware that the positivistic criterion of cognitive meaning which I have expressed here in a rather severe version has undergone a four-decade period of criticism by both positivists and nonpositivists and has emerged in a somewhat more liberal and chastened form. I have preferred to employ the earlier, tougher version of the criterion here because I feel strongly that theologians and philosophers of religion should undertake to meet the positivistic challenge head-on rather than attempt to escape the issue by resorting too readily to the niceties of logical and linguistic refinements that all too often enable them to hide the real problems.[6] The generality of religionists are philosophically naïve and pay little or no attention to matters of this kind; and some theologians seem to have been unaware of the positivist challenge to their product, or they have simply ignored it. Others, however, have faced the problem squarely and have engaged the linguistic and logical issues in religious discourse seriously and with strength. Still others have simply

[6] The "liberalization" of the positivists' criterion of cognitive meaning is best exhibited in the work of Carl G. Hempel. See especially his landmark essay "Problems and Changes in the Empiricist Criterion of Meaning," where he argues that there are degrees of meaning between sense and nonsense, and that significance should be determined in terms of systems of statements rather than single statements isolated from their context. *Revue Internationale de Philosophie*, vol. 4 (1950).

withdrawn deeper into the morass of irrationality, confusing theology with myth, abandoning philosophy for philology, turning away from science and its methods of achieving reliable knowledge to call upon the wisdom of the past, the dictates of mystic intuition, or the authoritarian pronouncements of religious leaders. In a time of great enlightenment, when our instruments for knowing are honed to a fine edge, there is in religion a debilitating loss of faith in human capabilities, an increased reliance upon the arcane and esoteric, a trust in supernatural revelation.

I must here confront the charge that all these judgments are rooted in a severe cultural bias, that they indicate an inordinate attachment to an intellectual tradition that glorifies cognition, logic, theory, and discursive reasoning, a tradition that typifies the modern occidental mind whose norms and habits are due especially to its hellenic antecedents. Religion is not science, philosophy, or theology; it is not essentially a body of ideas and should not suffer the fate of being categorized, analyzed, generalized, and systematized. It is an experience of the numinous, a confrontation of the divine mystery, an ultimate concern and commitment, not a doctrine or dogma.

Now it is true that my statement reflects a strong cultural bias. We are all conditioned by the culture or cultures in which we have our identity; those who hold that they have escaped that conditioning or have fully overcome it simply deceive themselves. But it is possible to achieve some measure of understanding of our intellectual prejudices, to examine our own predicament critically, and to take a stand on matters of this kind that is not indifferent to the claims of opposing and conflicting values. To argue for reasonableness in religion does not mean that the fundamental character of religion must be violated. Occidental theistic religion is grounded in truth claims of various kinds and therefore it cannot escape facing fundamental problems relating not only to specific knowledge but as well to the ways of knowing, reason, cognitive meaning, and evidence. It cannot dispense with philosophy and, especially in Christianity and Islam, its own history has entangled it inextricably with theology. Without theology religion would dissolve into countless sects of believers caught up in the enthusiasm of passion and emotion, Theosophists and mystics searching for an esoteric knowledge, ascetics seeking release from the world, and do-gooders determined to usher in the Kingdom. But with theology theism is inevitably thrown into the middle of the perennial philosophical problems.

I am not unmindful of the important role which myth has played and continues to play in religion; or poetry and the techniques of allegory, metaphor, and analogy; or the profound importance to the religious life of ritual and private and liturgical symbolism. And I sense the dangers of an inordinate commitment to rationality that would subordinate religion to science and rob it of its proper autonomous claim upon certain facets of the thought and experience of the individual and society. To repeat, religion is not science, and it will never be scientific. Moreover, it is a gross error to overstate the capacity of science to fully satisfy the human mind and will and temper the passions and emotions. Science is a human creation and even it is not free from a kind of faith and certain species of myth. And it treats the world piecemeal while in religion there is a sense in which a person achieves a relation to the world as a totality. Religion is caught in a prevailing struggle between reason and superstition, science and magic, truth and nonsense. There will always be those who in desperation to protect their religious views resort to paradox and contradiction, and the devoutly credulous whose fears and ignorance expose them to the most abject falsehoods and ludicrous practices. But there are also others whose wisdom and passion for truth and love of knowledge may save religion from destruction by its own excesses and absurdities.

It would be a horrible thing if all the teachings of the churches were true, for then the world would be filled with logical and practical confusion and there would be even more cruelty and suffering. But if in its most profound meanings theistic religion were true, there would be a sure ground for the hope of an ultimate redemption from the tragedy of human existence. So it is not a trivial thing to ask whether the claims of religion are true. No question is more profound or momentous. It is a question that has not been made clear and entirely meaningful, and for those who must seek answers through the avenues of reason, evidence, and critical intelligence, it is perhaps a question without a final answer.

2

Religious Thought and Philosophy

In an analytical discussion as in ordinary discourse religion and philosophy should be defined independently — religion as a mode of sentiment and experience and philosophy as an intellectual endeavor. To fail to differentiate them generates confusion and misunderstanding. But, in fact, in actual experience religion often cannot be completely disengaged from philosophy. In certain respects they may be inextricably joined, as in religion's involvement in the pursuit of the good while philosophy attempts to define, analyze, and describe the good, or where religion is an experience of unity with the divine while philosophy inquires into the nature of ultimate reality.

The question of the relation of religion to philosophy is in part simply a matter of definition. With liberal meanings it is possible to find something like philosophical presuppositions and possibly elementary philosophical concepts even in the structure of quite primitive religions, and it is difficult to distinguish some instances of sophisticated, intellectualized religion from what is commonly called philosophy. In their actual history, religion and philosophy are sometimes virtually identical, and more often than not cultivated religion exists in close association with philosophy. Their relation, of course, depends very much on the nature of the culture in which they are rooted, especially its habits of thought and language and its intellectual style.

The philosophy of religion is a mature discipline, and theology, the intellectual core of traditional religion, is in principle a department of philosophy, a specialized branch of metaphysics. But neither theology, which undertakes to construct a meaningful and logically consistent body of ideas central to religion, nor the philosophy of religion, which critically examines the premises and methods of theology, is religion. Both of these, however, are basic connectors of religion with philosophy.

Unlike science, which can be pursued successfully quite independently of its historical development, both philosophy and religion carry the burden of their past; they cannot be fully understood in abstraction from their history. For it is only in their history that they are seen as basic forces in the movements of cultures, and it is here that their substance and structure can be studied. Those interested in modern metaphysical or theological systems or sacramental doctrines and practices, for instance, will fail to grasp their subject in its full implications if they ignore its history. It is in their history that the mutual interplay of philosophy and religion with their interdependencies, antagonisms, and contradictions is best exhibited.

Philosophical elements are clearly important in the structure of any religion which has achieved an appreciable degree of intellectual cultivation, and through much of its history philosophy has had a relation to religion which has varied from near identity to aggressive opposition. In the Upanishads, for instance, the elementary foundations of Hindu philosophy are not fully distinguishable from the beginnings of sophisticated Indian religion. From the time of their composition until the present, with the exception particularly of the materialistic Cārvāka, the traditional Indian philosophical schools have been involved with religion. Indeed, in some instances, such as the Advaita Vedānta, Indian philosophies have been in a sense intellectualized religions, or what may be termed religious philosophies. The foremost historian of Indian philosophy, S. Dasgupta, even ties the primitive origins of Indian philosophy to the Rig-Veda, the earliest of the Aryan religious hymns.[1] Religious modes of thought are endemic to the Indian mind and are built into the Indian language and vocabulary. That religion and philosophy in India have often pursued common ends and followed the same course is a matter of ordinary knowledge. Unlike philosophy in the Occident, which arose largely from intellectual curiosity, philosophy in India seems to have had a practical origin in the experience of suffering and sorrow.

The early forms of Buddhism had philosophical characteristics, and even today the Hinayana is not improperly regarded as a philosophical system. Buddha himself must be listed among the great creative philosophers as well as with the foremost prophets and religious leaders — more philosopher, perhaps, than prophet, for his primary concern was inquiry into the problem of suffering existence rather than the pursuit or encouragement of religious worship. But while there is ground for holding that Hinayana is simply not religion in the traditional sense, much Mahayana Buddhism has similarities to occidental theism.

In the early Chinese philosophical Taoism and in Roman Neoplatonism, monism and absolutism had both a philosophic character and strong religious overtones, as in the practical naturalism of the *Tao Tê Ching*, the mysticism of the *Chuang-Tzu*, and the *Enneads* of Plotinus. Confucianism, which always exhibited a strong humanistic character with its primary concern for ethics and government, has commonly been regarded as a moral philosophy rather than a religion, except in the movement in the Han dynasty (ca. 208 B.C.– ca. A.D. 220) to declare Confucius a divinity rather than a sage, and in the nineteenth-century religious effort to counter the inroads of Christianity. Nevertheless, despite its quite consistent opposition to the supernaturalism that has commonly characterized religion, and which in the form of the Yin–Yang cult infected Taoism from an early date (a reaction especially to the introduction into China of Buddhism), philosophic Confucianism has always possessed certain qualities of a religious nature. The true sage achieves a level of

---

[1] Surendranath Dasgupta, *A History of Indian Philosophy*, 6 vols. (1922; Cambridge: Cambridge University Press, 1963); see vol. 1, chap. 2.

wisdom, insight, and experience that transcends morality and worldliness in the cultivation of spirituality.[2]

In contrast, hellenistic and Roman Epicureanism, which exhibited
some of the elements of religion — a founder, a prophet or two,
certainly an orthodoxy, and to some extent a "religious" fervor —
was from its origins a vigorous opponent of typical religion even
though it was an ethical philosophy. Some schools of philosophic
thought, as for instance the skepticism of the middle and later
Academy, the materialistic and hedonistic Cārvāka of India, or the
European and American logical positivism of the present century,
have been essentially free from religious involvement, or even a
direct religious interest, but their impact on religion has been considerable. The influence of logical positivism on religion, for instance,
has been especially strong in the area of religious or theological language and in the efforts of recent theologians to justify both their
non-empirical methods and their employment of metempirical sentences in theological discourse.

The origins of Greek philosophic thought were probably not
unrelated to religion, and religion and philosophy clearly intersected
in the pre-Socratics, but whether it is proper to describe the early
period as in principle religious or scientific has been a matter of
learned dispute. Theodore Gomperz accounts in part for the achievements of Greek philosophy by its independence of religion. "The
Greeks," he wrote in reference to the beginnings of the Ionian nature-
philosophy,

> were ever the favourites of fortune, and here again must be
> recorded what is perhaps the chief instance of their good luck.
> So far as the evidence of history extends, an organized caste of
> priests and scholars, combining the necessary leisure with the
> equally necessary continuity of tradition, was at all times indis-
> pensable to the beginnings of scientific research. But its begin-
> ning and its end in such cases were only too likely to coincide,
> for when scientific doctrines are mixed up with religious tenets,
> the same lifeless dogmatism will commonly benumb them both.

[2] See Fung Yu-Lan, *The Spirit of Chinese Philosophy*, trans. E. R. Hughes
(New York: Macmillan Co., 1948), Introduction.

... Thus we may account it a double blessing for the free progress of thought among the Greeks that their predecessors in civilization possessed an organized priesthood [i.e., the Chaldeans and the Egyptians] and that they themselves lacked it.[3]

Eduard Zeller agreed in principle with Gomperz in this matter: "The absence of a religious dogmatism favoured the formulation and dissemination of philosophic attempts at explanation of the world. At the same time, in the absence of an ethics founded on religious authority, practical philosophy filled a gap in the spiritual and moral life of the people, where in the same place other peoples had their belief in a religion based on revelation which also regulated their practical life." [4]

In his *History of Ancient Philosophy*, W. Windelband expressed the widely accepted view that Greek metaphysics developed from cosmological interests that had their roots in religion:

> The idea of the connection of things was no longer found after the models of mythology, but by personal reflection and meditation. . . . At first science treated the same problems that concerned mythological fancy. The difference between the two does not lie in their subject matter, but in the form of their interrogation and the nature of their reply. Science begins where a conceptual problem takes the place of curiosity as to sequences, and where, therefore, fancies and fables are replaced by the investigations of permanent relations." [5]

For the most part the biblical religious literature was comparatively free of what is commonly regarded in occidental culture as philosophical inquiry. There were exceptions, of course, as with Job, elements of Ecclesiastes, the Fourth Gospel, and the Wisdom of Solomon and Jesus ben Sira (Ecclesiasticus) in the apocryphal writ-

---

[3] Theodore Gomperz, *The Greek Thinkers*, trans. Laurie Magnus, 4 vols. (1901; London: John Murray, 1964); see vol. 1, p. 43.

[4] *Outlines of the History of Greek Philosophy*, trans. L. R. Palmer, 3d ed. (New York: Meridian Books, 1950), p. 20.

[5] Trans. Herbert Ernest Cushman, from 2d German ed., ca. 1900 (New York: Dover Publications, 1956), pp. 34f.

ings. Moreover, even the earlier biblical literature inevitably posed problems of a philosophical character. But from the beginning of the Common Era, as seen especially in Philo Judaeus and the Alexandrian theologians, there was a marked convergence of Semitic religion and hellenistic thought that set the pattern for the relation of religion to philosophy which was to dominate much of the intellectual life of Christian culture until the present and which had a most profound impact also on Judaism and Islam. First Platonism and Stoicism in their hellenistic and Romanized forms, and eventually Aristotelianism in its medieval form provided the philosophic reference for occidental theology. The ancient Skepticism and Epicureanism were in the environment of early Christianity, but their influence was largely the impact of the opposition.

From at least the second century B.C., Jewish culture was importantly affected by hellenistic thought, both in the Jewish communities of the Diaspora, particularly in Alexandria, and under the Ptolemies and Seleucids in Palestine. Even after the achievement of independence under the Hasmoneans, independence achieved by the revolt of the Hasidim and the Maccabees against the Greek Antiochus IV Epiphanes, the hellenistic influence in Palestine increased, increased with the virtual encouragement of Jewish monarchs and high priests with adopted Greek names and life-styles.[6] Both the extent and character of the hellenization of Jewish culture are impossible to assess fully, but the widespread use of the Greek Koine as a written language not only by Jews of the Diaspora, witness the

---

[6] In his *Hellenistic Civilization and the Jews*, trans. S. Applebaum (New York: Atheneum, 1970), Victor Tcherikover has analyzed with great thoroughness the relation of the Hasidic and Maccabean revolt to the Jewish hellenizing party and the edict of Antiochus IV proscribing the Jewish religion; see chaps. 4–6 of part 1. Tcherikover's entire volume, the work of a lifetime, should be read by anyone having a serious interest in the impact of hellenization on ancient Jewish thought and practice, both in Palestine and the Dispersion. *The Harvest of Hellenism* by F. E. Peters (New York: Simon and Schuster, 1970), is a valuable scholarly mine of information on all aspects of hellenization from "Alexander the Great to the Triumph of Christianity." See also W. W. Tarn's *Hellenistic Civilization* (1952), 3d ed., revised by the author and G. T. Griffith (New York: Meridian Books, 1961), for the background of Christianity in non-Jewish culture.

Septuagint, but in Palestine as well, as in the case of the New Testament, is in itself evidence of the probable depth of that influence. The use of Greek in preference to the Semitic languages, Hebrew and Aramaic, for literary purposes is a telling factor in the matter of the degree of cultural hellenization. Moreover, political and social institutions were affected as well as religion and literature. The negative effect of hellenistic thought and practice on Judaism was not the least of their influences, for their most important result was the reaction in the rise of the Hasidim and the flourishing of Pharisaism, which had an indelible effect upon the Judaism which was the foundation of primitive Christianity. By the second century of the Christian era, when Christian doctrine was beginning to take shape, the hellenistic versions of Greek philosophic thought had thoroughly permeated the eastern part of the Roman Empire and were powerful intellectual forces in the West. It was especially Platonism that affected the formation of Christian dogma, first in the writings of the Alexandrian theologians and eventually, at the close of the classical era, in the work of the greatest of the theologians, St. Augustine.

The impact of hellenistic religion and philosophy on the New Testament is difficult to assess, but it appears quite possible that the earliest of the extant Christian writings, certain of the epistles of Paul, were affected by the Stoicism which he had imbibed in his native city of Tarsus, the center of Stoic thought in the eastern part of the Empire. And it is probable that Greek ideas had an impact on the Gospel of John, composed near the end of the first century.[7]

---

[7] Recent scholarship is more cautious than that of a century ago (as in the Tübingen theological school) in attempting to identify Stoic elements in Paul, and it is far more conservative and guarded in its comparisons of Christianity with the Roman mysteries. Arthur Darby Nock, for instance, a leading authority on hellenistic Christianity, says in treating Paul's apparent Stoicism, "At most [Paul] has used Stoic material to construct his own system, and it is likely that in so far as he has used it it is through intermediary Hellenistic Jewish writings or discussion. It is not probable that he was widely read in Greek literature. In any case, some Stoic ideas were so widely current that an educated man could not fail to be affected by them." *Early Gentile Christianity and Its Hellenistic Background* (1928; New York: Harper & Row, 1964), pp. 95f. This reservation does not hold, however, in the matter of the influence of Platonism on the early theologians from at least the second

It is especially in the Pauline letters and the Fourth Gospel that the main foundations of Christian theology are laid.

But it was the Alexandrian theological school that best exhibited the influence of Greek philosophical thought on Christian ideas and beliefs. Here, of course, the intellectual format had already been well established by the Jewish philosopher and scholar Philo, who believed that through the employment of the method of allegorical interpretation he had exhibited that fundamentals of Platonic metaphysics already existed in the Hebrew Bible, especially the so-called books of Moses. This supposed conjunction of Platonism, the most important of the hellenistic philosophical schools, with the Hebrew scriptures — a joining of philosophy with revealed religion — became the model for Christian theology as it was cultivated by the Alexandrian theologians of whom Clement and Origen were preeminent in their influence on the course of Christian thought.

Philo's method and many of his conclusions are quite intolerable to the modern mind, but considering that his life, education, and intellectual interests belonged to two cultures, his attempt to achieve some kind of harmony and synthesis of those cultures, Judaic and Greek, is entirely understandable. Essentially the same factors conditioned the thought of the main early contributors to Christian thought, for although the employment of Greek ideas by the theologians was useful in eliciting favorable attention and even approval and conversions from the gentiles, the main ground for this pattern of thought is found in the extent to which the theologians belonged to two cultural worlds — the philosophical education of the Greeks and the powerful biblical tradition of moral and theistic religion

---

century. Edwin Hatch's work *The Influence of Greek Ideas and Usages upon the Christian Church*, his 1888 Hibbert Lectures (London: Williams and Norgate, 1907), is a classic study of the Greek impact of the early centuries. The earlier position with respect to the influence on Christianity of the mystery religions is best seen in the work of Franz Cumont, e.g., *The Mysteries of Mithra* (1902), trans. Thomas J. McCormack, 2d ed. (New York: Dover Publications, 1956). Those interested in changes in basic theories relating to the early development of Christian theology and the Christian church should read Frederick C. Grant's foreword to the 1957 edition of the Hatch work, which is entitled *The Influence of Greek Ideas on Christianity* (New York: Harper and Bros.).

inherited from Semitic origins. Despite the efforts of some Christian Gnostics, especially the Marcionites, to sever the ties of the Christian faith to its Jewish origins, the moral and religious tradition of the Bible triumphed and has dominated Christianity to the present. Nevertheless, Christian doctrine became and continues to be Greek in much of its form and substance.[8]

The theological task of constructing a reasonable intellectual formula capable of justifying the basic religious beliefs and providing interpretations sufficient to give them meaning in the thought and experience of the believer was facilitated by the employment of Platonic concepts in the Alexandrian school and by the less obvious but effective use of Aristotelian ideas by the Antiochene theologians. Platonism, particularly as Neoplatonism, its late antique form, was the chief philosophic influence in Christianity until the powerful infusion of Aristotelian thought in the thirteenth century.

The success of Platonism with early Christianity is not difficult to understand. In the first place, in various heterodox forms Platonism insinuated itself effectively and on a broad scale and at a fundamental level into the intellectual culture of the hellenistic world. Many ideas having at least a Platonic origin and flavor, as with much of Stoicism, were more or less taken for granted by persons of intellectual cultivation, as today we tend to take for granted such generalizations as evolution or the causal uniformity of nature. This general disposition favoring Platonism, which had affected hellenistic Judaism even before the rise of Christianity, was due in part to the attractiveness of the rationalistic and intuitive character of Platonic method and the literary quality of its productions. But it was influ-

---

[8] Edwin Hatch began his 1888 Hibbert Lectures, *The Influence of Greek Ideas and Usages upon the Christian Church*, with the statement: "It is impossible for anyone, whether he be a student of history or no, to fail to notice a difference of both form and content between the Sermon on the Mount and the Nicene Creed." That this contrast is a severe oversimplification of a complex matter has been quite clearly shown by historical and literary studies since Hatch wrote his famous lectures — studies relating, for instance, to Jewish sectarianism and Jewish and Christian eschatology, the origins of Gnosticism, and the dating of the Roman mystery religions. But that both Jewish and hellenic elements were built into the structure of Christian theology from at least the second century is entirely obvious.

ential also because of the general compatibility of Platonism with religion. That compatibility was crucial to Christianity in the Graeco-Roman world if the religion were to endure the quite highly intellectualized atmosphere into which it had been introduced in the second half of the first century and in which it struggled for existence.

It is not improbable that the very survival of Christianity in the hellenistic world was contingent not so much upon its incorporation into the theology of ideas that were generally acceptable, but even more upon its acquiring grounds for philosophical and theological interpretations that would make beliefs acceptable that were otherwise intellectually distressing. At least this need seems to have been basic to much of the work of the apologists and early theologians, though there were, of course, exceptions. Of those exceptions, the third-century Latin theologian Tertullian was most in evidence. Although he exploited his own philosophical education where convenient or necessary, and was quite unable to escape his own Stoicism, Tertullian — who had made devastating attacks upon both the pagan critics of Christianity and the Christian heretics, especially the Gnostics — wrote brilliant polemics against philosophy and the philosophers. Christ did not come, insisted Tertullian, to bring the uncivilized into civilization, but rather to bring those who are already civilized to salvation. Philosophy has a corrupting influence on the pure orthodox doctrine, which calls for revelation, not natural knowledge. Undisturbed by paradox and contradiction, he defended belief in the impossible and irrational. Redemption is by faith, not knowledge. "What has Jerusalem to do with Athens," asked Tertullian, "the Church with the Academy, the Christian with the heretic? Our principles come from the Porch of Solomon, who had himself taught that the Lord is to be sought in simplicity of heart. I have no use for a Stoic or a Platonic or a dialectic Christianity. After Jesus Christ we have no need of speculation, after the Gospel no need of research." [9]

This setting of faith against knowledge, so evident in Tertullian, has been, of course, the basic format of modern religious existen-

[9] *The Prescriptions against the Heretics*, in *Early Latin Theology*, vol. 5 of The Library of Christian Classics, trans. S. L. Greenslade (London: SCM Press, 1956), p. 36.

tialism and dialectic theology. It is very pronounced in Kierkegaard, Dostoevski, Berdyaev, and Barth, and the numerous writers who have been influenced by them, all of whom reacted vigorously against the Hegelian rationalism and the scientism of the nineteenth century and set themselves against the mainstream of the tradition of cognition that had progressively invaded religion from the Renaissance to their own time and had, they insisted, destroyed the faith and subjectivism that lie at the heart of religion. In the foreword of his *Athens and Jerusalem*, the Jewish-Russian existentialist Lev Shestov asserts this thesis as boldly as did Tertullian centuries earlier. "Within the 'limits of reason,' " says Shestov,

> one can create a science, a sublime ethic, and even a religion; but to find God one must tear oneself away from the seductions of reason with all its physical and moral constraints, and go to another source of truth. In Scripture this source bears the enigmatic name "faith," which is that dimension of thought where truth abandons itself fearlessly and joyously to the entire disposition of the creator. . . . Human wisdom is foolishness before God, and the wisest of men . . . is the greatest of sinners. Whatsoever is not of faith is sin.[10]

But in his opposition to Greek and Roman philosophy Tertullian was not typical of the early theologians, even though Shestov is a good index to much of today's theology. More representative was Origen of Alexandria, a devout Christian who held that revelation is essential to knowing God, but who insisted that intellectual inquiry is essential to religion. Origen wrote extensively on the Hebrew and Christian scriptures, but he reasoned and wrote in the logical mode of discourse appropriate to the Greek philosophical schools, and the substance of Greek thought is much in evidence in his books. His systematic work *De Principii* and the impressive defense of Christianity against its chief pagan philosophic critics, the *Contra Celsus*, not only exhibit high competence in Greek thought but the employment of Greek rhetorical forms and linguistic usage as well. Not simply Platonism but Stoicism and Epicureanism and the minor

---

[10] *Athens and Jerusalem*, trans. Bernard Martin (New York: Simon and Schuster, 1968), pp. 67–70.

schools entered into his argument and example. It was especially the
concept of the *logos* (λογος), mediated to the Alexandrian school
especially through Platonism and Stoicism, and employed so extensively by Philo, that had captured the imagination of Origen and
provided the vehicle for his treatment of the problem of God and
the world and his doctrine of Christ.

The impact of Platonism on Christianity was probably already
present to some extent in the Fourth Gospel, as seen especially in the
logos doctrine of the prologue.[11] The importance of the concept of
logos for the Christian religion was not only its value in relating the
world and the human soul to God through the mediation of Christ,
but perhaps even more in the general idea that reality is infused with
mind, purpose, and action — a metaphysical doctrine that was a quite
common ground for the more cultivated forms of hellenistic religion
and was basic to Stoicism.[12]   Although it would be erroneous to
attribute the *logos* metaphysics simply to Plato, for the concept of
logos certainly antedated Plato and was a part of his own philosophical inheritance, it was especially through the wide diffusion of Platonism and Stoicism that it was transmitted through the hellenistic era
and became almost a staple of thought in the Graeco-Roman intellectual world. Even before Origen, Justin (d. ca. A.D. 165), and
Clement of Alexandria had approached Christianity from a background of Greek paideia with the presumption — common to the

---

[11] Whether John's employment of the concept of the Word (1:1–5) followed the Greek *logos* theory, which descended at least from Heracleitus, or
was based on the Hebrew *memra* has been a matter of some controversy. It
is clear, however, that in the Alexandrian school the employment of *logos*
was in the Greek mode. It cannot be established that the appearance of the
logos in John's prologue was due to the influence of Philo, but the chronology, of course, is favorable to that possibility as the Fourth Gospel was probably not composed before the beginning of the second century and Philo,
whose writings were extensive and may have been rather widely disseminated,
probably did not live beyond A.D. 54.

[12] In treating the Johannine *logos* doctrine, Christian scholars in the past
have probably overstated the degree of God's transcendence in first-century
Jewish theology. This emphasis on transcendence, which justifies the *logos*
as mediator, may have been due to the impact of Philo on the Christian understanding of the rabbinical theology.

hellenistic apologists from at least the middle of the second century — that Christian faith and doctrine not only were not in principle antithetical to the hellenic tradition, but both could and should recognize an important kinship with the dominant Platonic intellectual forms of that tradition, an attitude that in its more sanguine expression represented Plato as a revelator of the truth even before Christ. The scriptural forms of Christian belief were honored for their simple and forthright declarations of faith, but the apologists and the later Fathers turned to their Greek intellectual ancestry when the occasion demanded defense or explanation.

While the success of the apologists in their defense and advocacy of Christian doctrine was due in no small part to the Greek elements in the substance of their message and the Greek techniques in their explanation, analysis, and argument, for these gains Christianity clearly paid a considerable price on its Hebraic side at the point of the simplicity of its message and the straightforward literalness in its reading of the Jewish sacred books and its own authoritative literature. But it is an inexcusable error to interpret the history of ancient Christianity in its Graeco-Roman context as an invasion of a pure Judaic Christianity by Greek and Roman intellectual, liturgical, and administrative forces and forms to produce a bastardized and apostate religion and church. The mainstream Christianity that is known to history was never a pure Judaic faith to begin with. When Paul and the hellenizers preached Christianity in the synagogues of the Dispersion and established churches in the cities of Asia, Macedonia, and Greece, they were laying the foundations of a religious movement which was inevitably Greek and Roman as well as Jewish. It was a Jewish invasion of the Graeco-Roman culture, a Jewish intrusion into the intellectual and religious life of the Empire, a transplanting of the Christian message into a different and foreign world that saved Christianity from oblivion as a Jewish sect destined for virtual extinction with the destruction of the Second Temple.

It was the Platonic element in Neoplatonism from the third century that was to be the chief philosophic influence on Christian doctrine. Like Origen, Plotinus (A.D. 205?–70), the foremost philosopher of the Roman era and the chief representative of Neoplatonism, was a student in Alexandria of the Platonist Ammonius Saccas. Although neither Ammonius nor Plotinus was Christian, in Alexandria, unlike Athens, Pergamum, and the intellectual centers of Syria, where Neoplatonism was intensely anti-Christian, Christianity cultivated a compatibility with that philosophy that in some measure lasted through late antiquity, the Middle Ages, and into the Renaissance and modern times. The Neoplatonism of Plotinus and his philosophic descendants was, of course, by no means a pure Platonism — far from it. It was a variable synthesis of Platonism, Aristotelianism, Neo-Pythagoreanism, and Stoicism, but it had a strong Platonic flavor; and as a philosophy it had remarkable powers of adaptation and endurance and became the dominant intellectual religion of late pagan antiquity and — despite the opposition to Christianity of such powerful adherents as Porphyry (ca. 232–ca. 306) and Proclus (ca. 410–485) — the philosophic companion and support of Christian theology.

The general compatibility of Neoplatonism with Christian theology seems to have been due especially to its theory that reality is essentially of the nature of mind as well as to its gradations in the levels of reality, providing a metaphysical context for Christology and for the relation of angels, the human soul, and other creatures to God, to say nothing of its capacity for covering the fall and incarnation. However, this apparent harmony should not obscure the very important areas in which Christianity and Neoplatonism were in strong opposition. Here I have in mind especially the Christian belief in creation, a doctrine of far-reaching importance for theology, as opposed to the Neoplatonic concept of the eternity of the world, and the theory of the emanation of the lower orders of reality, including matter, from the One. There are basic differences also in the concepts of the soul and matter. Although both the orthodox Christian theologians and the Neoplatonists, especially Plotinus, wrote vigorous attacks on Gnosticism, they differed importantly in their treatment of matter. Despite the common hellenistic disparagement of matter and their own not uncommon inclination to describe it as a source of evil, the theologians generally regarded matter as both real and in principle good, a creation of God, while Neoplatonism commonly saw it as at best the indeterminate and diminishing edge of reality and the principle of evil. The general tendency of Neo-

platonic metaphysics was toward a quite extreme monism which had
the basic characteristic of pantheism — a position abhorrent to the
Christian theologian, whose doctrine of creation placed God ontologically over against the world of his creation and made their identification an intolerable error.

It was in the work of St. Augustine (354–430), of course, and
later in Boethius (ca. 480–ca. 524) and St. Anselm (1033–1109),
that Platonism, mediated by Neoplatonism, was most clearly exhibited in Christian theology and philosophy.[13] Augustine, who was the
chief link of ancient with medieval thought, was much involved with
Neoplatonism before his conversion and baptism in 387. Indeed, it
seems to have been the Neoplatonic Christian theologians, particularly Ambrose, the Bishop of Milan, and Victorinus Afer, who
effected his conversion, and in all probability it was his commitment
to Neoplatonism that led to his acceptance of Christianity.[14] Augustine was more theologian than philosopher, and for him philosophy
was the servant of theology and religion; revelation was superior to
reason, but reason supported the revealed truth and was essential to
the quest for practical wisdom and the eventual state of blessedness
that comes through God's saving grace.

In his *Soliloquia* Augustine said, "I desire to know God and the
soul, nothing more." And it was the concepts of God and the soul
and their interrelationship that tied him and the entire Augustinian

[13] There has been considerable dispute over whether Anicius Manlius
Severinus Boethius was actually a Christian, a dispute generated especially by
the absence of Christian reference from his *De Consolatione Philosophiae*,
the most influential of his writings, which has well-defined Platonic and Stoic
elements. The dominant opinion today, however, is that at least some of the
Christian theological writings traditionally attributed to him are authentic.

[14] In his own account of his conversion, book 5, chap. 10 to book 9,
chap. 6 of the *Confessions*, Augustine reveals the Platonic basis of his involvement with Christianity and his esteem for the Neoplatonists as compared to
other non-Christian philosophers. See especially book 8, chap. 2; here, referring to Semplicunus, the father of Ambrose, he wrote in part, "[Semplicunus]
congratulated me that I had not fallen upon the writings of the other philosophers, which were full of fallacies and deceit, after the rudiments of the
world, whereas [the Platonists], in many ways, led to the belief in God and
His word."

philosophical tradition to Platonism throughout the Middle Ages and into modern Christian theology. The Christian concept of an immaterial immortal soul was essentially Greek in origin, not biblical. Belief in a bodily resurrection was a Jewish inheritance, from Jesus and the Pharisees, but the immortal soul was essentially Platonic. In the *Phaedo* especially, Plato was rhapsodic in his description of the soul and advanced several arguments for its immortality that became staples in Christian apologetics, particularly the case for the imperishability of a simple entity.

It would be difficult to overstate the impact of Platonism on the conception of God as that achieved maturity in Augustine's work, notwithstanding the fact of the crucial basic differences which separated Platonic metaphysics from Christianity, differences which centered especially in the impersonal and nontemporal nature of the ultimate reality in Platonism and Neoplatonism in contrast to the biblical concept of God as a personal, living being. Despite these differences, there was the general religious disposition of Platonism, its rationality and methods of argument, its commitment to mind, its monistic and mystical inclinations, and the moral absolutism guaranteed by its theory of value universals. There is justification for holding that perhaps most of the basic problems in Christian theology even today are the result of the synthesis, which matured in the work of Augustine, of hellenistic and Judaic theological ideas that eventually proved to be incompatible. The fusion of those ideas was a natural consequence of the process of Christianizing the Roman world, as was the growth of the Catholic church on the pattern of the Roman polity, but there were hidden incongruities and contradictions. I have in mind particularly the employment of categories generated for the impersonal absolutism of the Neoplatonic "One" in describing the personal God of the biblical tradition. Here, at the very heart of the theology, there were built-in difficulties that would inevitably surface and cause trouble — the relation of God to the world, for instance, the question of the timeless God and human history, the problem of divine absolutism and human freedom, of absolutism and the reality of suffering and evil, and eventually the passionless God of the creeds in a religion of compassion and redemption.

Nevertheless, on balance the Platonic philosophy served Christianity well, and even with the large infusion of Aristotelianism in the late twelfth and thirteenth centuries it continued to be the main intellectual understructure not only of the theology and religion but of the culture generally, providing, for instance, the mathematical ingredients for the development of modern science.[15] The Platonic virtues were built into the moral structure of Christianity, buttressed by the absolutism that was secured by Augustine's view — which was not original with him — that the Platonic forms, the universals which for Plato had an independent reality over and above all particulars, are thought eternally by the mind of God. While Augustine is often seen as primarily a voluntarist because of his very strong emphasis on the moral will, both divine and human, he was in principle an intellectualist, for in his theology the mind of God ultimately controls the divine will. But among those who are justifiably seen as inheritors of an Augustinian tradition, as for instance the Franciscans, there was often an intense voluntarism, as in the case of Duns Scotus and William of Ockham, who held that the divine will has a sovereign power over the intellect. Voluntarism in the conception of God was to become a major factor in Protestant theology, especially in Calvin and Calvinism.

The most important facet of Platonic metaphysics was its realism, the theory of the reality of the forms or Ideas, the independent and autonomous reality of universals. There is not a more basic problem in philosophy than the question of the ontological status of universals — basic not only to theology but to the whole of metaphysics

[15] While Platonism was the primary intellectual foundation of medieval culture, its influence continued with varying force into the modern era. At times it was incorporated in more or less organized philosophical movements, as in the Renaissance Florentine Academy founded by Marsilio Ficino (1433–1499) under Medici patronage, and the resurgence in England in the seventeenth century under the Cambridge Platonists, anti-Calvinists whose ranks included Henry More and Ralph Cudworth. Wherever Platonism flourished it was as a commitment to reason and to the rationality of religion. Although the flavor of Plato or at least Plotinus was always present in the historical forms of Platonism, in rational method, emphasis on universals, and concern for high morality, there was rarely a fully satisfactory attempt to understand Plato or to faithfully subscribe to his philosophical system.

and the many branches of thought that have metaphysical bearings —
and it was this problem that occupied much of the philosophical
talent of the Middle Ages. The controversy between realists and
nominalists, with conceptualists in the middle, sharpened the intellectual tools of the theologians and philosophers of religion and
honed their disciplines to a fine, if sometimes inordinate, subtlety.

There were Aristotelian influences upon the development of
Christian thought from the early period, as Aristotelian and Platonic
ideas, notwithstanding fundamental differences and conflicts, were
generally congenial companions in the movement of intellectual culture. Aristotle and Plato merged quite effectively in Christian theology where God conceived on the pattern of Aristotle's pure thought
or intellectual activity as the highest reality was also Plato's absolute
Good, the ultimate intelligible reality, God as both knower and
known, as the supreme subject and supreme object. And for the
Christian theologians, supreme person. Of course, Plato and Aristotle were concerned with many of the same problems, and due
to their close personal association inevitably there was much common
ground in their treatments of those problems. The differences, however, were often very basic, Plato's rationalism inclining him toward
a primary interest in being and the independent reality of universals,
while Aristotle's empirical temperament led him to concentrate his
metaphysics more on particulars and the processes of becoming. Here
in the problem of being and becoming was a large and fundamental
issue which the Greeks bequeathed to later centuries and with which
our theologians and philosophers are still struggling.

Except for his logic, the *Organon* — important elements of which
were available in Latin to western Christianity, together with commentaries — Aristotle was commonly known even in the East in
Neoplatonic versions that often distorted his original ideas.[16] It

---

[16] Porphyry, the anti-Christian Neoplatonist of the third century, wrote
extensively on Platonism and Aristotelianism, but of this material the main
survivor is the *Isagoge*, an introduction to Aristotle's *Categories*. In the sixth
century the Christian–Stoic–Platonic scholar Boethius produced Latin trans-
lations of the *Isagoge* together with extensive parts of Aristotle's logic, making most of that corpus available to medieval Latin scholars and thereby providing important logical foundations and methods for Christian theologians

was especially in Syriac versions of Aristotle, produced by Nestorian Christians, that the Muslims encountered the Peripatetic philosophy following the rise and spread of Islam in the seventh and eighth centuries. In Arabic translation, mainly but not exclusively from Syriac texts, Aristotelian thought in its Neoplatonic form was widely disseminated as the chief philosophical foundation of Muslim culture, a culture which eventually reached from India across Persia, the Middle East, and North Africa to Sicily and Spain.[17] The impact of Aristotelianism on Arabic thought was overwhelming, and due to the close involvement of Jewish learning with Muslim intellectual centers, it inevitably had a profound effect upon Jewish philosophy and theology. When it reached western Latin Christianity in the twelfth century, especially through Arabic and Jewish scholars in Spain, it had a powerful influence on Christian theology and philosophy of religion.

Islam, with its absolute commitment to monotheism, a position due largely to its initial contacts with Judaism and the Old Testament, was not occupied with theological problems on the order of the Christian christological controversies or the trinitarian disputes. And since it accepted creationism, it was firmly opposed to the Neoplatonic doctrines of emanation. But in its early period it was deeply involved with such matters as the reconciliation of divine absoluteness with human freedom, justice, and the existence of evil. Somewhat like the Christian Platonists of Alexandria, the earliest of the theological (Kalamite) schools, Mu'tazilah, employed Greek philosophic resources in explication and justification of Muslim beliefs in confrontation with the opponents of Islam, especially the Christians. And not totally unlike Tertullian, and more recently Kierkegaard and Barth, the Mu'tazilites engendered philosophical reactionaries who stood firmly on the ground of faith and opposed recourse to reason in religion. While the Mu'tazilite Kalām continued in influence through the eleventh century, the anti-philosophical movement,

---

and philosophers; he translated the *Categories, Prior Analytics, Posterior Analytics, Sophistic Arguments*, and *Topics*.

[17] The main period of the Arabic translation of Greek works was the late eighth and the ninth centuries.

the Ash'arah, has endured to the present. Like other sophisticated opponents of philosophy, the Ash'arites have, of course, employed philosophical arguments to advance and defend their own anti-philosophical position.

During the long career of Islamic philosophy, which extended beyond the medieval period of western Europe, some of the most illustrious names pursued their philosophic interests quite independently of Kalām, with more concern for basic metaphysical, epistemological, ethical, and logical as well as scientific questions than for theological and religious interests. Of these certainly among the foremost were the Arabian al-Kindi (c. 801–866), and the Persian al-Fārābi (870?–950), both Aristotelians affected deeply by Platonism and Neoplatonism. The greatest of the Aristotelians, the Persian scientist ibn-Sīna (Avicenna, 980–1037), brought the Peripatetic philosophy to a systematic climax, not only as a foundation for Islamic culture, but also as a heritage to Christianity upon which Roger Bacon in the twelfth and the scholastics of the thirteenth century and later constructed much of their argument for Christian theology.

The work of ibn-Rushd (Averroës, 1126–1198), of medieval Arabic philosophers the best known in the West and the most influential on Christianity, was in part directed against the critique of philosophy developed by al-Ghazzāli (1058–1111) in his *Tahāfut al-Falāsifa*, a Latin version of which, entitled *Destructio Philosophorum*, was read by Christian theologians in the thirteenth century. When made available in Latin translation, the writings of Averroës, in which he attempted a reconciliation of philosophy and religion by defining and limiting their cognitive fields while establishing that they are not contradictory, contributed greatly to the intellectual crisis in predominantly Christian Europe, a crisis that brought Aristotelian natural science and metaphysics into an arena dominated by traditional Platonism and a platonized theology.

In the academic centers of Catholicism, especially the University of Paris, the Aristotelian metaphysics in the Averroist interpretation encountered severe opposition as an extreme threat to the Christian faith. The opposition was directed especially toward the ideas of the unity of a single immortal intellect, which contradicted the doctrine of individual immortality, the eternity of the world, which denied creation, the perfectibility of man, which made salvation through grace unnecessary, and the denial of divine providence. Among those who attacked the work of Averroës were Albertus Magnus and Thomas Aquinas, both of whom were to be greatly affected by their own study of Aristotle. It was against Averroism that Aquinas wrote his great *Summa Contra Gentiles.*

At the death of Averroës, which occurred as new life was being breathed into Christian thought, the great era of Arabic philosophy came to a close. Thereafter the course of Islam was comparatively free from either philosophical encumbrance or creative philosophical inspiration and support.

Despite the fact that Jewish thinkers of major stature are prominent in the history of occidental philosophy — Philo, ibn-Gabirol, Maimonides, Spinoza, Mendelssohn (1729–1786), for instance — there is not a tradition of philosophical thought associated with Judaism as a religion or even as a cultural tradition in quite the way that philosophy and religion have been related through the mainstream history of Christianity, or even to the extent of the Mu'tazilite Kalām in Islam. Neither Judaism nor Islam was "philosophized" or "theologized" to the extent that this is true of Christianity; this is due in part to the difference in their social and general cultural relationships with the hellenic intellectual world and due also to the simplicity of their strict monotheistic doctrine as compared with the problems raised by Christology and Christian trinitarianism. In the case of Judaism, it was especially the Torah as the foundation and substance of faith and morals that wrapped a cloak of practicality around the religion which protected it from the ravaging refinements of the theologians' intellect. Except for Job and Ecclesiastes in the Old Testament and Ecclesiasticus and the Wisdom of Solomon in the apocryphal literature, there was little philosophic disputation in the ancient Jewish writings; and Philo, though he laid the formal foundations for Christian theology, was of little interest to the Jewish rabbinical leadership, whose concern after the destruction in A.D. 70 was the preservation of the people and the faith through the Mishnah and Midrashim.

Philo's philosophic interests were basically metaphysical, especially his concern with the problem of the relation of the absolutistic transcendent God to the world of space and time — a problem that did not occupy a large place in the rabbinical religion. The Diaspora Jews for whom such matters *were* a problem, as in Alexandria, were perhaps assimilated in large numbers into Christianity, whose theology was much involved with the question of God and the world and with speculation on mediation through the *logos*–Christ. But when Jewish and Islamic culture became closely related in the ninth and tenth centuries, both Jews and Muslims were engrossed by a common philosophic interest which centered especially on problems pertaining to revelation and natural knowledge, with the result that their theological and philosophical work even into the thirteenth century exhibits reciprocal influence. In this period of considerable freedom and creativity, when most Jewish philosophers wrote in Arabic, Jewish philosophy moved from Arabic Kalām through Neoplatonism to Aristotelian metaphysics — or at least what passed for Aristotelian metaphysics — despite fundamental differences of the philosophic from the biblical and Rabbinical tradition, as in the matter of the emanation of reality from its source and the doctrine of the world's eternity. It was essentially a quest for an intellectual bridge between rational knowledge and faith in revelation and an attempt to reconcile human freedom of will and the fact of evil with divine justice. Saadia Gaon of Sura (near Baghdad, 892–942) followed the traditional Mu'tazilite theology. He argued in his *Book of Beliefs and Convictions* for the compatibility of human reason and belief in normative doctrines received through the prophets, holding that the divine will can be known only through the authoritative scripture. Saadia held to the doctrine of the creation of the world and derived from the creation his arguments for the existence of God, whose unity, he insisted, is not compromised by the fact that our knowledge of him is through the multiplicity of his attributes. God has foreknowledge, but this does not negate the free will of man.

Solomon ibn-Gabirol, an eleventh-century poet (ca. 1021–ca. 1070) who was probably the first Jewish philosopher of Spain, had inherited a strong tradition of Neoplatonism, which is expressed in his Arabic work *The Well of Life* (*Fons Vitae* in the Latin translation of the twelfth century). His Neoplatonism appears especially in his acceptance of the emanation of the world from its divine source — a view contrary to the orthodox Jewish concept of creation — and in his agreement with the theory of levels of reality. The poet Judah ha-Levi (ca. 1075–ca. 1141), also a Neoplatonist, set revealed religion over against the severe limitations of human reason which were evident in every attempt to treat the question of God philosophically. Intensely Jewish in his viewpoint, ha-Levi held that knowledge of God comes only through reflection on God's dealings with man in Jewish history.

It was in the work of the foremost of the Jewish philosophers, Moses Maimonides (1135–1204), that Jewish thought achieved its highest level of maturity in the Middle Ages, employing both Neoplatonic and Aristotelian tools in its efforts to reconcile rational metaphysics with biblical faith. In *The Guide for the Perplexed*, Maimonides confronted the problems that had become traditional in the attempt of Arabic philosophy to square revealed religion with Aristotle. Here it was the religion of the Judaic tradition, the Hebrew scriptures and the Talmud; a reconciliation of the moral law with an intellectualized ethics; the moral lawgiver with the processes of reflective thought; the creation of the world from nothing with the eternal (Neoplatonic) emanation from God; the immortality of the individual soul with the single, all-inclusive active intellect; the practical religion with the contemplative ideal. Needless to say, Maimonides did not succeed in preserving either Judaism or Aristotle's metaphysics entirely intact, and even today the full meaning and historical import of his work is debated. But his was quite clearly the most effective and influential effort to bridge the wide gulf between the philosophical tradition and the Torah. Maimonides' entire attempt to describe the nature of God was against the Neoplatonic background of *negative* theology, the doctrine found in Philo and well established in Christian theology that it is possible not to know what God *is*, but only what he is *not*.

It was in thirteenth-century Catholic scholasticism, especially the work of Thomas Aquinas, that philosophy achieved its strongest ties with theology and religion. Here the relationship was one of rigorous reasoning and systematic application, with philosophic speculation supporting theology and religion while yet, within the bounds of religious assumptions, standing on independent ground. Despite strong opposition, not only against the "invading" Aristotelianism with its Arabic commentaries, but even against the philosophic tradition as a whole — opposition which eventually brought results in the Protestant revolt — Aquinas straightforwardly employed basic premises, principles, and methods of Aristotle along with his philosophical and theological inheritance from Augustine, the Fathers, Plato, and the Bible. He developed a remarkably ingenious and effective synthesis of disparate and sometimes quite incongruous elements to produce the most impressive intellectual system ever constructed to reconcile the sacred and the secular, the religious and the scientific, and to explain the relation of God to man and the world by justifying both divine revelation and natural knowledge.

Those who have not closely examined the work of Aquinas cannot fully appreciate the extent of his effort to construct a synthesis of Pauline–Augustinian religion with the natural science and philosophy of Europe's hellenic inheritance. Wherever one looks in his writings, there is evidence of that synthesis with its ingenious employment of the Aristotelian philosophy. The basic format is the dualism of the realm of grace and the realm of nature, of the domains of faith and natural knowledge, of the soul's salvation and human achievement, of the divine virtues of grace — faith, hope, and love — and the natural, moral virtues — prudence, fortitude, temperance, and justice. Even the dianoetic or intellectual virtue of Aristotle, the special virtue of rationality, is sandwiched into the system.[18] Aquinas' treatment of the relation of the Christian to the dianoetic and cardinal virtues is a quite remarkable exercise in cross-cultural synthesis. But this apparent harmony is actually forced by Aquinas' introduction of principles or premises which are contrary if not contradictory to Aristotle's position, where they are necessary to the synthesis, as, for instance, ideas pertaining to personal immortality and the achievement of blessedness as against eudaemonia as the proper end of human life.

[18] *Summa Theologica*, part 1 of part 2, ques. 56–62.

I find it quite impossible to accept Aquinas' system, basically because although it is imbued with Aristotle's brand of empiricism, it is still a product of the pre-scientific age and fails to satisfy our more rigorous methodological strictures upon speculative thought. But I am reasonably sure that it is not at all probable that there will appear another Christian philosophy that will surpass or even equal Aquinas' in its capacity to satisfy the intellectual inquiry of those who are committed to the preservation of human reason in matters pertaining to religion, while at the same time asserting the superiority of revelation over natural knowledge.

Those receptive to Thomism in the thirteenth century immediately encountered difficult obstructions from those who were accustomed to the intuitive rationalism of the semi-mystical Christian Platonism and were understandably opposed to the humanistic and empirical inclinations of Aristotelianism. Through the succeeding centuries Thomism experienced both fortune and misfortune, its standing usually alternating with that of Platonism. From the fourteenth century to the nineteenth Thomism, opposed by Duns Scotus and the Franciscans, by Ockham and the nominalists, by Luther and the Protestant revolution, by the growing tide of humanism, and, after Galileo and Newton, by the growing respect for empirical method and the natural sciences, suffered a considerable decline. But since the issue of the encyclical *Aeterni Patris* of Leo XIII in 1879, it has had quite remarkable success as the primary philosophic bearer of Catholic faith, doctrine, and morals through a difficult period of onslaught from scientific thought and naturalistic humanism. Such a pragmatic success, of course, is not an evidence of the truth of Thomism; but it is an important testament of the practical strength of that philosophy as an intellectual support for theology and religion. Those who disparage the value of philosophic activity in strengthening both the intellectual foundations and the superstructure of religion should consider the remarkable degree of integrity which characterizes Catholic religious thought at the present time in contrast to the confusion that reigns in Protestantism. Nevertheless, I must warn again that it is not an indication of the truth of Thomism that it has served Catholicism well in at least slowing if not preventing its progressive dissolution by the acids of modernity.

I cannot subscribe to an essentially pragmatic approach to the meaning of truth. And besides, there are strong indications now in the very camp of the neoscholastics that the ancient substantive categories which treat both metaphysical and theological questions in terms of absolute being are failing to satisfy the requirement for a more dynamic metaphysics which will accommodate descriptions of the world in terms of time and movement. Accordingly, there is a growing interest especially in the process philosophy of Whitehead. In a sense, a departure from Aquinas in favor of Whitehead would be a shift of philosophical foundations from Aristotelianism back to Platonism; but in another sense it would be a radical movement of occidental religious thought toward something less dependent on its antique beginnings.

It is unlikely that genuinely new philosophic problems will arise within the arena of religious thought. There will probably always be those who incline toward methodological problems and are concerned with the ways of knowing; some will convert philosophy into an analytic format, either logical or linguistic, or both, as was done in both ancient and medieval times and is now done in our own era. Others will concentrate on substantive issues in the theory of reality, or value theory. Still others will take the anti-philosophical position of Tertullian, Luther, Kierkegaard, and Barth. New refinements in the theory of knowledge will follow developments in the psychology of the knowing process, and unexpected nuances will appear in analysis. But the fundamental substantive problems will probably remain. The question of the ontological status of universals was basic in Plato and Aristotle, basic in Augustine's concept of God, basic in the early medieval conflict over realism and nominalism, basic in the metaphysics of Aquinas, Duns Scotus, and Ockham; and in this century Bertrand Russell, a philosopher not given to looseness or excess, has held that the way universals are to be treated is still the basic philosophical problem. Even Luther in his opposition to the strong Greek element in the thought of the church was involved with a dissident metaphysics and theory of knowledge pertaining to universals, Ockham's nominalism. Every serious anti-philosophical movement seems to be inevitably philosophical in its own way.

Whether a theistic religion can survive and thrive without the support of a philosophy that provides at least a theory of knowledge that effectively treats the problem of faith and reason and a metaphysics that accounts for such matters as the place of universals in the structure of reality is a complex problem that raises questions concerning the extent to which particular religions are involved substantively and traditionally with theology, the nature of both the religions and their theologies, and the character of the cultural contexts of the religions as they are actually practiced, whether the culture generally complements or in principle contradicts the faith. The only effective way to inquire into these matters is to examine religion historically to see it in process within its cultural context and over a substantial period of time.

It seems quite obvious to me, as I have already indicated, that Christianity would not have survived its early period if it had not developed a considerable intellectual apparatus, both theological and philosophical. If Christianity had remained an eschatological Jewish sect, as it began in Palestine under the leadership of the original apostles, very simple and familiar doctrinal interpretations of Judaism and its fulfillment by the Messiah would have sufficed. But in all probability it would have virtually disappeared at the destruction of Jerusalem by Titus in A.D. 70 while it was still in its primitive beginnings; and if not then, it would quite certainly have been extinguished by the destruction under Hadrian a few decades later. As a Jewish sect, Christianity found its meaning essentially in its conformity to the Torah, the prophetic–pharisaic tradition, the synagogue, the community, and especially in the expectation of the end, the dawn of the Messianic aeon. There was no need to add materially to the frugal, simple theology of ethical monotheism which was the intellectual framework of the religion then as it is now, for the Jewish religion was not geared primarily to a set of theological beliefs that required technical intellectual formulation. The need was, rather, the conduct of life in conformity to the divine law, written and oral. The primitive Palestinian Christianity apparently had no disposition to move out of and away from that Judaism. The primitive Christian requirement was not the acceptance of a philosophical system or a set of theological dogmas, but rather conformity to the law, with faith in the purposes of a God whose existence and concern for Israel were not in question, and to the belief that his anointed had come with the message that the Kingdom of God was at hand.

But the fortunes of the Christianity that survived as the mainstream of European culture were quite a different matter and, as I pointed out earlier, both its internal development in directions indicated by the teachings of Paul and the hellenistic philosophical and gnostic and mystery cultic environment within which it was nourished inevitably produced an elaborate theological and philosophic structuring.

Considering the early date of the Greek conquest of Palestine, more than three centuries before Christ, and the continued Greek cultural impact on the Jews and Judaism — even during most of the Hasmonean period prior to the Roman conquest in 63 B.C., and throughout the Herodian–Roman era to the destruction under Hadrian — it is a fair question to ask why Palestinian Judaism was not influenced by hellenistic culture in a manner at least comparable to its influence on Christianity. As a matter of fact, the hellenistic influence was very great, but it was the Judaism of that large segment of the Jews in Palestine which was committed to religious isolation and resistance to foreign cultural forces, the Judaism of rabbinical pharisaism, that survived the Roman destruction and eventually joined with Babylonian Judaism in establishing the centers of Jewish learning in Mesopotamia.[19] It was this anti-hellenic Judaism of which the primitive Palestinian Christianity was an eschatological sect, a Judaism which effectively built around itself an insulating wall of law that preserved it from the modifying impact of gentile philosophy. Its intellectual environment did not require, and its internal character did not permit, the development of a distinctive philosophical system designed as an intellectual foundation and interpretation of the religion.

Apparently it was the close and quite positive association of Jewish and Muslim culture in Mesopotamia, North Africa, and Spain

---

[19] The Patriarchal office in Palestine was discontinued about A.D. 425. The Babylonian Talmud was probably completed by the end of the fifth century.

that turned Jewish thought toward systematic philosophical activity. In general, the form and the substance of Jewish and Muslim philosophy were similar and at times identical, a condition not difficult to explain considering the common ground of the two religions, with their foundations in strict monotheism, their emphasis on the moral law, and the commitment of both to authoritative scripture. There was undoubtedly considerable reciprocal influence between the Jewish and Muslim philosophers, but the chronology of events seems to indicate that the prior philosophic impact was Islam upon Judaism. There is no evidence, however, that philosophic analysis and speculation played as large a role in the life of either of these religions as they did in Christianity. In the Middle Ages, the period of their chief philosophic activity, neither Judaism nor Islam was confronted as was Christianity in its early centuries with a philosophically oriented culture against which it was forced to struggle for existence. Neither faced enemies comparable to the Roman philosophical schools of the first three centuries, and certainly neither encountered anything quite like the massive onslaught of Gnosticism, which required Christianity to enter vigorously into a doctrinal struggle not only in relation to Christology but also in the definition of its position on the world, matter, and evil, and to preserve its continuity with the biblical tradition. The importance of the confrontation with the mysteries or with Manichaeism probably cannot be fully determined, but there is no question that the conflict with Gnosticism was a life-and-death affair, one which required theological and philosophical doctrine for a successful resolution.

3

Modern Philosophy and Liberal Religion

For the past century and more the intellectual burden of religion has been borne in our culture in considerable part by the idealistic metaphysics whose chief technical foundations were laid by Immanuel Kant. This has been the case, at least, in the Protestant segment of the culture for those who have been concerned with the philosophical foundations of theology. Kant's *Critique of Pure Reason* was an attempt to establish the boundaries of knowledge by defining the relationship of reason to sensory experience and determining the relation of the knowledge process to the object known. This critical analysis of knowledge, which, due especially to Hume's influence, had a strong empirical bent, resulted in a thoroughgoing agnosticism in metaphysics. The traditional cosmological and teleological arguments for the existence of God, upon which religious philosophy had for centuries been partially predicated, were declared by Kant to be invalid because of their lack of experiential grounding.[1]

---

[1] *Critique of Pure Reason*, Transcendental Doctrine of Elements, Transcendental Dialectic, chap. 3, The Ideal of Pure Reason, sec. 3–7. Kant, of course, also rejected the ontological argument which, although it has persisted to the present, has enjoyed less standing than the cosmological and teleologi-

But while the critical philosophy held that God's existence cannot be proved, by the same arguments it held that the non-existence of God cannot be proved, leaving the matter open for belief or faith. The effect of the later *Critique of Practical Reason*, in which Kant affirmed God as a moral postulate, was to bring the doctrine of man to the center of religion.[2] Whereas formerly — as even today in typical Roman Catholic philosophy — acceptance of the possibility of a rational theology assured the centrality of the concept of God for the philosophy of religion, in the aftermath of the two Kantian *Critiques*, God as an object of knowledge was replaced by God as an object of faith, and a greater degree of subjectivism than it had known before was introduced into theology. Perhaps in part because both Calvinism and Lutheranism were already committed to the Augustinian approach to religion, which was grounded strongly in beliefs about the nature and predicament of man, Kant's position with its strong subjective elements eventually prevailed for most Protestantism. The result was an intellectual context for religion that was conducive to the development of both nineteenth-century religious liberalism and twentieth-century theological existentialism.

---

cal arguments. The attempt of Anselm to achieve a rational proof of God's existence that is completely free from experiential elements made the ontological argument entirely unacceptable to Aquinas and to Catholic philosophers and theologians generally.

[2] For Kant's discussion of God, freedom, and immortality as postulates of the pure practical reason, see the *Critique of Practical Reason*, part 1, book 2, chap. 2, The Dialectic of Pure Reason in Defining the Concept of the Highest Good, 5, The Existence of God as a Postulate of Pure Practical Reason.

> The postulate of the possibility of a highest derived good (the best world) is at the same time the postulate of the reality of a highest original good, namely, the existence of God. Now it was our duty to promote the highest good; and it is not merely our privilege but a necessity connected with duty as a requisite to presuppose the possibility of this highest good. This presupposition is made only under the condition of the existence of God, and this condition inseparably connects this supposition with duty. Therefore it is morally necessary to assume the existence of God. [Trans. Lewis White Beck]

But it must be noted that Kant does not adequately justify the "presupposition" of the possibility of the highest good upon which he constructs his case for the necessary postulate of God's existence.

By his critique of knowledge Kant laid the groundwork for the classical non-Catholic resolution of the conflict between religion and science. By grounding religion on faith rather than knowledge, he in effect insulated it against the possibility of scientific attack or successful rational refutation. Reality was divided between the phenomenal and the noumenal — roughly between science and religion — with each realm guaranteed a certain immunity against the method of the other. It was a neat arrangement and profoundly argued, and it appeared on the surface at least that both the scientists and the theologians should be satisfied, convinced that they were entirely secure in their own territory.

The subjectivism of Kant's epistemology, that the phenomenal world — the world of space, time, and matter known through the senses — is not objectively real in the way that it appears to be but is actually in part the product of its being known — the product of the knowing mind — became in the nineteenth century the groundwork for the elaborate structure of idealistic metaphysics that swallowed up both science and religion and everything else within an absolutistic framework. This metaphysics was generally congenial to religion although in a radically unorthodox way. Idealistic absolutism — the product in its formative stages of the German idealists Fichte, Schelling, and Hegel, and in its later maturity and declining era of the English-speaking idealists, especially Bosanquet, Bradley, and Josiah Royce — in effect appointed itself the philosophical patron of religion and wrapped its protective cloak around the religious tradition.[3]

Whatever justification there was for this presumption of religious proprietorship lay in the fundamental affinity of idealistic metaphysics for the religious conception of the world. It seemed obvious that if it is true that reality is of the nature of mind and rational process rather than matter and mechanism, religion in some basic and precious sense may be true, because such a universe should be congenial to God and the Soul, certainly more congenial than a

---

[3] F. H. Bradley, whose *Appearance and Reality* is the most closely reasoned and persuasive case for absolute idealism, was not a defender of religion in any conventional sense, but his logic and metaphysics were placed in the service of religious philosophy by others.

mechanistic, materialistic world. Idealism came equipped, moreover, with high technical skill in logic and a disposition and capacity to maneuver the concepts of science in the service of metaphysics, usually a metaphysics at least congenial to religion. Indeed, when the physical sciences broke through the nineteenth-century physical synthesis, with its rigorously deterministic implications and its presumption in favor of mechanistic materialism, idealists were in the forefront of those philosophers who declared that the new physics, with its electronic conception of matter, relativity, and quantum mechanics, spoke eloquently of the freedom, meaning, purpose, and divinity resident in the universe. Where for centuries it had been fashionable to believe in God because the universe has an orderly causal structure, for many philosophers and theologians who interpreted Heisenberg's Uncertainty Principle as proof of indeterminism, it now became evident that there is a God because the universe is *dis*orderly. At least disorderly because on the subatomic level it does not behave in the traditional manner prescribed by Newtonian physics.[4] Fortunately for their case, there was an ample supply of high-level scientific talent prepared to support the claim of indeterminacy in the world at the level of subatomic particles. Although many religionists having some degree of scientific and philosophical sophistication rushed to establish an alliance with science, among philosophers it was especially the idealists who found, or thought they found, support from the new physics. Indeed, many physical scientists, among them such eminent figures as Arthur S. Eddington, James Jeans, and Robert A. Milliken, found a ground in physical science for idealistic metaphysics that would support the claims of

---

[4] Virtually all works in the philosophy of science treat the uncertainty principle and the claims of indeterminacy which are based upon it. A brief description of the principle is found in Bertrand Russell's *Human Knowledge: Its Scope and Limits* (New York: Simon and Schuster, 1948), chap. 3. In his *Philosophical Foundations of Quantum Mechanics* (Berkeley and Los Angeles: University of California Press, 1944), Hans Reichenbach develops a three-valued logic on the basis of the idea of physical indeterminacy. In Reichenbach's view, propositions are of three logical types with indeterminateness added to the traditional values of truth and falsity (high or low probability).

religion at least to the extent of belief in a universal mind.[5] Sir James Jeans, writing in 1930, summarized the claim that physical science was moving toward metaphysical idealism:

> Today there is a wide measure of agreement, which on the physical side of science approaches almost to unanimity, that the stream of knowledge is heading towards a non-mechanical reality; the universe begins to look more like a great thought than like a great machine. Mind no longer appears as an accidental intruder into the realm of matter; we are beginning to suspect that we ought to hail it as the creator and governor of the realm of matter — not of course our individual minds, but the mind in which the atoms out of which our individual minds have grown exist as thoughts.[6]

But many religionists failed to recognize that at best Jeans's *mind* was hardly the God of religion. In the next paragraph he continued, "We discover that the universe shews evidence of a designing or controlling power that has something in common with our own individual minds — not, so far as we have discovered, emotion, morality, or aesthetic appreciation, but the tendency to think in the way which, for want of a better word, we describe as mathematical."[7] Like many modern physical scientists, Jeans was a Pythagorean for whom the world is essentially a mathematical phenomenon.

Idealism was commonly closely tied to religion in part because it provided a metaphysical foundation for human values and in part because along with its concern for the cosmic process it had a special interest in values and in the development of culture, human institutions, and human affairs. In this century's controversies over the value–fact issue, the question of the status of value judgments in relation to factual propositions — a matter of the most basic impor-

---

[5] See Arthur S. Eddington, *The Nature of the Physical World*, the Gifford Lectures for 1927 (New York: Macmillan Co., 1933).

[6] *The Mysterious Universe* (New York: Macmillan Co., 1937), p. 186.

[7] Ibid.; for a competent critique of the idealistic leanings of early twentieth-century physical scientists, see L. Susan Stebbing, *Philosophy and the Physicists* (1937; New York: Dover Publications, 1958).

tance to value theory — it has been mainly the idealists who have held, on both metaphysical and logical grounds, that values are facts.[8] Contrary to the pragmatists, who have in a sense inclined toward the position that facts are values, and contrary as well to the positivists, who have insisted on a rigorous fact/value bifurcation, many idealists have held that normative value judgments are in principle true or false. The compatibility of this position with the absolutistic ethics of typical religion is entirely obvious.[9]

But if idealism partially succeeded in protecting the foundations of religious philosophy from the onslaught of materialism, mechanism, and secularism, its kiss was the kiss of death for orthodoxy; for in subtle ways idealism provided much of the rational acid that inevitably eroded the traditional beliefs and creedal forms of the faith while it encouraged and underwrote the formation of the liberal spirit and much of the liberal scholarship that was to dominate the course of religion in the early decades of this century.

Several facets of idealism contributed to the decline of orthodoxy. There was the consuming interest in cultural history generated by the Hegelian philosophy, largely, it appears, because this history is a reading of the autobiography of the absolute in its more respectable phases. But nothing is more devastating to a religious orthodoxy than a close and comparative look at its own history, a serious attempt to discern its origins and reason and measure it against other orthodoxies. It was, to say the least, disconcerting to discover, for instance, that many of the supposedly unique elements in Christian beliefs were in various guises the common property of many and at times widely separated religions, or to uncover the mythical foundations

[8] For the idealistic position on the logical status of value judgments see Brand Blanshard, *Reason and Goodness* (1961), and Wilbur Urban, *Valuation: Its Nature and Laws* (1909).

[9] This is not to say that all idealists have employed their logic, epistemology, and metaphysics in support of religious philosophy in the traditional sense. Bradley, J. M. E. McTaggart, and the American philosopher Brand Blanshard are important exceptions. Among American idealists who have brought their philosophy to the support of religion are Josiah Royce, Borden Parker Bowne, William Ernest Hocking, Ralph Tyler Flewelling, and Edgar Sheffield Brightman.

of time-honored doctrines or to expose the often crude origins of traditional ritual.

The main impact of historical study was at the point of the biblical scholarship which combined literary with historical analysis in a serious effort to find out what was meant by what was written in the scriptures. For the most part the results were destructive of orthodoxy because the orthodox faith was too deeply rooted in a tradition of literal and verbal inspiration to withstand the shock of discovering such elementals as the documentary structure of the Pentateuch, the composite authorship of Isaiah, the interdependence of the Synoptics, or the apparent hellenistic character of the Fourth Gospel.

Another threat to orthodoxy from the idealistic camp was inevitably resident in the absolutistic character of all forms of Hegelianism. Both Christianity and Judaism were rooted in the biblical theism that demanded a rigorous ontological distinction between God and the world, the creator and the creatures, a distinction that demanded a large measure of transcendence in the description of God and set established religion in opposition to every threat of pantheism. Calvinism, which placed great stress on the moral sovereignty of God, ran the risk of deism by exaggerating its transcendentalism, but Lutheranism, in satisfying its subjective and mystical inclinations, held strongly to the immanence of God in the world. Its risk was the threat of pantheism, a pantheism that was eventually embraced in the German absolutistic metaphysics. In the metaphysical systems that issued from German idealism, God or the absolute included the totality of reality. Here all relations were internal to the divine nature, a concept which not only denied the ontological distance between God and his world that was so evident in the scriptures and so basic to the reformers, but that even compromised the concept of the divine personality. The very meaning of personality, whether human or divine, entails the possible reality of something other than a single person, an environment of at least another person.

Idealism was as heavily involved in the construction of liberalism as it was in the destruction of orthodoxy. Immanuel Kant had already subordinated religion to morals by declaring that religion is "the recognition of all duties as divine commands," and the chief

advocates of idealism repeatedly grounded religion in moral experience or even identified religion with morality. It was here that the
liberals, unable to accept the traditional doctrines but too possessed
by piety and sentiment to extricate themselves from their religious
inheritance, made their stand — on a positive affirmation of moral
religion. The liberal religion was a joint product of Enlightenment
philosophy and the romanticism of the idealists. With a militant
determination to salvage the moral message of religion, it rejected
the negative orientation of Christianity that was grounded in the
dogma of original sin and made the affirmative assessment of man
the foundation of the faith.

In Germany, where advanced religious and moral thought belonged to the universities, the liberal movement, which had a long
history especially in the development of Ritschlian and Friesian theology, was essentially academic, with little relevance to the churches
or to civic affairs. It was expressed through a multitude of scholarly
works, historical, exegetical, and theological, of which the writings of the great Berlin historian Adolf Harnack are representative.
Harnack's analysis of early Christian doctrine revealed the extent
of the intrusion of Greek metaphysics into Christian thought, while
his examination of the meaning of Christianity celebrated the moral
teachings of the Gospels to the subordination or exclusion of matters
of doctrine.[10] The extent of the liberalization effected by German
scholarship is indicated by Schweitzer's complaint that the obvious
eschatological character of the Gospels had been denied and a distorted portrait of Jesus had been drawn on the lines of an upstanding
nineteenth-century Christian liberal.[11]

In America, where religious thought has been less academic and
closer to the life of the church, the liberal religion combined with
democratic social conscience to produce a religious demand for social
action. Embarrassed by both the eschatology of the New Testament
and the Pauline and Johannine doctrine of Christ as Savior, the

---

[10] See especially Adolf Harnack, *History of Dogma*, 7 vols., 1886–1890,
English trans. Neil Buchanan (London: Williams and Norgate, 1896).

[11] *The Quest of the Historical Jesus*, 1st German ed. 1906, English trans.
W. Montgomery (New York: Macmillan Co., 1961).

liberals attached themselves especially to the Old Testament prophetic religion in their efforts to secure the biblical foundations of
their faith. Unable to accept the Christian doctrine, they nevertheless sought and found inspiration in Christian origins.

Idealism has had a varied career in its courtship of American
religion. A secondhand Hegelianism done up in attractive literary
form by the New England transcendentalists played a prominent role
in delaying the development of a full-blown humanism in some
intellectual circles by directing the energies of intellectual and spiritual rebels toward a refined and more-or-less innocuous speculation
that was aesthetically satisfying and morally inspiring while still
enjoying a large measure of affiliation with the religious tradition.
When the real thing made its appearance at Harvard, however, in
the form of the technically argued absolute idealism of Josiah Royce,
America's pluralistic sensitivities were deeply offended. Royce struggled, especially in his 1899–1900 Gifford Lectures, *The World and
the Individual*, to preserve the individual from complete absorption
by the absolute, but his metaphysics elicited from William James
his most brilliant polemic — that by its very nature absolutism denies
the possibility of moral discrimination in human experience — and
generated his most stimulating religious doctrine — the finiteness of
God.[12] Here in James's pragmatism was a theology that should have
had a strong appeal for American religious liberals — radical, earthy,
in every way moral and practical, and with a deceptively empirical
odor gratifying to the methodologically sensitive.

The reality of evil in human experience, insisted James, is not
to be denied, either by a philosopher's absolute God who so totally
includes the world in his own being that moral distinctions are
unreal, or by the God of orthodox theology, who enjoys absolute
power over a world groaning with failure and suffering. The only
God worth our worship, says James, is a God who is in the midst of
the world's evil, struggling to overcome it, who conceivably may even
go down to failure but would not turn away from the sufferings of
his creatures. James's world was one in which human freedom,

---

[12] See William James, *Pragmatism* (1907), *Essays in Radical Empiricism*
(1912), and *A Pluralistic Universe* (1909).

human effort, and human achievement count for something in the total outcome of things. Supported by impressive arguments for a nominalistic and pluralistic metaphysics, his doctrine was easily the most important contribution of American philosophy to theology. It deserved a larger influence because it was probably in principle as near the truth as theism is likely to come. But James's philosophical descendants on his pragmatic side were naturalists, such as John Dewey and George Herbert Mead, who were devoted especially to the strengthening of the foundations of humanism, while on his realistic side they were psychologists and epistemologists who for the most part could not become excited over religion. The liberal religionists in the meantime, though not unaffected by pragmatism, lusted for the fleshpots of absolutism, determined to make it a case of all God or none. Like the orthodox, they found it impossible to place their trust in a finite deity who has problems of his own.

Neither James nor Royce, of course, held views compatible with orthodoxy. James made no pretense to defending Christianity, but had a strong commitment to theism and even a marked sympathy for mysticism. Royce, on the other hand, saw himself as a philosopher for Christianity with his concept of the community and religion as loyalty. His philosophy of religion, whose influence was largely academic, was concerned with such matters as guilt, atonement, and salvation, but its sophisticated idealistic formulation bears little resemblance to the traditional Christian doctrine.[13]

More successful with the clergy in America were the personalists, idealists of a somewhat pragmatic stripe, who had inherited the German idealistic tradition through Rudolf Hermann Lotze in Germany and Borden Parker Bowne at Boston University. More than any other person, Bowne gave to American liberal Protestantism a technical philosophical foundation of genuine intellectual strength. He and his philosophic offspring seized upon personality not only as the foundation of value but also as the key to the mysteries of reality. Convinced that only the reality of a personal God as the ground of

[13] See esp. *The Problem of Christianity*, with an introduction by John E. Smith (1968). Smith's introduction is a valuable treatment of Royce's philosophy of religion.

the world can adequately account for the data of experience, they offered at the same time a solution to the age-old metaphysical antinomies of unity and plurality and being and becoming, as well as a framework for theistic religion.[14] Always the personalists were plagued by the spectre of the absolute, but they devised various means for drawing its sting. Ralph Tyler Flewelling, a leading personalist, complained, "In my youth I was tarred with the Hegelian stick, and I have spent a lifetime getting it off." For Flewelling, as for most personalists, God, the creator and sustainer, has by his creative process imposed limitations upon himself, especially the limitation resulting from the reality of other free persons, and it is by these limitations that both natural and moral evil must be explained.[15] Edgar Sheffield Brightman, Bowne's other leading disciple, held the quite original idea that the source of both moral and natural evil is a "given" in the very constitution of God, an internal irrationality that God progressively struggles to overcome.[16] But in neither Flewelling's nor Brightman's metaphysics is there an environment that stands genuinely in opposition to God as in the theodicy of William James. They were too much under the spell of absolutism to settle for James's style of pluralism.

The personalistic movement was strong in Europe, especially in France, but it was less systematic, less committed to metaphysics and theology, certainly less affected by absolutism and more closely tied to existentialism than in America. The personalistic tradition of French thought, independently of the main thrust of French theology which has been a captive of organized religion, has a strong history back through Charles Renouvier and Maine de Biran at least to Pascal and extending in this century to Emmanuel Mounier and the Catholic existentialist Gabriel Marcel.[17] It is a tradition that opposes the entrapment of the individual person, his spiritual life, and his freedom in the web of a metaphysical system, either materi-

[14] Borden Parker Bowne, *Metaphysics* (1882), *Philosophy of Theism* (1887), *Personalism* (1908).

[15] See *Creative Personality* (1926), *The Person* (1952).

[16] See esp. Brightman's *A Philosophy of Religion* (1940).

[17] See Emanuel Mounier, *Le Personnalisme*, 2 vols. (1949).

alistic or idealistic. But neither French nor American personalism, despite the obvious affinity of both for the basic values of occidental religion, had an impact on general religious thought comparable to the existentialist movement that drew its inspiration especially from the nineteenth-century Danish theologian Sören Kierkegaard, to a lesser degree from Friedrich Nietzsche, and from such ancient sources as St. Augustine.

In the meantime, of course, other strong intellectual forces were at work in religion. Idealism, though the dominant influence, was simply the primary expression of the rationalistic philosophical tradition, while its personalistic offspring, especially in America, was more than anything else a revolt against the loss of personality and individualism in the absolutistic, idealistic metaphysical system. But in a world becoming increasingly conscious of the pitfalls of rationalistic method, there were already groping efforts to ground religion more adequately on experiential foundations, but usually with vague or ambiguous meanings for both experience and empirical method. Such attempts often yielded quite negative results, as in the extreme instance of the religious psychologism that had been served up by Ludwig Feuerbach, whose materialism was a left-wing inversion of Hegel's objective idealism. For Feuerbach, "God, considered in his moral or spiritual attributes . . . is nothing other than the deified and objectified mind or spirit of man," and theology is anthropology and physiology.[18] Sometimes those attempts were little more than scientifically grounded cosmological treatises saturated with piety, or mystery, or, more than anything else, with a mixture of mysticism and dogmatism. Often, however, they were competent efforts to establish the possibility of a natural theology, and always they expressed a serious interest in reconciling religion to the demands of an increasingly secularized culture or in establishing its independence and autonomy.

In his treatise *On the Bondage of the Will*, Luther, opposing Erasmus' rational and philosophic treatment of religion, had insisted that faith must be grounded in a nonintellectualistic apprehension

---

[18] *Lectures on the Essence of Religion* (1846), trans. Ralph Manheim (1967), Third Lecture, p. 21.

of God, in a religious experience that is independent of both speculative and moral considerations. This position was intensified by Schleiermacher in his *Addresses on Religion to Its Cultured Despisers*, where religion is conceived in the romantic style in terms of feeling. Intending to establish the autonomous life of religion, Schleiermacher nevertheless compromised the meaning of religion by declaring that its domain includes the entire gamut of feeling, for this made it difficult if not impossible to distinguish religion from art. As a good romantic, Schleiermacher was saturated with pantheism, and even in his later *Dogmatics*, where he limited religion to the feeling of dependence and did his best to preserve the redemptive character of Christianity, his thought was still permeated with ambiguity and far removed from the central power which had moved Christianity as a historical religion.

It remained for Rudolf Otto in our own century to adequately refine the Lutheran insight in his *Idea of the Holy*, possibly the most profound phenomenological analysis of religion since Augustine.[19] In an attempt to guarantee the full autonomy of religion, Otto identified it as a unique experience which is not a synthesis of non-religious elements but must be distinguished rigorously from science, art, and morality. For Otto, a religious a priori than which there is nothing more primary in experience is built into the structure of the human soul as a category of both meaning and value. Here is the immediate apprehension of the sacred in the experience of the numinous, a fearful compounding of mystery and awe that possesses the creature in the presence of the wholly other.

Drawing on the extensive data not only of both Testaments but also of worldwide religious biography, Otto employed ingenious talent in exploiting the technical Kantian analysis of subjective creativity and summarizing the labors of Augustine, Luther, Schleiermacher, Ritschl, Fries, and Troeltsch. He demanded recognition of the unique character of religion against the traditional tendencies to confuse it with metaphysics, art, or morals — tendencies found in both idealism and naturalism, as for instance in John Dewey's anal-

---

[19] *Idea of the Holy*, from *Das Heilige* (1917), trans. John W. Harvey (1923).

ysis of the religious as a quality that may characterize any experience whatsoever.[20] In exploiting the nonrational facet of religious experience, Otto struck a major blow against the dominant rationalistic tradition which had threatened the particular and the individual in religion and had diluted the character of religion as personal encounter while imposing upon it an architectonic of speculative ideas.

With the decline of scholasticism after the fourteenth century, a decline occasioned in part by the victories of nominalism and pantheism, into the nineteenth century Catholic thought, long characterized by an objective realism, was increasingly affected by independent and sporadic outbursts of idealism. But from late in that century, with Christianity seriously threatened by Hegelianism, materialism, and general cultural secularism, scholasticism, with its roots in Aristotelian and Thomistic realism, made rapid gains within Catholicism. In the 1879 encyclical *Aeterni Patris*, Pope Leo XIII established scholasticism as the chief foundation of Catholic thought and education, a position repeated by Pius X in 1907 in the encyclical *Pascendi Gregis*, which dealt a death blow to modernism among the Catholic clergy. In 1923 Thomism was again confirmed as the basis for Christian theology by the encyclical *Studiorem Ducem* of Pius XI.

Especially under the influence of Cardinal Mercier at Louvain, scholasticism was deliberately revived as an instrument for the reconciliation of religion and science through the construction of a realistic philosophical synthesis of the traditional realms of nature and grace together with a technical definition of the domain of revelation and the limitations of human reason. Its revival contributed greatly to the intellectual strength of the Church in its remarkable capacity to resist the onslaught of secularism, the modern subjectivisms, the new fundamentalism, and the historical disillusionment which followed the First World War. The Church has even demonstrated some capacity for encompassing within the Thomistic framework the outcroppings of a Catholic existentialism which have appeared especially in France, as in the work of Gabriel Marcel.[21]

[20] See John Dewey, *A Common Faith* (1934).

[21] See Marcel's *Metaphysical Journal* (1927), trans. Bernard Wall (1952), and *The Mystery of Being*, 2 vols., trans. G. S. Fraser and René Hauge (1950).

Jacques Maritain, foremost of the recent Catholic philosophers, has stood as an impressive bulwark against idealism and subjectivism as well as relativism and nominalism. His realism in both metaphysics and epistemology is a defense of an ordered structure of external reality which is discoverable by human reason and is the foundation of natural law, the objectivity of truth, and absolute value. Catholic doctrinal and sacramental orthodoxy, which long ago was accommodated to metaphysical support and protection, enjoys nothing but the best relationships with this neoscholastic realism. Even in the present anti-Thomistic stirrings in Catholic philosophy, influenced by existential thought as well as by current philosophical analysis, it is the process philosophy of Whitehead, a realistic metaphysics and epistemology directed to the problem of God's relation to the temporal world, that holds the largest promise of making effective inroads on Catholic scholasticism.

Realism in its several forms has appeared in many parts of the world in opposition to the subjectivism of the idealistic theory of knowledge — as a theory of logic freed from psychology and metaphysics, and as the metaphysical ground of value and science. Sometimes it has been cultivated as the rational foundation for religion, setting itself in vigorous opposition to idealism and pragmatism as well as traditional materialism. More often it has had a more effective affiliation with science than with religion. A forerunner of today's realism was the so-called common-sense philosophy that from the time of David Hume to the present dominated philosophic and religious thought in Scotland, the center of a long tradition of vigorous reform theology. The impact especially of Thomas Reid's criticisms of idealism was felt throughout the English-speaking world. Reid's philosophy was based on the contention that the mind is stocked with common-sense principles that provide a direct apprehension of the external world, the soul, and moral values. But realism did not achieve strength in England and America until the turn of the last century. Again it was mainly a reaction against the subjectivism and absolutism of idealism, a movement in league with empiricism and naturalism. The turn toward realism in American philosophy was prompted especially by William James's 1904 essay, "Does

Consciousness Exist?," which opposed the mind–matter dualism that had dominated philosophic thought since Descartes.

Realism was in many ways more congenial to the American temper than idealism. Less concerned with the subject and more with the object, less rationalistic and more empirical, less pious and more amenable to scientific findings, realism was often the ground for a religious philosophy for the unchurched who saw or thought they saw in idealism an epistemology and metaphysics outmoded by science and outraging common-sense, still clinging on tenaciously through the machinations of its logic long after it should have forfeited its proprietary hold over the spiritual life. Yet American realism as a technical philosophy was for the most part naturalistic and made few constructive contributions to theism.[22]

A most notable exception was the work of William Pepperell Montague, who perpetuated both the finitistic theology and sympathy for mysticism of his teacher, William James. But Montague, who was one of the original "six realists" of the New Realism, was strongly opposed to institutionalized religion and unfortunately had little impact upon it. A lovable dissident, Montague held that Christian orthodoxy is essentially a life-denying affair. For him all churches looked more or less alike, and all were devoted primarily to the obstruction of human happiness. All of them failed to grasp fully the positive factors in human experience and aspiration, so engulfed were they by their concern for sin and redemption.[23]

Somewhat more acceptable in liberal circles was the work of the Canadian–American realist Douglas Clyde Macintosh, who suffered from a chronic unhappiness over the fact that much Protestantism

[22] I have in mind here the thought of those in American philosophy who are commonly regarded as realists rather than the movement in theology which is often described as religious realism, as in the case of Walter M. Horton. There are important exceptions, such as the Swedish-American philosopher John Elof Boodin, and, of course, Jacques Maritain and Alfred North Whitehead, whose later lives were spent in this country and whose views are treated in this essay.

[23] Montague's religious ideas are best expressed in his *Belief Unbound* (1930) and "Confessions of an Animistic Materialist" in *The Ways of Things* (1940).

had, with Kantian agnosticism, abandoned the claim to religious knowledge and accepted faith as the basis for religion. Macintosh devoted his years to the elaboration of a unique realistic theory of knowledge which combined the monistic elements of the New Realism with the dualistic epistemology of Critical Realism to produce what he, and few others, regarded as a puncture-proof, empirically grounded theory accounting for a genuine knowledge of God. God, the object of religious knowledge, he held, can be known with as much certitude as the objects of science and by the same empirically grounded method.

The realism of England was associated with logic, psychology, and philosophical analysis; and through the work of Bertrand Russell, Alfred North Whitehead, Samuel Alexander, G. E. Moore, and others, it contributed importantly not only to the technical foundations of metaphysics but as well to the philosophy of science. As for religion, Bertrand Russell is perhaps without peer among its more brilliant, though sometimes superficial, critics. But Russell's criticism of religion has little relevance to his technical philosophy. It is more a critique generated by a naturalistic temperament than a technically argued case. Alexander's work is an excellent example of that combination of evolutionism, religious liberalism, and physical science which produced in the English-speaking world so many cosmologies touched with emotion. There may be some truth in Russell's quip that the divinity was included in the title of Alexander's *Space, Time and Deity* to enable its author to qualify as a Gifford lecturer, because certainly he (or it) bears virtually no resemblance to the deity to whom Judaeo-Christian religion had become accustomed. God, for Alexander, is simply the next step ahead in the course of cosmic emergent evolution. But Alexander's work, a most distinguished metaphysical treatise, symbolizes the degree of departure from the traditional meanings of religion to which modern philosophy has at times been willing to accommodate the concept of deity.

Something of this is encountered in the theological constructions of Alfred North Whitehead, certainly one of the most creative minds ever devoted to the rational justification of religion. In his 1925 Lowell Lectures, *Science and the Modern World*, Whitehead had written that Aristotle's metaphysical thought "did not lead him very far towards the production of a God available for religious purposes" (p. 249). Having apparently satisfied his earlier interests as mathematician, logician, and philosopher of science, to the consternation of his more cautious friends and the delight of the more literate religionists everywhere, who more than welcomed such eminent support, Whitehead set himself the task of succeeding where Aristotle had failed. But his friend and early colleague Bertrand Russell was among the more dubious. In 1926 Russell commented on Whitehead's thesis that God is a metaphysical principle: "I must confess with regret that I have failed to understand Professor Whitehead's argument on this important subject, and, speaking generally, I cannot persuade myself that his logical reconstruction of physical concepts has any such tendency as he attributes to it, to restore the consolations of religion to a world desolated by mechanism."

Whitehead's 1929 Gifford Lectures, *Process and Reality*, were his most thorough treatment of philosophical theology. His cosmology, grounded in a dynamic organic conception of reality, requires a highly sophisticated metaphysical concept, God's *Primordial* nature, to account for the universe being what it is instead of what it isn't. So far, however, as Whitehead's critics have pointed out, there is little reason for believing that this philosopher's God listens to anyone's prayers or takes the slightest interest in ecclesiastical affairs. Besides, there is the problem of whether he is the creator of evil. To solve this problem, Whitehead had discovered an entirely new side of God's nature, his *Consequent* nature, describing him now as the creator of good and the conserver of value.[24] Here, of course, is the God of religion, who indeed saves the world but saves it mainly by regarding it as an object of aesthetic delight. To confront the problem of evil, Whitehead described God in relation to good and evil as finite, opposing with the most vigorous language the idea of a creator of absolute power:

> Among medieval and modern philosophers, anxious to establish the religious significance of God, an unfortunate habit has prevailed of paying to Him metaphysical compliments. He has been conceived as the foundation of the metaphysical situation

[24] *Process and Reality* (New York: Macmillan Co., 1941), pp. 523–33.

with its ultimate activity. If this conception be adhered to, there can be no alternative except to discern in Him the origin of all evil as well as of all good.[25]

But there still remains the question of God's relation to the supreme values of the individual finite person, whether even in his finiteness our moral values are his concern. "The teleology of the Universe," he wrote in 1933, "is directed to the production of Beauty. Thus any system of things which in any wide sense is beautiful is to that extent justified in its existence. . . . Beauty is left as the one aim which by its very nature is self-justifying. . . . The real world is good when it is beautiful." [26] The question is whether our world, the world of individual persons, is really the real world, and whether Whitehead's treatment of the problem of evil and suffering is not basically a transmutation of moral into aesthetic distinctions. All in all, nevertheless, Whitehead's God is available for some rather unorthodox purposes, but it is not at all clear that his more available side is an implicate of the data of experience rather than the product of his author's piety and religious disposition. But whatever the verdict of time in judging his religious metaphysics, it is not likely that the defense of religion will attract a greater intellectual talent than that of Whitehead.

Contemporaneous with the work of Whitehead was that of the Cambridge theologian Frederick R. Tennant, who erected on essentially realistic foundations perhaps the most impressively constructed empirically- and scientifically-oriented rational theology. Tennant examined with minute care not only the foundations of knowledge and the nature of causation, natural law, and scientific explanation, but also the concepts basic to classical theism: creation, eternity, infinitude, the divine personality, evil, perfection, and revelation. And though far removed from orthodoxy, he concluded that a careful control of the data of experience justifies intellectual assent to the existence of a God not unlike the God of the religious tradition.

[25] *Science and the Modern World* (New York: Macmillan Co., 1927), p. 258.

[26] *Adventures of Ideas* (New York: Macmillan Co., 1933), pp. 341–42, 345.

That justification is essentially a teleological argument. Of Tennant's great work, the *Philosophical Theology* (published in 1928 and 1930), Britain's scientifically-minded C. D. Broad wisely wrote, "If a system of speculative philosophy cannot be established by Dr. Tennant's method, I agree that it is still less likely to be established by any other. . . . Dr. Tennant's method at least ensures those who use it against nonsense, enthusiasm, and credulity; it leads to a form of theism which is intellectually and morally respectable and in practice inoffensive . . . ."

Reinhold Niebuhr's *Moral Man and Immoral Society* was published in 1932. It was the beginning of a brilliant, sustained polemic against liberalism which kept him thereafter in the center of religious thought and action in America and which has played a major role in the reevaluation of liberalism and the redirection of Protestant thought along more traditional lines if not toward actual orthodoxy. Disillusioned by the failure of religion to move society toward genuine social justice and convinced that the liberal conception of man fails utterly to assess the essential egoism in human nature and the complex demonic forces in history, Niebuhr declared that in liberalism Christianity had sold its soul to the secular culture, duped by the belief in the redemptive process of human history — a process, it was claimed by the liberals, that steadily and inevitably moves man toward whatever goals are worth achieving. Embarrassed by the Christian belief in a unique revelation and the doctrine of original sin, and by the absolute moral demands of the gospel, modern man, said Niebuhr, placed his faith in the progressive revelation of history and, with pride in his reason and his moral perfectibility, denied his creaturely contingency and limitations. Niebuhr insisted that it is in the biblical Christian view which places sin at the center of the self that the truth about man and his world is to be found, as it is only by a miraculous transhistorical gift of salvation that redemption comes.[27]

[27] See esp. his *Moral Man and Immoral Society* (1932); *Reflections on the End of an Era* (1934); *Beyond Tragedy; Essays on the Christian Interpretation of History* (1937); *The Nature and Destiny of Man*, 2 vols. (1941 & 1943); *Faith and History; A Comparison of Christian and Modern Views of History* (1949).

The anti-liberal return to a form of biblical orthodoxy or near-orthodoxy within the context of sophisticated thought and scholarship was already well established in Europe when it took root in America. In Europe it was clearly a crisis theology produced more than anything else by the destruction and disillusionment of the First War. Best expressed by Karl Barth, who was dominated by the Calvinistic dogma of the divine sovereignty and who undertook to reestablish religion on the indisputable word of God, it was an anti-philosophical, anti-scientific, anti-cultural movement that reveled in paradox, dogmatics, and subjectively interpreted revelation.[28] Human nature, declared Barth, echoing the reformers and, he believed, Paul's Epistle to the Romans, is in every way perverted, and human reason and all cultural achievements are grounded in sin. Under the impact of the depression of the thirties, Barthianism became influential in the English-speaking world, but whatever its appeal in a world that was anxious to retreat from reason, common sense, and faith in itself, it lost heavily when Barth refused to lead continental Protestantism in a commitment against the threatening spectre of Communist power. It was a repetition of the neutral stand he had taken in the early days of Nazism, declaring that the gospel of Jesus Christ is irrelevant to the temporal problems of men and the course of human history. A more moderate, less anti-philosophical defense of the new orthodoxy than Barth's was that of the Swiss theologian Emil Brunner, whose dialectical theology had important similarities to Barth's. Dialectical theology held the theological paradoxes, such as the contradiction of God's will with the reality of evil, to be indicative of the insufficiency of philosophical reason to replace the personal encounter of revelation as the foundation of religion and theology.[29]

The anti-liberal movement, of course, has been culture-wide; it is in no way confined to religion. Its chief, but by no means only, philosophical expression is existentialism, the technical outlines of

[28] See Barth's *The Epistle to the Romans,* trans. 1933; *Church Dogmatics,* trans. 1936.

[29] See Brunner's *The Christian Doctrine of God,* trans. Olive Wyon (1949); *Man in Revolt,* trans. Olive Wyon (1939); *The Philosophy of Religion,* trans. A. J. D. Farrer and B. L. Woolf (1937).

which were constructed in Germany amid the ruins of the First War on foundations laid by the nineteenth-century Danish theologian Sören Kierkegaard and the philosophical poet Friedrich Nietzsche.[30]

Existentialism is a philosophy of the human predicament. It cares nothing about things but only about the honest facts of existence — freedom, decision, hope, frustration, and death. The liberals were optimistic, it says, because in their high intellectualism they dealt only in abstractions and generalities; they knew man only as a universal, as a species, or as human society. But nothing important ever really happens to these, because they don't authentically exist. Liberalism knows nothing of the individual: the universal is an intellectual figment; the species goes on forever; society survives indefinitely; but the individual, the truly existential reality, lives the dreadful life of moral freedom, suffers anguish, and dies.

Existentialism drew heavily on psychoanalytic theory and the new developments in depth psychology, all of which encouraged it in its creation of a vigorously negative conception of man and the human condition. It is here, of course, that it made its appeal to anti-liberal theology. They were two of a kind and in various ways and in varying degrees they joined hands to attempt a clean sweep of liberalism and reestablish sin at the center of the religious consciousness and theological doctrine.[31]

A major intellectual interest of the twentieth century has been the analysis of meaning, an investigation which has moved in many directions and has had a varied impact on religion. In the hands of logicians and radical empiricists, for instance, it resulted in the logi-

---

[30] See Kierkegaard's *Either/Or*, 2 vols.; vol. 1 trans. D. F. Swenson and L. M. Swenson (1941), and vol. 2 trans. Walter Lowrie (1944); *Fear and Trembling*, trans. Walter Lowrie (1941); *The Concept of Dread*, trans. Walter Lowrie (1944); *Concluding Unscientific Postscript*, trans. Walter Lowrie (1941); and Neitzsche's *Thus Spoke Zarathustra, Beyond Good and Evil*, and *Toward a Genealogy of Morals*.

[31] See Mary Frances Thelen, *Man as Sinner in Contemporary American Realistic Theology* (1946), for a useful discussion of this movement. *Types of Modern Theology: Schleiermacher to Barth*, by Hugh Ross Mackintosh (1937), contains a valuable treatment of the rise of neo-orthodoxy in its chapters on Kierkegaard and Barth.

cal positivism that denied the cognitive meaningfulness of the fundamental propositions of cultured theology. The positivistic critique of theology — which was based upon a rigorous criterion of factual meaningfulness that denies the possibility of any substantive metaphysics — was in principle the severest blow yet received in the attempt to construct an intellectual foundation for religion. It is no doubt far less discomposing to be told that one's philosophy is false than that it doesn't make any sense.[32]

There was, however, an important positive impact on religious thought effected by the logical and linguistic analysis of meaning, the impact of a large concern for the nature and the uses of signs and symbols. In several philosophers of great stature, notably Charles S. Peirce, Alfred North Whitehead, and Ernst Cassirer, the role of signs and symbols in the life of man and his culture was examined on a profound level, and the result for conservative religion was genuinely encouraging.[33] This inspired a great devotion to many of the religious forms of the past which had been branded as outmoded by liberalism and encouraged the neo-orthodox to look with some favor on symbolic formulations which could be interpreted to mean what the original users often did not intend; it also justified them in much of their obscurantism. All of this was convenient and useful for persons who were returning to what they regarded as truths of the Bible too profound to be articulated in straightforward language and were therefore properly set forth by the biblical myths.

[32] A. J. Ayer's *Language, Truth and Logic* is a classic statement of the positivist position on metaphysics, theology, and ethics; see the second ed., 1946. Rudolf Carnap's *The Logical Syntax of Language*, trans. Amethe Smeaton (1937), is the most important single technical work setting forth the logical foundations of logical positivism. Ludwig Wittgenstein's *Tractatus Logico-Philosophicus*, in German and English (1922), was an important background for the work of the Viennese Circle in developing the groundwork of positivism, as were the logical writings of Bertrand Russell.

[33] See the *Collected Papers of Charles Sanders Peirce*, ed. Charles Hartshorne and Paul Weiss (1931–35); a useful collection of Peirce's work in one volume is *The Philosophy of Peirce: Selected Writings*, ed. Justus Büchler (1940). See also Ernst Cassirer's *An Essay on Man* (1944); *The Philosophy of Symbolic Forms*, 3 vols., trans. Ralph Manheim (1953–57).

It was useful especially for those who believed the Bible but did not believe much of what was written in it. With these theologians myth is again having its innings — not myth confused with history, but myth as expressive of meanings not otherwise adequately expressible.

Paul Tillich was an existentialist of uncommon talents who brought the findings of depth psychology to his fundamentalistic description of human existence and, with extensive scholarly and philosophic erudition, imbued the whole affair with a rough semblance of Christian orthodoxy by a sophisticated employment of symbolism and myth. No believer in the Garden of Eden, he yet believed profoundly in what he regarded as the truth of the story, that man in his existential predicament is fallen from his true nature and is estranged from God, from the world, from his fellowmen, and from the ground of his own being. In this fallen condition he suffers the anxieties which are inevitably engendered by his consciousness of his own finiteness, his ontological contingency which renders him totally dependent in his being and precarious in his existence — the anxieties of the meaninglessness of life, the inevitability of moral guilt, and the constant presence of impending death.[34] Redemption is possible, but not through human history — rather by the divine miracle of saving grace.

Unlike Barth, Tillich was not anti-philosophical nor did he attempt to abstract religion from the context of culture and history. His doctrine has both intellectual strength and prophetic vigor, and if he is mentioned with the neo-orthodox, his orthodoxy consisted more in his unliberal concept of man than in his concept of God; for in spite of his biblical pretensions, Tillich's God is not the God of the biblical tradition; he is not a personal living being. He isn't *a* being of any kind. He is simply *Being* itself.[35]

Tillich, who died in 1965, was the last of the major theologians of this century, a theologian whose thought is a remarkable com-

---

[34] See esp. the section on Types of Anxiety in *The Courage To Be* (1952) and the section The Marks of Man's Estrangement and the Concept of Sin in vol. 2 of *Systematic Theology* (1957).

[35] See *Systematic Theology*, vol. 1 (1951), part 2, Being and God, 2B, The Actuality of God.

plex of scholarship, piety, philosophy, liberalism, and heresy. His thoroughly unorthodox Christianity combined with his existentialism and biblical faith to produce a theology which on a high intellectual plane exemplifies the present state of sophisticated theology — an attempt to sound the depths of religion and religious belief by employing the experience and wisdom of the past in combination with the analytical tools of the present.

The major trends in the development of modern religion which eventuated in the liberalism of the first half of this century involved much more than technical philosophy. Perhaps the primary factor in that process was the rationalism which first achieved articulate expression in the deism of the Enlightenment and thereafter effected the attempted accommodation to the sciences which characterized the career of much religion in the nineteenth century. Enlightenment religion was at once an Arminian revolt against the Calvinist orthodoxy, with its doctrines of absolute divine sovereignty and divine election; a declaration of the autonomy of reason; and an affirmation of the positive worth of man. Historically it was inseparable from those forces that produced the early modern culture of which it was integrally a part and with which also it must be in some measure identified: the scientific spirit, method, and knowledge; the increasing hegemony of the middle class and the competitive spirit of the capitalistic economy; the revolt against aristocratic authority, both civil and ecclesiastical; and the broadening intellectual and cultural horizons which invited change and reform and encouraged an imperious faith in the future. The Enlightenment demanded a religion of nature and reason, one that recognized the universe of law and order, squared with the new physical science, hated ignorance, superstition, and tyranny in all their forms, and enjoined virtue in obedience to the moral law. The nineteenth-century extension of the Enlightenment effected a refinement in natural religion and rational theology which was produced by the impact of the particular sciences, notably physics and biology, and of scientific disciplines of peculiar importance to religion, especially comparative and historic anthropology and biblical literary-historical criticism. In the first decades of the twentieth century the refining process was intensified by the impact on religion of descriptive psychology and normative sociology. The former influence gave theology and religious philosophy that intellectual respectability which is achieved only through an intimate association with science and respect for its methodology; the latter gave a rational interpretation to religion as psychological and social fact and encouraged its commitment to the improvement of society.

But infusions of reason and science by no means tell the whole story of the growth of liberalism in religion. Despite its obvious attractiveness, Enlightenment deism was satisfying to only a comparative few, and for most of these, serious religious thought was at best only incidental to a primary interest in physics, politics, or social theory. The creation of the liberalism that achieved its maturity in our own time depended as well on that second basic factor in the growth of modern thought, which was frequently an enemy of reason, namely, the spirit of romanticism, which, though generated on the continent, permeated American religion and philosophy both indirectly through English poetry and directly through French social philosophy and German idealistic metaphysics.

The sensitive romantics refused to accept the world of either the orthodox or the deists. To orthodoxy they opposed unitarianism; against the transcendent creator of deism, they set the immanent God of theism; to science they opposed poetry; against sensory empiricism they championed intuitive imagination; the natural world they denied, ignored, or consumed in pantheism as the temporal yielded to the eternal; to the search for truth and goodness they added the quest for beauty; against mechanical determinism they championed creative freedom; personal mystic communion replaced rational theology; knowledge ceased to be description and became creative process; and reason yielded to faith. The rebellious romantics created the world of their hearts' desire.

Now, it was the interplay of rationalism and romanticism, here contending and there cooperating, which defined the general development of religion and theology into the present century. These functioned not as abstract intellectual disciplines only, but as expressions of a genuine interrelationship of philosophic thought with the complex milieu of personal experience and social process as well, the whole inspired and directed by a growing moral consciousness. The end product was liberal religion, that complex of attitudes, ideas, and actions which future historians must recall as one of the highest, most heroic, and perhaps most tragic expressions of the human ideal.

It is religion as thus defined in terms of reason, creativeness, and the positive worth of man which has been under fire in our century. As an optimistic faith in the perfectibility of human nature and human society it received a death blow in Europe at the hands of the First World War. The comfortable circumstances of America's middle class sustained it in this country for more than a decade, but with the economic depression of the thirties and the Second War, together with the more recent wars and the disheartening failures attending the efforts to establish the peace, it has suffered a severe disintegration. We have been losing that faith in ourselves and in our powers of reason to discover and solve our problems which for some time appeared to be a chief glory of modern occidental culture.

An examination of the causes of the decline of liberalism reveals several important factors. There never was a unified liberal faith. Rather it existed in varying degrees, ranging from a half-hearted orthodoxy on the one hand to a reluctant humanism on the other, while its form and content were determined variously by the diverse temperaments and several interests of its advocates. Biblical criticism, concern for the historical Jesus, the social gospel, social psychology, natural science, technical metaphysics, historical criticism, and later medical psychology, each produced a phase of liberalism. The philosophical defense of liberal religion was primarily by the grace of the idealists, but among its advocates realists and pragmatists were not wanting. The strength of the faith was its unity of spirit and purpose. The absence of unity in method and content was a source of richness but has contributed to liberalism's comparatively low resistance to the onslaught of practical adversity. Moreover, the masses of religious persons were at most only indirectly affected by the liberal faith, and the fundamentalist forces organized with skill and determination and did not fail to seize every opportunity to generate a revival of orthodoxy.

On the other hand, the humanists, who had surrendered entirely the basic categories of traditional religion, abandoning faith in God in favor of a naturalistic interpretation of man and his universe, cultivated an even more positive and aggressive program of human action. They, with the general though indirect support of secularized public education, made a vigorous appeal to the liberals to accept the conclusions of their own logic, muster the courage of their convictions, and declare themselves free from the religion of the past which still held them in its embrace.

But a factor of far more significance than these, one which has set for liberal religion much of its problem, has been the spirit of self-criticism which has been articulated within its own ranks. It is the recognition of grave intrinsic deficiencies in the liberal doctrines themselves, deficiencies which were made evident by the stern realities of war and economic and social chaos in an age of science, education, and suffrage. The most radical among the critics in American theology followed the European irrationalists, though haltingly, in the creation of a new orthodoxy designed to correct the ills of the liberal faith. A new era has dawned in Western culture, was the claim, an era which demands a more realistic theology and more genuine spirituality. Liberalism with its optimistic faith in man was shallow and superficial in its failure to recognize the egoism, selfishness, and sinfulness which characterize human nature; its happy hopes for human society were naïve failures to face the political and social realities which now are so evident to all; its easy doctrine of progress was the pleasant illusion that good will, education, and the sciences could deliver men from the social evils that must take their toll in bloody suffering; the liberal faith in a pleasant finite God failed to assess the demonic in human history and the utter tragedy of human existence. So the liberal walked with an easy conscience, enlightened, naïve, and innocent.

No one who faces these charges candidly can deny that they were not entirely groundless. In becoming intellectually respectable and socially responsible, liberal religion lost much in spiritual dynamic and moral depth. But now what are the options? Can there be a return to the fundamentalism which substitutes the authority of creeds for the autonomy of reason, legend for history, and myth for science? Or can one follow the path of the neo-orthodox and declare anew the absolute sovereignty of God and the depravity of man and construct the entire edifice of religion upon a groundwork of irrational faith in indifference to science and philosophy? Or, with the humanists, is one to declare religion in the traditional sense a remnant of the past, pleasant in certain respects, but untrue, and unfitted either to the intellect of modern man or to the manifold practical problems to which he must now turn himself in the new spirit of science?

A return to fundamentalism is a turning of one's back on the human advancement which through generations of the most arduous toil has delivered men from the bondage of superstition and ignorance and the grip of moral and spiritual servitude. To declare with the new orthodoxy is to confess frustration and despair and in defeat to place the dead hand of the past upon the culture to hasten its day of doom. To abandon all vestiges of the traditional faith and settle for a naturalistic humanism is a more inviting alternative; the atmosphere, if thinner, is yet purer, and the call to thought and action clear and definitive. But humanism is a denial of the highest hope of the human heart, a confession, to borrow the language of Professor Montague, that the voice of God which men had so often strained to hear was nothing but the ghostly echo of their own feeble and despairing cries.

Or is it possible that liberal religion possesses the powers necessary to its own resurgence; that it can preserve those elements of enduring value which it helped to create — the respect for experience, the search for truth, the demand for theoretical knowledge and social righteousness, the positive affirmation of man — and combine these with a more satisfactory metaphysics and psychology, a more realistic social and political analysis, and a deeper spiritual and moral insight, to produce a religion adequate to the challenge of the future?

That a renascence of what is basically liberal religion is a possibility is the implicit claim of the new "process theology," of which the American philosopher Charles Hartshorne is the most original, creative, and interesting representative. The process theology is attractive not only to Protestant theologians but also to many of those Catholic philosophers and theologians who find the Aristotelian-based metaphysics of Aquinas too deeply rooted in the nontemporal and impersonal categories of Greek thought to satisfy the religious requirements on the nature of God and his relation to the world and humankind. It continues the tradition that insists on a rational grounding of religious faith and belief and is in effect a liberal theistic reply to the strong trends toward humanism and neo-orthodoxy of the past half century. It seems to me that in its attempt to preserve a meaningful theism by redefining the conception of God, as an incidental matter the process theology largely disposes of the basic arguments of the recently popular death-of-God theology.

Hartshorne, who was an associate of Whitehead, recognizes that the basic weakness of the traditional classical conception of God is rooted in its uncritical absolutism and its eternalism which destroys the possibility of a theology that relates God to the world, especially to the human moral will, in the personal relationship meaningful to religion. In his impressive study *Man's Vision of God and the Logic of Theism* (1941), with uncommon insight and logical skill he formulated three theological alternatives, which he called "the formally possible doctrines." By critical analysis he disposed of the first and third, leaving the second as the only acceptable theology:

    I. There is a being in *all* respects absolutely perfect or unsurpassable, in no way and in no respect surpassable or perfectible. . . .

    II. There is no being in all respects absolutely perfect; but there is a being in *some* respect or respects thus perfect, and in some respect or respects not so, in some respects surpassable, whether by self or others being left open. Thus it is not excluded that the being may be relatively perfect in all the respects in which it is not absolutely perfect.

    III. There is no being in *any* respect absolutely perfect; all beings are in all respects surpassable by something conceivable, perhaps by others or perhaps by themselves in another state.

Hartshorne's theism (the Second Type), which he sometimes calls panentheism, is an attempt to define a position that preserves whatever is worth preserving in absolutism while accepting those relativistic factors essential to relating God to the world, and preserves the eternal values while seeking to find and cultivate them in the temporal order. It is an attempt to define being as becoming, as a process rather than something unchangeable, and to see God, therefore, not as the changeless, impassive, eternal absolute of the classical theism, but as living process and experience. Nothing that is genuinely real, Hartshorne holds, following the Law of Polarity enunciated by Morris Cohen, "Can be described by the wholly one-sided assertion of simplicity, being, actuality, and the like, each in a 'pure' form, devoid and independent of complexity, becoming, potentiality, and related contraries." [36] Both pantheism and the classical theism have adopted the one-sided position of absolutism without providing an adequate hearing for pluralism and change. But, insists Hartshorne, excellence is not to be found at only one pole of the polarity — God, for instance, is both active and passive, both one and many, both cause and effect, both actuality and potentiality, both eternal and temporal. Unless God is described in such an absolute–relative way, he cannot be conceived both as supreme being and the object of religious worship.

Hartshorne's philosophical theology, which exhibits the influence of the nineteenth-century German philosopher Gustav Fechner as well as of James and especially Whitehead, should be taken seriously by anyone who hopes for a strengthening of the rational ground of religion at a time when religion is sinking rapidly into irrationalism. His analysis has genuine logical strength and is supported by extensive studies in the history of both theology and philosophy. The James–Whitehead–Hartshorne theology may well provide the possibility for liberal religion to establish that it is not simply the route of an inevitable transition from orthodoxy to naturalistic humanism, that it is a religion of both faith in God and faith in man.

[36] *Philosophers Speak of God*, with W. L. Reese (Chicago, 1953), p. 2.

4

The Primary Forms of Religion in Judaeo-Christian Culture

The general study of religion entails the consideration of a vast confusion of sentiments, behaviors, symbols, and ideas whose very complexity makes description difficult and comparative and critical judgment hazardous. In this essay I intend to simplify the examination of religion in Judaeo-Christian culture by developing an elementary explanatory classification of its basic types. The format of this classification should facilitate the exposition of the primary facts of religion and provide a convenient basis for the analysis of the more common occidental religious forms, both theistic and nontheistic.

Depending upon the purposes and range of a study, the grounds for the classification of religions may extend from the concept of God or the doctrine of salvation to such facets of religion as the meaning of the sacraments or ecclesiastical polity. I will employ here the concept of human nature and the predicament of human beings, commonly referred to as the doctrine of man, as an especially useful principle of classification. The concept of man and the human predicament is a central factor in all occidental theology and religious philosophy and is basic to the character of religion in both its devotional and moral aspects. It can usefully serve, therefore, in the study of religion, whether as a critical analysis of theology or a phenomenological description of religious experience and behavior. This concept has both experiential meaning and immediate relevance to the qualities of the religious life, and it can be employed effectively for the classification of both theistic and nontheistic religions.

In employing the concept of man in the description of religion, I will make reference to the doctrine of man as an individual and as society, and to the doctrine of man as a natural being and as a being whose ultimate ground is supernatural.

The concept of man as a natural being refers to man described as a part of the natural order of the material spatio-temporal world, the world of ordinary experience, man as a possible object of scientific inquiry, as involved in the social and historical process. I have designated this concept of man as a natural being the *proximate* doctrine of man.

The conception of man as supernatural indicates that the natural character of man does not exhaust the fullness of his being, that he is immortal spirit as well as matter, eternal as well as temporal, and that his destiny is not fully encompassed by this life or by human history. This concept of man as a supernatural being, involved with nature but not defined totally by it, I have designated the *ultimate* doctrine of man.

Two related concepts are now added to the foregoing: *pessimism* and *optimism*. I will call a theory or doctrine of man *pessimistic* when its descriptions of the character and condition of man are fundamentally negative, especially when it denies the possibility of the achievement of genuine values by human effort. I will call a doctrine of man *optimistic* if its descriptions of the character and predicament of man are fundamentally positive in that it affirms the possibility of the achievement of authentic values by human effort.

The concepts indicated yield four logically possible combinations. These combinations define the four primary forms of religion in Judaeo-Christian culture. They are: (1) *Orthodoxy*, the conjunction of proximate pessimism with ultimate optimism; (2) *Liberalism*, the conjunction of proximate optimism with ultimate optimism; (3) *Hu-*

manism, the conjunction of proximate optimism with ultimate pessimism; and (4) *Existentialism*, the conjunction of proximate pessimism with ultimate pessimism.* The descriptions which follow will define these type names with more precision even though they are used here at the price of considerable ambiguity.

The four primary forms of religion indicated by this classification are not in any sense exact descriptions of actual religious systems. On the contrary, they are ideal constructions prescribing the logical possibilities of religion when defined by a single isolated factor, the doctrine of man. Living institutions never conform exactly to the theoretic structures employed in their classification or analysis. Religion is an affair of life and faith, not of logic, and even the most rigorous theological constructions are alarming in their inconsistencies. But the descriptions to be given are generalizations on religious beliefs and religious phenomena and, although inadequately, together they disclose broadly the character of religious thought and practice in Judaeo-Christian culture. The result is severe oversimplification, but simplification is necessary in any attempt to control an otherwise unmanageable body of materials. All efforts at cultural or historical classification and analysis result in gross distortions of the factual data and their relationships and yield results that at best are properly subject to continual reexamination and correction.

II

ORTHODOXY

Orthodoxy, the meeting of *proximate pessimism* with *ultimate optimism*, defines the general character of traditional, conservative religions of redemption. In its more extreme forms, especially in

---

* My use of the term "Orthodoxy" here is subject to objection. I originally employed the word "Fundamentalism," but was justifiably criticized for using a twentieth-century term coined to identify a religion of simplistic biblical literalism in designating the classical form of Christianity. "Orthodoxy" seems adequate when employed with reference to Christianity, both Catholic and Protestant, but of course it does not fit Judaism, where "orthodoxy" refers especially to observance of the Law and where a positive doctrine of man prevails generally. Moreover, in this essay, of course, "Orthodoxy" is not intended as a reference to *Orthodox* or *Eastern* Christianity.

Augustine, the Jansenists, Luther and Calvin, and the modern "fundamentalists," its negative concept of human nature describes man the individual as both sinful and helpless; by nature he is depraved and morally corrupt, his mind and will at enmity with God. In his debasement he is powerless to will the good; in his helplessness he despairs of all possibility of moral merit for his soul's salvation.

At least in those extreme forms, Orthodoxy gives an equally dark description of human society. The selfish, egocentric, sensuous, irrational, impulsive drives of the individual guarantee the eventual failure of every human effort to create a genuinely good society that will provide justice and make possible the achievement of authentic human happiness. The affairs of men are born in moral corruption and the social order is unalterably evil.

Without confidence in himself, skeptical of human reason, suspicious of every human effort, and afraid of contamination by the world's culture, orthodox man throws himself upon the mercy of God, prays for divine revelation and intercession, and begs for his soul's salvation. Or with a life-denying mystic and ascetic fervor he withdraws from the world and its corruptions and longs for the destruction of human society and the end of human history.

But pessimism is not the whole of Orthodoxy, for the natural man is not the whole of man. Man is a child of God. His flesh belongs to this world of time, but his supernatural spirit belongs to eternity. As sinful man he is lost, but in his unworthiness he is redeemed by a sovereign and merciful God. Without merit and convicted of utter depravity, he is yet saved and exalted by the free gift of divine grace. And not only does God by a divine and gracious miracle give undeserved salvation to the individual soul; he overthrows the kingdoms of the world, destroys human society, and by a miraculous imposition establishes the kingdom of heaven. The *proximate pessimism* of Orthodoxy is transmuted in its *ultimate optimism.* God is in his heaven and despite the evil of man and his world all is well.

The dominant tradition of the Christian church, from its beginnings as a non-Palestinian hellenistic religion to the present, is grounded in this orthodox faith. Its historical roots, predominantly hellenistic and non-Jewish, are found in the cosmology and redemption myths of Gnosticism, in the mystery cults of the dying and rising savior gods, to a minor degree in some forms of Jewish apocalypticism and rabbinic theology, and in the more negative expressions of Neoplatonism. Its chief creator was Paul and its ideational structure is articulated in his theology and in Tertullian, Augustine, Luther, Calvin, Jonathan Edwards, and Karl Barth. Its practical expression is seen in the self-effacing piety, devotions, and living faith of the countless multitude whose lives have been ruled by its proximate negations and ultimate affirmations.

The negative concept of man in Christian Orthodoxy is incorporated in the dogmas of the fall of man, original sin, and atonement through the blood of Christ. From Paul to the present, in various technical forms, it is always a doctrine of miserable, alienated man, who is under the irresistible and sovereign power of sin, helpless to save himself, worthy only of eternal damnation, yet saved by the grace of God. Becoming incarnate in Jesus Christ, God takes upon himself the sin of all mankind, to pay its penalty through a vicarious suffering that purchases eternal salvation for the sinner and gives him a newness of moral and spiritual life.

In the chief organon of Christian Orthodoxy, the Epistle to the Romans, St. Paul laid the foundations of the Christian theology: "Therefore being justified by faith, we have peace with God through our Lord Jesus Christ: By whom also we have access by faith into this grace wherein we stand, and rejoice in hope of the glory of God" (5:1–2). "But God commendeth his love toward us, in that, while we were yet sinners, Christ died for us" (5:8).

Of course, for Paul and the orthodox there are limits on the *ultimate optimism*, for not everyone is saved. Only those who believe, who accept Christ as their savior, enjoy the mercies of God. The remainder, always the majority, are consigned eternally to hell and damnation.

St. Augustine, the philosopher of Orthodoxy and the chief creator of its theological system, determined to glorify God by a complete and total debasement of his creature, robbed man of his last vestige of merit, the merit of faith in his savior. In the dogma of prevenient grace, even that saving faith is assigned by God to those whom he has elected for salvation and withheld from those whom he has created for damnation.

Not man alone, but the whole world is degenerate and evil because of Adam's sin. God's total creation has fallen from its initial glory to corruption. "For we know that the whole creation groaneth and travaileth in pain together until now" (Rom. 8:22). The world has become a kingdom of sin and Satan is its god. But all things conform to the purposes of the creator, and his earthly drama will have an end wherein the powers of evil will be bound and judgment will come upon the world and upon all men. Then the City of God will be established, and in eternal felicity, free only to know and do the good, unable to sin, the saints will know God and rejoice eternally in his presence. But nothing that human beings can do will hasten the coming of the kingdom. They can only passively wait for God to ring down the curtain on the temporal scene.

Since the time of Augustine, Catholic theology has subscribed to the main outlines of what I am calling the orthodox religion and it continues to do so today, but with numerous refinements that have compromised its rigor. The *ultimate optimism* is there, to be sure, and the *proximate pessimism* is by no means gone, but the doctrines of grace and the fall conspire with the theory of the efficacy of the sacraments to rob the pessimism of its sting. A profound respect for man's rational nature, a feature that characterizes the entire structure of Catholic thought — a classical inheritance incorporated by its philosophers into the foundations of the church's theology — has partially neutralized the negative force of the pessimistic dogma and has produced in Catholicism a practical, moderate Orthodoxy which has much in common with Liberalism. By the fall man lost the supernatural gift of sanctifying grace, but this is not a condition of total depravity. Human nature is wounded, but not corrupted, by the fall of Adam; nor is freedom of the will wholly lost. Man is saved by divine grace, but he has retained the powers of reason and is not totally without merit for salvation, and even grace is partially a response to his worthy disposition.

It is in the theology of the Reformation that Orthodoxy is found in its most rigorous and effective form. Both Luther and Calvin revolted against the liberalizing tendencies of scholastic philosophy and demanded a return to the foundations of Augustinism, imposing their commitment to the saving grace of Christ upon their doctrine of man. With a theological rigor unsurpassed in the history of religion, Calvin asserts in the *Institutes of the Christian Religion*:

> Therefore original sin is seen to be an hereditary depravity and corruption of our nature, diffused into all parts of the soul. . . . For our nature is not merely bereft of good, but is so productive of every kind of evil that it cannot be inactive. . . . Whatever is in man, from intellect to will, from the soul to the flesh, is all defiled and crammed with concupiscence; or, to sum it up briefly, . . . the whole man is in himself nothing but concupiscence. [Bk. 2, chap. 1, edition of 1559]

Again, the ultimate destiny of man is salvation for some and damnation for others, as both Luther and Calvin affirm the predestination which Catholic dogma had partially abandoned. The *Institutes* declare that:

> No one who wishes to be thought religious dares outright to deny predestination, by which God chooses some for the hope of life, and condemns others to eternal death. . . . By predestination we mean the eternal decree of God, by which he has decided in his own mind what he wishes to happen in the case of each individual. For all men are not created on an equal footing, but for some eternal life is preordained, for others eternal damnation. [Bk. 3, chap. 21]

Today Protestantism is torn apart by the conflict of Orthodoxy and Liberalism, a dissension that knows nothing of church boundaries and divides the clergy and laity alike. But Orthodoxy, though usually in greatly modified tones, still qualifies the lives of millions and may justifiably claim to be the bearer of the primary Christian tradition.

LIBERALISM

Liberalism, the union of *proximate optimism* with *ultimate optimism*, describes the religion of total affirmation of life. Its theology defines man as good rather than evil, or at least as morally neutral with a high potentiality for goodness. Man is inherently capable of achieving an abundant and happy life, not solely through his own effort, for he is not alone in the universe, but in cooperation with God, in whom he has his being.

Not only man the individual but man as society is capable of genuine and positive achievement. Man's selfishness and egocentrism are aberrations from his truer nature. He is educable to the good or the bad by the impact of his environment and the cultivation of his mind and spirit; he is perfectible socially as well as individually. Good will is not only a possibility; it is a reality. And good will with right effort under the cultivation of reason will bring the good society, the society in which the individual may realize the abundant life. But again, this achievement, which is a genuine social ideal and not simply an apocalyptic vision, is not the work of man alone; it is to be accomplished through a living faith in God, a God who works with man, and through him, to realize his divine purposes.

But this life and this world, whatever their possibilities, are for Liberalism not the entire story of man. For man is an immortal soul, God is real, and man's destiny is an eternal beatitude in communion with his divine creator. The liberal, no less than the orthodox man, belongs to eternity. But in *his* theology all men are saved, for the liberal has no hell. His eyes, nevertheless, are fixed upon nearer things, for his heaven depends upon what he does with himself and his fellow men in this world. The *ultimate optimism* of Liberalism is consonant with its *proximate optimism.*

The major tradition of occidental Liberalism has been borne by Hebrew prophetic religion and its inheritor rabbinical Judaism and by the Greek philosophic and scientific heritage that undergirds Western culture. But it has appeared also in Palestinian Jewish Christianity, in Pelagian, Socinian, and Arminian Christianity, in Renaissance humanism, in Enlightenment deism, and, with qualification, in Mormonism. Its full expression is in nineteenth- and twentieth-century social Protestantism and Reform Judaism. Its prophets have been Moses, Amos, Isaiah, Jeremiah, Hillel, and Jesus; its theologians Pelagius, Aquinas, Schleiermacher, Ritschl, and Harnack; its philosophers Socrates, Philo, Maimonides, Locke, Kant, Hegel, and William James.

As in the case of Orthodoxy, historical examples of Liberalism are varying approximations to the ideal type. Nor is full consistency to be found in the religions indicated; there are liberal facets in every orthodox faith. Paul, for instance, at times taught a doctrine of merit; and in his polemic against the Manichaeans, Augustine asserted an almost Pelagian moral freedom and responsibility. There are qualified liberal elements in Calvinistic puritanism in its principle of the sanctity of work and its doctrine of the saints' creation of the kingdom of God.

I have already mentioned the liberalizing facets of Catholicism. The rise of an aggressive cultural and religious Liberalism in the nineteenth century was not without consequence for the Catholic church. A liberalization of religion was established as the basic policy of Catholic education by Leo XIII through his endorsement of the scholasticism of Thomas Aquinas as a philosophy for the church, despite the effective suppression of modernist thought by the encyclical *Pascendi Gregis* of Pius X in 1907. Modern Roman Catholicism is in many respects a liberal religion in an orthodox theological setting.

Mormonism, which exhibits its nineteenth-century American origins, is in substantial agreement with typical fundamentalist Protestantism, as for instance its biblical literalism, its dispensation theory of history, and its eschatology. It has, nevertheless, a positive conception of human nature and a generally life-affirming quality that gives it a pronounced liberal character. The Book of Mormon declares that "the natural man is an enemy to God, and has been from the fall of Adam" (Mosiah 3:19). But such fundamentalist pronouncements have failed to persuade the Mormon theologians, who commonly interpret the fall as good rather than evil, as being necessary to moral freedom. Through the grace of God man is capable of meritorious works and these are necessary to his salvation, for there is no predestination or divine election, and salvation does not come as a free unmerited gift.

Judaism, which has been characterized throughout its history by the affirmation of life and a positive doctrine of man and human society, has known little but liberal religion. It is true that the Old Testament lays a strong emphasis on sin and that ancient apocalyptic Judaism as well as the early rabbinic doctrine of the fall were a part of the context in which Pauline Orthodoxy arose, but the idea that man by nature is evil or that his flesh is corrupt has never established itself in the Jewish faith. The instruction of the Torah, that "God created man in his own image" (Gen. 1:27), dominates the whole of Judaism from earliest times to the present. The Jewish Messianic ideal has been a national hope and aspiration, not a redemption.

It is in Protestantism that Christian Liberalism, as well as Orthodoxy, has achieved its chief expression. Rejecting the negativisms of Pauline and Augustinian Orthodoxy, Protestant Liberalism, whose historic roots are as old as the culture itself, but whose flowering belongs to the nineteenth century, has drawn its inspiration from the positive faith of the Hebrew prophets and Jesus. This it has combined with the spirit of science and with a democratic social conscience to produce a religion of faith and reason which believes that man with God can create a better world.

Any effort to account for the rise of particular religions must inevitably fail because of the impossibility of describing or adequately assessing either the entire character of a movement or the infinite variety of its environmental and causal factors. But it is not impossible to indicate general features of the cultural milieu of Orthodoxy and Liberalism that appear to have had a causal bearing upon their formation and nurture.

The origins of the *proximate pessimism* of Christian Orthodoxy are quite clearly related to the broad and deep sense of failure, loss of confidence, and moral despair which had characterized the hellenistic world for at least a century before the birth of Christ, turning men's thoughts to another and better world and their hopes to salvation by miraculous grace. Even Judaism, with its almost stern insistence upon human effort and this-worldliness, was mined with a rich apocalyptic literature whose eschatology was a major inheritance of Christianity, and indeed whose spiritual Messianic ideal gave initial meaning to the Christian message. The failure of the Greek polity and its cultural vision, the ecumenic quality of the Alexandrian Empire, the dying culture, and the rising civilization of Roman power brought a new world which the individual faced with fear and a faint heart.

Of course, even under favorable social circumstances Orthodoxy has continued to thrive, perpetuated by the natural conserving forces of religion, by the indoctrinating power of the literature and institutions into which it is incorporated, by its perpetual appeal to those who face life's common crises, and by whatever truth there may be in it.

But the *proximate optimism* of Liberalism reflects the life-loving confidence of the Greeks in the great fifth century, the creative faith of the Hebrews in the age of prophetic religion, or the new and spontaneous worldliness of the Renaissance humanists. The Liberalism of the present is grounded in man's faith in his own reason as that faith has justified itself in the achievements of modern science since Galileo and Newton. Its concept of man combines that faith with the profound sense of the ultimate intrinsic worth of human personality that was always the most precious possession of Orthodoxy, and with the new social conscience that expressed itself in the eighteenth-century Enlightenment and in nineteenth-century romanticism and liberal politics. Liberalism is the product of a world that believed it was succeeding, as Orthodoxy is the product of a world that believed it was failing.

Today Liberalism is disappointed and somewhat disillusioned; but Orthodoxy, for centuries the dominant faith of the Western world, is gaining new strength and aggressiveness, because economic catastrophe, two world wars and a host of others, together with a record of unspeakable human brutality are evidence once more that the world is failing. Men are losing their faith and their nerve and are again crying upon their gods.

HUMANISM

Humanism is defined by the junction of *proximate optimism* and *ultimate pessimism*. Humanism has no church, no ecclesiastical polity, no established creeds, no well-defined community. But it is not inarticulate; it speaks clearly in the literature of every age that knows intellectual and moral freedom, wherever men are not bowed under the yoke of official orthodoxies. It has no theologians, because it has no gods. But it has its prophets, poets, and philosophers — Democritus, Aristotle, Epicurus, Lucretius, Bruno, and Spinoza; Voltaire, Mill, Bertrand Russell, and John Dewey.

The life-affirming optimism of Humanism is not unlike that of Liberalism. Indeed, just as many liberals are on the borderline of

Orthodoxy, many are near the boundaries of Humanism, for Humanism, though having an ancient tradition of its own, results in modern times from the same positive forces that produce Liberalism; and as the children of the orthodox may be liberals, their grandchildren may be humanists. Moreover, Humanism is not easily distinguished from certain types of impersonalistic theism, and in its more sentimental forms it may be regarded as naturalistic pantheism and may have much in common with traditional religious mysticism. But in theory, at least, the humanist is more self-sufficient than the liberal and his optimism, therefore, more self-reliant.

For the strict naturalistic humanist believes that there is no God and there is no immortal soul. His *ultimate pessimism* is his denial that there is an ultimate. For him the proximate world exhausts the whole of reality and existence. There is no cosmic purpose, no genuinely telic process, no center of absolute meaning for the world and for man. There is no superhuman moral power that judges the thoughts and actions of men, no world spirit that moves their history, that seeks the triumph of righteousness, guarantees an ultimate justice, or comforts with an all-forgiving love. All of these are real for the orthodox and the liberal, who live out their lives under the guidance of a sustaining faith that gives them a sense of genuine shelter and security. But for the humanist there is no God, there is no savior, no redemption, and man is alone in the world. But it is a world of which he is genuinely a part and in which he is at home.

Now the life of the humanist is not devoid, because of his naturalistic philosophy, of moral and spiritual value. Like those who believe in God, he loves his wife and cherishes the fondest hopes for his children, he is concerned for the well-being of his fellowmen; like the theists, in his heroic moment he will give his life for another; he gazes upon the same art as they, communes with the same nature — his spirit uplifted by the same music, his will steeled by the same high resolve, his life shattered by the same tragedies. Atheism does not make the humanist morally bad; it cultivates in him the cosmic loneliness of those who believe that their only companions in life and death are their fellowmen and the mute world which has unknowingly cast them up, and will unknowingly reclaim them.

The strength of the humanistic religion is its supreme commitment to reason, its faith in man's creative intelligence — faith that he has the power to discern, articulate, and solve his problems. The humanist is confident that under the guidance of good will the patient processes of scientific thought may eventually win through for the amelioration of society and the achievement of human happiness. Nowhere is there a greater confidence in education, in man's power to affect his own character or to determine the course of history. Humanism denies that there are uniquely religious experiences and refuses to distinguish between the sacred and the secular. It declares instead that religion embraces every worthwhile human attitude and activity, and it grounds its moral ideals in the living experience of the individual and society. Man is the primary object of its interest and devotion. Its instruments are science and democracy, and its goal is the good life.

As a religion Humanism enjoins men to engage in the moral struggle to create the highest values. But it is a struggle that can know only momentary victory, for the universe is totally indifferent to man and his moral aspiration. Everyone must die; after a brief moment the race will perish and the drama of humanity will be ended without the slightest trace of memory that it ever began.

Some humanists are acutely conscious of the ultimate tragedy of human existence and their philosophy is characterized by sadness and melancholy. But more often Humanism sees the world as a confederate rather than as an enemy. Man is born of nature and belongs to nature. His life is a part of its life; his values are its values. Though blindly and unconsciously, and with no intent or purpose, nature has yet conspired to produce him, his creations, his culture. This life is all, but there is nothing to regret — for it is enough. The moral injunction is to live it fully and abundantly, and when the time comes to leave it, to die stoically, with resignation and without complaint. Tragedy for the true humanist does not consist in death; tragedy is to live a life that fails to achieve a genuine meaning and value.

EXISTENTIALISM

Proximate pessimism when conjoined with *ultimate pessimism* yields Existentialism, the religion of meaninglessness and emptiness and despair; the religion that offers no hope here or hereafter, that finds man in his anxieties and leaves him there, that describes him as appetites that cannot be stilled, as impulsive striving that cannot be fulfilled, as passions that find no satisfaction, as irrational action guided by no integrated purpose. This is the religion of those who look for the naked facts of existence, who define man not as a being whose essence is his soul, or his reason, or any substantial entity — but as existence itself. And that existence, they declare, is meaningless.

This is not the plight of the humanist, for even though he denies that there is a meaning given to man by God, the humanist yet finds the grounds for such a meaning in man's own nature and therefore pursues life in the belief that man can invest himself with purpose. He can create meanings that integrate his own life and the life of society, which order the course of his actions and give to his character and that of his community their stability and moral discipline. But the pessimism of Existentialism is proximate as well as ultimate, and for the existentialist life is without a center for genuine integration, for he holds that his existence precedes his essence and that man is therefore only what he makes of himself.

Now Existentialism is of two kinds, secular and theistic. The Existentialism under discussion here and defined by *ultimate pessimism* as well as *proximate pessimism* is, of course, the secular variety. Theistic existentialism enjoys the *ultimate optimism* afforded by belief in God, and is, therefore, with its *proximate pessimism*, a variety of Orthodoxy, a Neo-orthodoxy. For it the estrangement of man from himself, from other men, and from the world is overcome by the act of faith in God which alone conquers the anguish and despair that mark the real character of existence. Lying near or at the heart of the recent resurgence of orthodox religion, theistic existentialism is a powerful factor in the new life of Protestant theology and has produced a significant theological and philosophical awakening in both Judaism and Catholicism.

In its more technical formulations, Existentialism is a recent development, but it has an ancient though ill-defined heritage. The psalmists, Socrates, Paul, Augustine, and Pascal contributed to its foundations. The creators of modern theistic Existentialism are Sören Kierkegaard, Dostoevski, Berdyaev, Jaspers, Gabriel Marcel,

Martin Buber, and Paul Tillich. Of secular Existentialism the prophet is Friedrich Nietzsche; Martin Heidegger is its philosopher and Jean-Paul Sartre its high priest. Because it fears that its living concreteness is lost in the abstractions of philosophic discourse, Existentialism often finds expression in the mythological representations of religion, in fiction, poetry, and drama, and in studies in psychopathology.

A comparative consideration of the origins of Humanism and Existentialism reveals a situation somewhat parallel to that of Liberalism and Orthodoxy. The story of Humanism is the story of secularizing and naturalistic tendencies and movements throughout the history of the culture: Athenian sophistic philosophy, Greek and Roman Epicureanism, Roman skepticism, Renaissance this-worldliness, eighteenth-century Enlightenment philosophy, the French Encyclopedia, nineteenth-century German materialism and British utilitarianism, Marxism, and American pragmatism. The modern secularization of politics, the achievements of industrial technology, and the democratizing of social institutions were positive factors in the cultivation of Humanism's affirmative and aggressive attitudes toward life. But above all, Humanism was a long-range response to the remarkable achievement of seventeenth- and eighteenth-century physical science in constructing theoretical explanations of the causal order of the universe which broke the back of religious supernaturalism. Thereafter, nineteenth-century physics, evolutionary biology, cultural history, and twentieth-century experimental psychology established naturalistic philosophy on enduring foundations.

The history of Existentialism is a different story. While Humanism has had a social orientation and interest, Existentialism has been a highly personalized and individual philosophy. And where a radical disparity between itself and all forms of supernaturalism has marked the history of humanism, it is only the recent forms of Existentialism that have been entirely naturalistic and secular, and even here, as in Jaspers, the issue is at times ambiguous. Moreover, where Humanism cultivates scientific intelligence as a precious instrument, Existentialism treats it with at best a tolerant indifference. Despite the importance for Existentialism of psychological analysis, science and the scientific spirit do not lie at the foundations of Existentialism as they do for Humanism.

Of course, the familiar explanation of Existentialism is that in both its secular and theistic forms it is a product of socio-cultural failure. Its technical philosophical structures were created in the ruins of Germany during and after the first war, while its initial but modified impact on England and America coincided with the depression of the thirties. With the rise of nazism it gained in strength and it was born as a popular religion in the confused milieu of lost nerve and iron courage in Occupied France. After the second war its influence grew steadily in America as well as on the European continent, and although today it is declining in influence as a distinct philosophical position, no one with a serious interest in contemporary culture can afford to ignore its claims or its impact upon the thought and spirit of this century. But if social failure is invoked to explain the Existentialism of this century, what was the occasion for Nietzsche and Kierkegaard? Here again the usual answer is a ready one: These were men of genius, but with sick minds; like an ailing society, they were producers of a diseased philosophy. But such simple explanations are quite inadequate, and whatever their worth as a partial account of origins, they leave unanswered the large questions of the truth and adequacy of the existentialist philosophy and religion.

III

Any consideration of the theoretical or practical implications of the concept of man is complicated by the obvious fact that this concept combines with other and variable factors of both a practical and a doctrinal nature to produce different results under different circumstances. Countless problems arising from the complex interrelationships of the multiple facets of religious life and thought are a definite hazard for any effort to comment generally and comparatively on the character of the four primary forms of religion which I have described. But I will risk this hazard and make a few more evaluations, even though this essay will not permit adequate reference to the great amount of evidence necessary to support and justify them.

An assessment of Orthodoxy as a religion involves its doctrine of man and, of course, the various associations of that doctrine, such as its characteristic theology, its biblicism, its eschatological sense, its morals, and its attitude toward culture. Orthodoxy's concept of God is quite consistent with its central dogma of man, for where man's finiteness, contingency, impotence, humiliation, and sin are exaggerated and magnified, the opposing qualities of God, his power, knowledge, and glory are absolutized. The dogma of the fiat creation guarantees that God is everything, and that, except for the divine grace, man is nothing. However much he has been celebrated with moral descriptions, the God of the fundamentalist is an arbitrary tyrant. He is sublime, majestic, transcendent, sovereign, inscrutable, and wholly other; he has created a world that groans with pain and suffering, accepts the blood of his own son as payment for his mercy, and creates souls to burn in hell eternally. The pages of orthodox theology and history are full of vigorous descriptions of God's inhumanity to man. In orthodox Christianity God is the symbol of power and force and dominion; Christ and the Virgin are the symbols of mercy and love and grace.

Orthodoxy, with its absolutistic and amoral doctrine of God, generates, of course, an authoritarian religion — the authoritarianism of the power of priest or church, or the ascendancy of a book and a tradition — the dominion over men of forces that are from without rather than from within. The orthodox live with their minds on the past, and the strength of their inspiration is measured by the antiquity of its source. Yet they have no real sense of history. They do not distinguish between the past and the present. They ignore the most obvious evidences of historical process, of real growth and development, in favor of a static world conformable to their absolute God. Lacking both the disposition toward and appreciation for historical criticism, they confuse prehistory with history, and myth, legend, and poetry with historical fact. Their historians are thinly disguised theologians whose cosmic schemata tyrannize over every attempt to examine objectively the course of human events. They fail to see that prophets speak to their own people in their own times, that the universality of their message is simply the depth of their insight into human problems and human affairs. They read the present into the past, and the past into the present — always with their thoughts geared to a golden age near the beginning and to the coming destructions that will mark the end — never fully aware of the abundant evidences of intellectual, moral, and spiritual progress that mark the pages of their own scripture. The orthodox cooperate fully in that retrogressive conspiracy which elevates the folklore of one age into the divinely ensured dogmas of later ages and restrains men under the dead hand of the past by demanding their submission to the hypotheses of their ancestors.

The orthodox believer fears contamination from the world's culture, which for him is often a symbol of human pride and arrogance. It is not simply that his morals may be ascetic and life-denying, or that his mind is fixed on another world, for he does not turn down his share of the world's material goods. But he senses the disintegrating powers of the culture, disintegrating to the rigid and dogmatic structure of his orthodoxy. The orthodox of today, like their ancient duplicate Tertullian, fear the secularizing force of philosophy and strengthen their fortifications against it by a determination that faith is in no need of reason and absurdity should be no deterrent to belief. They are suspicious of science. Although they enjoy the fruits of technology and openly rejoice in whatever alliances with theoretical science they may be able to negotiate, they nevertheless do not enter sincerely and affirmatively into the spirit of the scientific enterprise, nor do they accept its methods as the final instruments for adjudicating knowledge.

Being unaware of the cultural determinants that largely account for their religion, the orthodox are without sufficient perspective for an adequate appraisal of the religions of foreign, and for them inferior, cultures. They are confused and embarrassed by other religions' similarities to their own and regard their devotees at worst as heathen and at best as deluded prospects for conversion. Sometimes Orthodoxy has accomplished a transformation of the culture; often it has attempted to escape the impact of the culture. But no religion can successfully insulate itself against the world.

Yet Orthodoxy has remarkable powers of endurance, for today it is not only the predominant form of occidental religion, but it is enjoying a vigorous recrudescence under the stress of social crisis. Its unusual powers of indoctrination are not sufficient to account for its perennial strength. This can only be explained by its adequacy in satisfying basic religious interests and needs.

The cruel events of recent decades have dealt staggering blows to the optimism of both Liberalism and Humanism and quite surely have been fuel for the fires of orthodox pessimism. For the disillusionment is not only of society and its possibilities, but of individuals as well, countless millions of whom have suffered the desolation of their souls because of man's brutality and indifference. It is hardly to be wondered that where these salvage their faith in God, it is often under the conditions set by Orthodoxy. Nor is it surprising that a resurgence of the sense of sin and depravity and of human helplessness and inadequacy should follow in the wake of war with its myriad destructions and its ominous threat of future annihilation.

The meaning of Orthodoxy is not exhausted by its pessimism. Its strength as a religion lies not simply in its recognition of evil, in its refusal in spite of its own absolutistic theology to deny the realities of human corruption. It is this together with the ultimate faith which declares that whatever the failures of men may be, however tragic the character of existence, the failure and the tragedy eventually must be transmuted, and not merely for the universe, but in the very life of the individual who now suffers. This surely is the secret of the strength of Orthodoxy, that though it discerns the radical disparity between human aspiration and human ability, and knows that life which must end in death is tragic, it yet denies that tragedy with an ultimate faith which frees its votaries from both guilt and suffering and invests their lives with meaning and consecration. Whatever the advances of science, or however strong the naturalistic persuasions that follow in their wake, this kind of religious faith in a divine alchemy that transmutes death into life will never perish.

The strength of Liberalism lies in its confidence in human reason and in its commitment to the moral transformation of society. In the first instance it achieves at least an apparent compatibility with science, as in the problem of organic evolution, and effects various alliances with non-naturalistic philosophy. Although it continues in the cultural tradition established by Orthodoxy, it cultivates the instruments of rational analysis, such as historical and literary biblical criticism, which give it historical discernment and liberate it from the myth and legal forms of the past. Liberalism enjoys a high degree of historical and cultural sophistication.

In its moral commitments, Liberalism draws its chief inspiration
from the social prophetic religion of ancient Israel and Judah and
from the moral teachings of Jesus. It has acute sensitivities to human
suffering and social injustice and, unlike typical Orthodoxy, its loyal-
ties know nothing of national or racial barriers. Again unlike Orthodoxy, which has been an important contributor to the rise and preservation of capitalistic economy as well as to the formation of the
modern nation-states political system, Liberalism has identified itself
with the interests of the laboring classes and with progressive social
programs generally. Indeed, Liberalism has been a vital force in
producing social legislation in this country during the past several
decades and a major creator of the attitude of internationalism that
makes possible today a forum of international deliberation. The
general spirit of Liberalism is progressive and ecumenical; that of
Orthodoxy is conservative, reactionary, parochial, and sectarian.

The theology of Liberalism has much in common with that of
Orthodoxy, though it varies widely from a position approaching
Orthodoxy to an almost complete involvement in Naturalism and
Humanism. It may abandon belief in the resurrection but not belief
in an immortal soul. It may relinquish the virgin birth and divinity
of Christ but be reluctant to surrender the belief that Jesus is a genuine revelation of the character of God. And some liberals may even
agree with the orthodox that in Christ the eternal God entered into
the temporal order of human history. Both Jewish and Christian
liberals have strong attachment to the Bible and draw heavily upon
it for their inspiration, but for them it is in no sense an infallible
revelation or instruction. The liberal accepts the scientific verdict
of the orderly processes of nature and expects no miraculous inter-
ventions, yet he often prays and his prayers may be for intercession
as well as communion.

Like the God of the orthodox, the liberal's God is a person; he
is a living being who thinks and feels and acts; his moral will legislates for mankind, and his moral purposes are the framework of
human history. Unlike the God of Orthodoxy, he is not a tyrant;
his love and compassion are his essential character. He is less an
absolute sovereign and more a loving companion, less transcendent,
more immanent and approachable. He predestines no one to damna-

tion, but saves all. He is an ever-present partner in the moral enterprise of life and of history.

In its technical philosophy Liberalism tends to move away from absolutism and toward finitistic and temporalistic descriptions of God. Under the impact especially of Kantian criticism and moral philosophy, it has largely abandoned theocentric religion in favor of an anthropocentrism that makes man and his moral experience the basis of theology, requiring the conception of God to square with the realities of free will and genuine moral struggle. Although in its search for philosophical foundations Liberalism has exploited rationalistic method, in alliance especially with German idealistic metaphysics and theory of knowledge, in Britain and America it has cultivated experiential approaches to the problem of God and the soul and has associated with both realism and pragmatism.

The most effective critique of Liberalism is that offered by the recent resurgence of Protestant evangelicalism, the Neo-orthodoxy that came to life on the continent at the close of the first war, whose quickening was felt in Britain and America during the thirties, and which since the second war has virtually breathed new life into the Christian religion. This Neo-orthodoxy, which is beyond question the most important religious development of the present century, is a compound of existentialist, liberal, and traditionally orthodox elements. A product in part at least of social catastrophe and personal crisis, it is a renewal of the orthodox faith of the reformers and a reaction against nineteenth-century rationalistic philosophy and sociohistorical optimism. Its theologians, representing independent viewpoints, are Karl Barth, Emil Brunner, and Reinhold Niebuhr; its philosopher is Paul Tillich.

Neo-orthodoxy is the religion of liberals who have criticized the content of the liberal faith and found it largely empty of the original message and power of the Christian religion. Within the framework of contemporary culture, accepting such modernisms as evolution, higher biblical criticism, and the new psychology — and with a cultural and historical awareness that distinguishes it clearly from earlier Orthodoxy — it has proclaimed with new vigor the primary doctrines of Orthodoxy: original sin, the saving grace of Christ, the special revelation of God in biblical history, and the Christian eschatology. Neo-orthodoxy proclaims that the Liberalism of the social gospel era is dead — dead by its own hand; it charges that in its efforts to conform to the scientific temper, Liberalism had not only accepted the findings of the sciences themselves, but had compromised itself with scientifically inspired naturalistic philosophy — a naturalism which disposed of the supernaturalisms resident in the very heart of the Christian message. Likewise in its comparative and critical biblical analyses it had not only, and justifiably, overthrown the literalism that plagued the old Orthodoxy, but had expelled as well the revelation of God which, though not in the book, was in the historic events recorded in the book. Where Liberalism escaped naturalism, the neo-orthodox insist that it sold its soul to rationalism and idealism — philosophies soon to be discredited — always because it was searching for a philosophical support for religion to replace the biblical foundations from which it had been torn.

Unable to accept the orthodox biblical religion *about* Jesus, the liberals had turned to the religion *of* Jesus. Having denied him as the savior of men's souls, they accepted him as moral teacher and prophet, and refusing to recognize the eschatological character of the gospels, they mistakenly attempted to deduce from them a system of social ethics for modern times. In the hands of the liberals, God lost his awful holiness and Christ his divinity; religion became a moral idealism and salvation the progress of society. "Sin" and "redemption" were words dropped from the liberal's vocabulary, and pride ceased to be a deadly evil.

Now whatever one may think of Neo-orthodoxy as a constructive religion which has returned to the foundations of Orthodoxy, he can deny only with difficulty that there is much truth in this critique. Indeed, few liberals will now deny that their somewhat sentimental and optimistic assessments of both the individual and society were excessive, that their moral idealism failed to face the stern and brute realities of political action and of the perversions of individual moral freedom. And not only this, but the liberals now realize that if the strength of their religion was in its commitment to social ends, its weakness was in its neglect of the individual. Liberalism has learned that education and idealism are not sufficient guarantees of social progress and that social progress even when real will not compensate for the neglect of the spiritual needs of the individual.

But although many liberals may now concur with Brunner, that "the real theme of the gospel is eternal salvation, eternal life in Christ — not 'social salvation,' " only the reactionaries abandon their liberalism to agree with him that "the central fact of human existence is that sin separates us from the holy God." Only the youthful reactionaries yield to the allurements of the eschatology which tells them that unless history has an end it has no genuine meaning. Because it is a religion of reason, Liberalism is self-critical and self-corrective, and far from being dead, as some of the neo-orthodox aver, it is realigning its forces on a new level in the hope of escaping the pessimistic exaggerations of the old Orthodoxy and the secularism of Humanism. It has taken a fresh look at society and the individual and at the history of religion and the Bible. Wiser now than a few decades ago, it has learned much from politics and from the depth psychologists and has a better understanding of the nonrational life of man; it has learned much from the philosophers of language and has a deeper appreciation of the role of myth and symbol in religion; its attitudes toward the ceremonial forms of the tradition are most generous and, as in the temples of Reform Judaism, it has made at least a partial return to the richer liturgies of orthodoxy.

Now, the humanist looks upon all of this with much disdain. Akin to Liberalism in his *proximate optimism*, the humanist is inclined toward contempt for what he regards as the liberal's lack of courage, the courage to assert his freedom from the bondage of pre-scientific thought by abandoning every vestige of cosmic supernaturalism, by breaking the bonds that tie him sentimentally and morally to the forms of the past. The liberal, he believes, is attempting the futile task of rationalizing an outmoded theology in terms of a modern world view with which it is totally incompatible. The humanists join the neo-orthodox in convicting the liberals of professing a Christian faith while at the same time abandoning those very beliefs in redemption which have made Christianity a world religion and which throughout its history have been the chief source of its strength.

Humanism has a quality of tragic heroism. Its tragic character is its belief that there is no ultimate meaning in human existence, that men must struggle alone to create and support their world of values, and that someday they all will die and everything they have created will die with them. The heroism of humanism is that believing this dreadful thing to be true, men will yet struggle valiantly to create such a world and conserve it for others yet unborn, and that even the heartbreaking disappointments of the past decades have not completely disillusioned them. For Humanism grounds its philosophy in an uncompromising denial that morality requires a theistic sanction or that secularism in principle is inimical to the full pursuit of high personal and social values. Morals, it declares, can and should be cultivated independently of belief in God. A person should be moral for no other reason than that he is a human being. Replying to the claim that the moral structure of society, involving those very values which the humanist himself cherishes, is the product of theistic religion, the humanist points to the broad differential between actual practice and the absolutistic ideals of theological ethics and arraigns that absolutism as a major cause of today's moral confusion. Or he calls attention to the long history of Chinese culture and its moral institutions that were for many centuries successfully grounded in Confucian humanism, or to the humanist saints of every society who have lived and died by high moral courage.

Today's criticism of Humanism comes largely from conservative religionists who often see it not only as a purposeful attack upon piety but as a conspiracy against personal morals and even against democratic society. In the most extreme instances they may insist that its agnosticism and atheism are one with the godlessness of Marxist communism. They fail also to realize that the evil in Soviet communism does not follow inevitably from its atheism, but rather from its false religion. Communism is not a true Humanism; it is an idolatrous religion in which men worship the false god "Dialectic," a religion which gives a pseudo-divine approval to the consummation of their own interests and creates in them a fanatic devotion to a perverted moral idealism. The result is the monopoly of power by a single group, and it is from this that the evils of the police state ensue. The democratic institutions of Western society are in part a product of a fortunate conjunction of theistic moral religion and eighteenth-century humanistic secularism, as indicated in the confluence of Calvinism and deism in the founding of the American republic. History provides overwhelming evidence that democracy does not follow necessarily from theism, nor tyranny from secularism.

It is the fate of the humanists to be judged by their disbelief in God rather than by their faith in man, and the condemnation is most rigorous from the camp of those who have abundant faith in God but little or no faith in man. This is the injustice of judging men by their disbeliefs without inquiring into their beliefs. It is not atheism but the positive affirmation of life and human values that lies at the heart of Humanism.

But if the humanists are misjudged by the conservative theists who fail to recognize them as a creative moral force in society, it is equally true that the humanists err in their assessment of traditional religion, which they regard largely as a drag on cultural progress. Too often the humanist sees religion in its role of conserver but does not appreciate its creative powers. He sees its legal and sacramental forms and assumes that they cannot embody a genuine spirit; he is justifiably sensitive to its superstitions and its myths, but he may fail to see the profound meanings that are sometimes conveyed by them. Too often he concludes that historical, social, and psychological explanations of the origin and development of ideas of God, the soul, or immortality are proof that those ideas are false. Or he assumes unjustifiably that a mystical passion for communion with God and the feeling of dependence upon him are evidences of weakness or fear. The humanist revolts against the dogmatisms of typical theism but does not admit the dogmatisms that plague his own system.

The chief strength of Existentialism is its demand that philosophy be a philosophy of the individual, its insistence that man has occupied himself far too much with system, with ideas and things, and far too little with himself. And it is not man as an animal species, or as collective society, or as an abstract universal that concerns the existentialist. It is man the individual, the living, concrete, existing reality; the actual individual who is thrown upon the tide of time and is here for a moment, and then gone; the individual of anguish and decision who must create himself by his free choice, who would escape his dreadful freedom but cannot; the individual of impulse, passion, reason, and anxiety — who suffers, aspires, fails, despairs, and dies.

But if it is the merit of secular Existentialism to grasp concrete human existence unclothed by the raiment of ideas and reveal it in its nakedness, it is also its weakness to appraise that existence from a standpoint which encourages an obsession with the nonrational and irrational facets of human nature, conceals the genuineness of reason and its integrating power over the individual and society, and distorts the positive quality of life by a morbid preoccupation with death. Here is a secular religion which in its popular forms, at least, celebrates whatever there is in life that disintegrates, fragments, deteriorates, and degenerates. It describes reality as nothingness, the quest for the moral life as lost in a congeries of meaningless choices; it sears the brand of nihilism on all that it touches — and says that the meaning of life is found in death.

Or if it is to the credit of Existentialism that it defines man as creative freedom and insists that he cannot escape the responsibility of that freedom, and enjoins him to throw off the shackles of institutionalism and social inhibition, it is its great weakness to fail to recognize and adequately value the realities of genuine moral solidarity. For the existentialist does not appreciate the possibilities for an objective structure of reasoned values, or the organizing powers of moral custom and habit. Or, finally, if it is merit in Existentialism that it advocates a subjective method to counteract the objectifying techniques of science and of rationalistic philosophy, it is quite surely demerit that fails to capitalize on the abstractive powers of the mind to achieve a genuine body of public knowledge.

Now, much credit is due Existentialism for its depth of insight into the character and predicament of man, and certainly admiration for the raw, uninhibited courage of its partisans. One may even indulge the existentialist aesthetes whose moral holiday fails to recommend their sincerity. But surrender to such a religion is submission to a philosophy that is not a product of balanced and integrated thought and therefore distorts the character of man's existence. It fails to grasp the full positive powers of rationality and of man's achievement of an adequate habitation through his socializing and culture-creating powers. Existentialism is an effective deterrent to the oversimplifying and at times superficial propensities of Humanism and Liberalism, but its negations cannot satisfy as a lasting religion.

IV

Religion is man's ultimate concern and commitment, a living experience that sounds the deep mysteries of his own being. But it is an experience that becomes involved in countless relations with other personal and social factors and forces. It would be quite impossible to overstate the power of religion as a complex of ideas, attitudes, and symbols to affect men's minds and conduct. When organized with access to its traditional instruments of indoctrination and education, it can become the most efficient and powerful weapon for controlling thought and political action. Religion can command endlessly the emotional resources of the individual and of society and can fortify these with inspiration drawn from the ancestral past or with apocalyptic visions of things to come. It can cause men to look forward, or backward, to love the things of this world, or to despise them.

Religion can induce in men the most dedicated moral commitment, recommend them to lives of utter and selfless devotion and denial, or move them to supremely heroic action. It can deepen their aesthetic apprehension and appreciation, strengthen their moral perceptiveness, and refine their moral sensitivities. It can elevate them to the loftiest idealism and broaden their perspectives to create a genuine ideal of community. Religion can free men's minds from superstition, from bigotry and moral blindness, and it can cause them to look upward and outward in an honest search for truth, to become aggressive enemies of evil and injustice and courageous advocates of righteousness. And it can cultivate a deep and sensitive spiritual awareness that enriches experience and imparts a quality of radiance to the whole of life.

But if religion can create, it can also destroy and enslave. For religion can confound the reason and stupefy the moral sensibilities. It can and often does enslave men's minds to the superstition, magic, and primitive science of their remote ancestors. It can and often does enslave their wills to the most crude and elemental moral principle and practice of the past. It can blind them to the realities of moral evolution and rob them of the full value of their moral heritage. There is no social evil or injustice that has not at some time enjoyed the sanctifying approval of religion. Religion can involve men's theology with their basest moral prejudices, and when it encourages passion to dominate reason, it can bring them in the name of God to commit the most heinous crimes. Religion can and often does destroy the joy of life by its ascetic negations. It can enslave the personality to legalistic codes and sacramental forms that are an abortion on the spiritual life. It can convince men that conformity in belief is better than the creative search for truth, or the guaranteed performance of ritual than a living communion with God. Under the motive of religion, scholars will prostitute their scholarship, and disguised and protected by its halo, statesmen will ruthlessly pursue power over their fellowmen. Religion can convince men that their highest virtue is obedience and that submission to their priests is conformity with the divine will. It can delude them with the superstition that their good fortune is the result of divine approval and can deceive even the seeming righteous into the sin of identifying their own selfish interests with the will of God.

Unlike men in bondage under the less popular forms of slavery, those enslaved by religion do not know that they are not free. This can be religion's most subtle evil, for because of it men are often robbed of their dignity without knowing what they have lost.

Religions are not made to order, nor are they created in a day. They issue from the long slow processes of cultural growth that relate man's rise from his primitive origins to whatever cultivation he has realized. From the crude tribal beginnings of animism, magic, and blood penalties to the high achievements of ethical monotheism and the religion of reason, religion is the story of man's effort to relate himself adequately to the world in which he lives, to interpret its phenomena in relation to his own life, and to come to satisfactory terms with himself and with his fellowmen. Into it are woven the incantations of priests, the inspiration of prophets, the disputations of theologians and philosophers, the ecstatic fervor of mystics, the blood of martyrs, the denunciations of reformers, and the piety of saints. But these are not the real creators of religion. Religion is born out of the milieu of the living experience of the masses of men and women who are caught in the maelstrom of economic and political conflict, in the crosscurrents of cultures, in the rise and fall of civilizations, in the perennial struggles with life and death.

No one by taking thought can create for himself a religion into which he can withdraw and thereby escape from the errors of others. And no one can live in complete detachment from the religious culture, for long before he seeks to escape, it has impressed itself indelibly upon the total character of his life and thought. But if religion can be neither voluntarily created nor escaped, it can yet be met with a dedication to those high resolves and consummate ideals by which every person of intelligence and good will must judge the ideas and institutions to which he commits himself or which he commends to others. Today religion is moving once more toward the twin evils of irrationalism and authoritarianism, and only those who set themselves firmly against these corruptions are faithful to the high estate to which humanity has finally come.

In its ideal form religion is committed irrevocably to the intrinsic worth of every human soul, not only as a principle of moral thought, but as a positive guide for every course of action. It is committed to the community of all mankind, is inclusive rather than exclusive, unites men rather than divides them, and creates genuine sympathy and understanding among them. It has a social conscience that commits it to equality for *all* men, and it sets itself as a courageous critic against every form of political and economic injustice that corrupts the social order and defends at whatever cost the rights of every person against the coercive power of men and institutions.

The world is in need of religion that is committed to the genuine affirmation of life and is relevant to the whole experience of man, religion that sanctifies both his work and his play and enters aggressively into his quest for happiness. It must be religion that cultivates the attitude and technique of self-criticism, that is available to every possible source of new insight and inspiration, that insures to men the heritage of their tradition without enslaving them to the past, that encourages conviction without dogmatism. It must produce an ever-increasing awareness of beauty in all its forms and enrich life by its encouragement to artistic creation and enjoyment. It must quicken moral sensitivity, intensify the perception of right and wrong, and inspire men as advocates of righteousness and destroyers of evil.

The only religion which can fully satisfy today's ideal is a religion that is committed sincerely to the search for truth, that refuses to ground faith on naïve credulity, that refuses to prostitute learning for the defense of belief, that encourages rather than condemns genuine and uncensored scholarship, that is not afraid of what men may learn in their quest for knowledge. It is a religion of freedom that is committed to the destruction of every form of tyranny over the minds and souls of men.

Religion should bring consecration to life and direction to human endeavor, inspire men with faith in themselves, dedicate them to high moral purpose, preserve their natural piety in the presence of success, and give them the strength to live through their failures with nobility and face with high courage their supreme tragedies.

5

Time, History, and Christianity

The central problem of contemporary theology is the relation of God to the world. Beyond its theoretical interest, this issue has practical implications relating to the meaningfulness of religion, to freedom, and to the religious sanction for morality.

The problem is not the relation of God to space and matter. This question is of little or no religious interest. It is rather his relation to time and events — to human history and to the purposed and free actions of human beings.

It is common to regard the scientific conception of the world as the prime embarrassment to Christianity, but this is not the case. Whatever the theoretical difficulties for supernatural religion in its confrontation with natural science, those who on practical grounds are inclined toward belief will find a way to some accommodation. The fundamentalists will either renounce scientific intelligence, as some have always done, or resort to any number of well used but transparent devices of reconciliation. The liberals will continue to deceive themselves in thinking that they can reconstruct Christianity within a scientific framework while still preserving the essential elements of the religion. And the neo-orthodox, the most sophisticated of all, will take the only safe route: they will continue to ignore science and the scientific world-view as if they did not exist or had no relevance whatsoever to religion.

The real offense to Christianity, and to theistic religion generally, does not lie in science. It is found, rather, in that very area where science is most deficient, in human motivation and action, in the large movements of history which determine the character of societies and cultures.

My thesis is that in the matter of history Christianity, with its roots in the biblical religion and hellenistic intellectual culture, has placed itself in a compromising predicament that is now a leading cause of its own deterioration. Christianity was a major contributor to the conception of history that is now a dominating influence over the mind and spirit of the Western world, a concept that has large implications for the whole life of man. But the religion is basically incompatible with its own creation, and this incompatibility has added to the contradictions and confusions that currently obtain in religion and morals, and in the general culture.

I refer to the doctrine of historical progress which captured the mind and imagination of the eighteenth and nineteenth centuries and has exerted a large impact upon the twentieth down to the present. It was basically an unchristian idea and was never fully accepted by Christianity. But it was, nevertheless, in part a product of Christianity, and when it fell into disrepute, as recently as our own time, confusion and frustration followed in its wake. The Christian world, deceived by the false optimism of its own faith in progress, could not return to a genuinely Christian view of history, so strong was the grip of modernism upon it.

I believe that much that disturbs the world at the present time, in political and social affairs and in personal experience, has its ground in this predicament. With the decline of the orthodox Christion faith, with its supernatural cosmology and its preoccupied concern for the soul's salvation, a new faith emerged — the so-called liberal or modernist religion. It compensated the loss of eternity with a powerful commitment to humanity, to the world and its future, and it tied the search for meaning and moral purpose to the progressive movement of social history. As religion became increasingly secularized, the faith in humanity and history gathered strength from the dramatic successes in human accomplishment — until in our own century, first in Europe and now in America, the hollowness, the deceit, the frustrations that darken our hopes and feed our fears and anguish cannot any longer be suppressed. They cannot any longer be disguised by the successes of history when the failures of history have become so obvious.

When we glance at the hellenic and hellenistic backgrounds of Christianity, we immediately encounter the theory of historical cycles which dominated much of ancient thought and has in various forms enjoyed a brilliant renascence in our own time. There were some among the Greeks, the atomists, for instance, who held that time is infinite and non-cyclical, or Xenophanes, whose treatment of human affairs did not entirely conform to the cyclical pattern. And in Xenophanes there was even a conception of progress. But in general the cyclical theory furnished the framework for much Greek philosophical thought, both cosmic and social. As is well known, both Plato and Aristotle described the nature of governments against a cyclic background of the degeneracy of better forms to worse, and in the *Timaeus*, the most influential cosmological work of antiquity, Plato described the Great Year when "the perfect number of time fulfils the perfect year when all the eight revolutions [sun, moon, fire, planets, and fixed stars] having their relative degrees of swiftness, accomplished together and attain their completion at the same time" (39a). Here Plato was expressing an idea familiar in the antique world in India, Babylon, and Persia. It was current among the pre-Socratic Greeks and was yet to become a favorite dogma of Stoic philosophers and Roman poets.

It was a doctrine that expressed the sense of ultimate sadness and futility that held the ancient world in its grip. It is seen, though entirely out of character, in the Hebrew Bible. "Vanity of vanities, saith the Preacher, vanity of vanities, all is vanity. What profit hath a man in all his labour which he taketh under the sun . . . the thing that hath been it is that which shall be; and that which is done is that which shall be done; and there is no new thing under the sun."

Or, in the soliloquy of the Stoic Emperor Marcus Aurelius Antoninus in his tents on the Danube struggling to stay the barbaric invasions that would eventually crush his Empire and bring to a close the brilliant civilization of the classical world:

> [the rational soul] traverses the whole universe, and the sur-
> rounding vacuum, and surveys its form, and it extends itself into
> the infinity of time, and embraces and comprehends the periodical
> renovation of all things, and it comprehends that those who come
> after us will see nothing new, nor have those before us seen any-
> thing more, but in a manner he who is forty years old, if he has
> any understanding at all, has seen by virtue of the uniformity that
> prevails all things which have been and all that will be.
>
> [*Meditations* 11:1]

The Greek conception of cycles enjoyed the best of all possible technical supports, the idea that time itself is cyclical. Aristotle clearly relates the circular notion of time to the historical cycles when he asserts in the *Physics*: "This also explains the common saying that human affairs form a circle, and that there is a circle in all other things that have a natural movement and coming into being and pass-ing away. This is because all other things are discriminated by time, and end and begin as though conforming to a cycle; for even time itself is thought to be a circle" (4:14, 233b 24–30). Time, said Aris-totle, is circular because it is the measure of circular motion, and circular motion is the measure of time.

Plato, somewhat more poetic but with a clear intention, described time as the "moving image of eternity," an instrument employed by the creator to bring the world of becoming, the imperfect world of change and process, into a closer imitation of the world of being, the reality that suffers no change, that knows neither motion, nor growth, nor decay. Being is the eternal timeless world of all absolutes and all values. Because of time, this world of process, of physical nature, is a better approximation to its eternal model. Why is this so? Because the regular measure of time is a circular motion, and a circular motion is the motion which most nearly approximates motionlessness. There-fore time, being circular, is an image of eternity. Cyclical time is the nearest temporal approximation to timelessness, the eternal.

Behind this idea of Plato's were the metaphysic of his early and middle dialogues and the strange and intricate cosmological speculations of the *Timaeus*, the speculations on process of Heracleitus, the massive metaphysic of being of Parmenides, Orphic myth, and Pythagorean mathematics. And ahead of it lie centuries of thought which were to be dominated by a yearning for the timeless, motionless eternity in which there is no historical movement, no genuine event, no progress — centuries for which the Platonism of the eternal absolutes that are the highest value and the highest reality and the Greek theories of time and timelessness were the chief technical foundation.

The positive roots of the modern linear historical consciousness, which is the framework for the doctrine of progress, are found mainly in the Hebrew scriptures. Whether for causes of migration, geography, political and military involvement, native characteristic, or divine inspiration, the ancient Hebrews possessed a strange sensitivity to time that cultivated in them a faith in a historical vocation and a talent for written history that made of them the most uniquely historically minded of all people and of their Bible the most remarkable of all early historical records. Like Midas whose touch changed everything into gold, the Hebrews, whether poets, prophets, or statesmen, changed everything into history. Here was no mystic or ideational quest for a timeless, motionless eternity, but an aggressive acceptance of the temporal world and a faith in a temporal God whose holy and moral purposes are fulfilled by human decision and action in time. The hope for salvation, whether in the prophetic religion or the apocalyptic, was not for a blessedness in eternity, but for a happy future in time.

The Hebrew faith was not free from the idea of the past golden age, and in the later Old Testament are the roots of the restorationism that was to greatly affect Christian thought. But there was nevertheless a persistent hope, expressed in the ideas of the Day of the Lord and the Messiah, that a new and lasting age of moral prosperity would come for Israel and through Israel for the world. Although extreme political and economic adversity produced a Jewish eschatology that envisioned an end to human history and placed the fulfillment in a new world beyond (the eschatology within which Christianity was born and originally nourished) the general form of the Hebrew view of history remained unchanged — a movement forward and upward toward a positive goal.

The belief that the world had a beginning in creation at the hand of the same God who established the end combined with the social and moral inclination of the people and with their affirmative assessment of human nature to produce this view of history which is so clearly the ancestor of the doctrine of progress that we have known in our day.

The biblical religion was involved to a remarkable degree with time and history. The God of the Hebrews was the Lord of History, whose divine will was enforced in the movement of history toward a final goal. It was a religion grounded in time rather than space, its God coming to be identified with the whole of history rather than with the geographic space occupied by his chosen people. The "turning point" in religion, the death of polytheism, Paul Tillich held, was the words of Amos declaring that God would destroy his nation without thereby destroying himself, words which released him from the bounds of space and identified him with the totality of time.[1]

In Christianity, born in Jewish eschatology and established in the eclectic religious and intellectual culture of the hellenistic age, the Greek preoccupation with eternity and the Hebrew commitment to time were brought together in an uneasy union that ever since has plagued Christian theology with its most difficult and persistent problems. For here the impersonal definitions of timeless, eternal, motionless being, fashioned by the metaphysicians as representations of the ultimate reality, were employed as descriptions of the personal, living, moving God of time and history. This is the main source of theological trouble today — how can a God whose ultimate nature is described primarily by a metaphysic of being which failed to provide for the movement of history, for whom there was no genuine historical telos, for whom the passage of time brought the world no nearer to the fulfillment of its purpose, for whom, indeed, there was no historical purpose — how can such a God be related to the world of human history, the world of human striving, failure, and fulfillment; how can he be involved with a world in which the urge to establish meaning in life and human endeavor centers in the cumulative events of history?

[1] *Theology of Culture* (New York: Oxford University Press, 1964), chap. 3, "Time and the Prophetic Message."

In both the theologies and creeds of Christendom, the Hebraic
religion has at times challenged the Greek metaphysics in the description of God. But in the theological clutch, the Platonic ideas have
usually won out over the biblical personalistic categories. In Augustine, the greatest of the theologians, the mind of the biblical God was
stocked with the Platonic universals; they were both the nature and
the content of his intellect.

But in the first century, long before Augustine, Philo Judaeus —
who established at Alexandria the Jewish philosophical school that
was to dominate the construction of technical Christian theology —
had attempted his celebrated synthesis of Platonic philosophy and
Mosaic religion by impressing eternity and its absolutes on the God
of time and relative events. "For the living God," said Philo, "inasmuch as he is living, does not consist in relation to anything; for
he . . . is sufficient for himself, and he existed before the creation of
the world, and equally after the creation of the universe; for he is
immovable and unchangeable, having no need of any other thing or
being whatever." [2]

Philo came to grips with the issue of time and eternity in a manner that became classic for occidental theology. "But God," he said,
"is the creator of time also . . . so that there is nothing future to
God, who has the very boundaries of time subject to him; . . . and in
eternity nothing is past and nothing is future, but everything is present only." Both Origen and Augustine later asked the obvious and
difficult question, what was God doing before he created the world?
And they gave the answer of Philo, that there was no "before" the
creation of the world, as God created time when he created the world.
Eternity has no past and it has no future. Indeed, it is even meaningless to say that eternity is a constant present. For "present" is a
temporal term and it has no meaning apart from "past" or "future."

It is clear that in describing God as eternal the classical Christian
theologians intended to remove from him the distinction of past,
present, and future, though this is occasionally denied today. St. Augustine held that "The eternity of God is his essence itself, which
has nothing mutable in it. In it there is nothing past, as if it were

[2] *Works of Philo Judaeus*, trans. C. D. Yonge, vol. 2, p. 243.

no longer; nothing future, as if it were not yet. In it there is only
'is,' namely, the present." [3] Later, St. Thomas Aquinas, following
Boethius, defined eternity as the "simultaneously-whole and perfect
possession of interminable life," and argued that in eternity there is
no temporal succession.[4] And in his *Institutes*, Calvin held that
"when we attribute foreknowledge to God, we mean that all things
always were, and perpetually remain, under his eyes, so that to his
knowledge there is nothing future or past, but all things are present.
And they are present in such a way that he not only conceives them
through ideas . . . but he truly looks upon them and discerns them
as things placed before him." [5] Those who have difficulty with the
problem of free will and God's foreknowledge have only touched
the edge of the issue. It is a question not of God's foreknowledge,
but of his fore-experience, of his having all experiences in one immediate, constant, simultaneous present — to use illicit terms which all
belong to the context of temporality.

This does not mean that time with its past and future is not real
to God. The time of the world of motion, of growth and decay,
change and historical events is not an illusion; it is a genuine reality.
Its reality depends upon the creative act of God. God has no past
and no future because he is not in time. Time is subject to him. There
is a question of the relation of God to history, but not of the reality
of history.[6]

[3] *Expositions on the Psalms*, 101:2, 10.

[4] *Summa Theologica*, part 1, ques. 10, art. 1. Aquinas adds to Boethius'
definition, "Further, *those things are said to be measured by time which have
a beginning and an end in time*, as it is said in *Physics IV*, because in everything which is moved there is a beginning, and there is an end. But as whatever is wholly immutable can have no succession, so it has no beginning, and
no end."

[5] *Institutes of the Christian Religion*, book 3, chap. 21, 5.

[6] For a discussion of the idea of God's timelessness and the reality of
time, see Paul Tillich's *Systematic Theology*, vol. 1, part 2, Being and God,
2 B 6, God as Related, and vol. 3, part 5, 3 C, The Kingdom of God: Time
and Eternity. Tillich holds that eternity should be defined in terms of neither
timelessness nor endless time. "Neither the denial nor the continuation of
temporality constitutes the eternal" (vol. 3, p. 419).

The crux of the matter in the Christian religion is that in Jesus Christ the eternal God entered the world of human history. In this intersection of eternity and time, history has its meaning. That Christianity as a religion has been essentially a concern for the salvation of the individual soul does not mean that for it the importance of history has been lessened. On the contrary, the soul's salvation through God incarnate in Christ is the central meaning of history.

Considering the general pessimism that pervaded the world of antiquity, it is no wonder that Paul reminded the Christians of Ephesus that when they were pagans they were without hope. But the hope that he offered them was for the salvation of their individual souls for eternity, not for this world. Nor has the Christian religion, which was born out of the despair of the hellenistic world and took its refuge in the apocalyptic promises of the Jews and the redemption hopes of the mysteries, ever cultivated a genuine and full doctrine of temporal progress based on an affirmative assessment of human nature and human possibility. Always its foundation commitment to the sinful quality of humanity and the necessity therefore of salvation as a free gift from God has dominated its attitude toward this world and its civilization, toward human institutions and human history. Even the optimism associated with liberal Christianity through the past century and into the present was only partially and indirectly a product of the religion. It was to a considerable degree the product of those very secularizing forces that are today the chief destroyers of religion. Tertullian stated the case for the church most effectively when he insisted that Christ came to bring salvation to those already civilized, not to bring civilization to the uncivilized.

But where then is Christianity's impact upon the doctrine of history, if its main concern is not with the progressive achievement of society and culture? It lies in this, that when in Christianity the biblical religion confronted the hellenistic culture, the temporal concern of the God of the Bible broke the back of the dogma of historic cycles which so completely dominated the ancient world and infused into it the dread incubus of futility and fate. Though the Orient even today is more often than not under the rule of timelessness and cycles of time, the biblical religion destroyed this dogma as a foundation of occidental culture.

The key to the matter was the doctrine of creation. A world that has a beginning is expected to have an end. And a world that has a beginning and an end is a world in which events are moving toward a goal. Here there was no repetition. What has happened is past. It will not occur again. And what has not happened is future. It has not occurred before. As St. Augustine wrote, with an impact that is still felt in Western culture, "For once Christ died for our sins; and, rising from the dead, he dieth no more."

It was in St. Augustine that the Christian philosophy of history became articulate, and with his greatest work, *The City of God*, he established the pattern that has dominated the religion even to the present time. But for Augustine the end which God has purposed for the temporal world is not the creation of civilization and culture, but rather the cultivation of the saving knowledge of God. The battles with evil and the powers of darkness were already fought and won in Christ. The task now is not to create a better world, but through faith to learn to live in the world that God has prepared. In his *Soliloquies*, his first treatise after his conversion, St. Augustine assured himself: "I desire to know God and my soul. And nothing more." And yet he moved the conception of history closer to the typical modern view: first, by dealing a major blow to the theory of historical cycles, affirming the linear doctrine of historical process which insists that whatever happens is genuinely new; and second, by moving beyond the parochialism of both Greeks and Jews, conceiving of history as the history of the totality of the human race.

Still, for Augustine human history, moving under the dominion of divine purpose, was largely a story of the preparation of the soul for its salvation, a drama staged and witnessed by a God who stood outside of time and only once entered into it. It was a drama that might be brought to a close at any time by the intervention of the apocalyptic miracle, since the incarnation disclosed the full meaning of history and because it was not human society or human culture that was moving horizontally toward an important goal. The movement that counted was rather the verticle passing across the line of history of the lives of the saved and the damned. Certainly it was not the story of the progress of mankind.

This Augustinian formula on history has in varying degrees dominated Christian thought to the present and is cultivated even more intensively today than it was a century ago. Here, as in so many other things, the dead hand of the church's greatest intellect — who stood firmly against much of what describes modern culture and who laid the foundations of medievalism on the ruins of antiquity — yet closes its grip tighter upon us as our own society grows fearful of the faith in progress to which it was so recently committed.

The long and slow emergence from medievalism of the modern idea of progress is in large part the story of the gradual disintegration of this Christian concept of history, a process identical in some respects with the decline of orthodoxy itself. More than anything else the change was the abandonment of the negative conception of man associated with the dogma of original sin in favor of a more optimistic doctrine that not only affirmed a natural goodness of man, whether conceived as a child of nature or of God, but insisted as well that especially in his capacity of reason man has the potential to move his race, generation by generation, toward a better life in a better world.

There were radical implications for theology in this new and positive estimate of man, involving the doctrines of the absoluteness of God, salvation by grace, the freedom of the will, predestination, and the entire theory of the church, its authority and sacraments. In some places and with some populations orthodoxy survived relatively though not entirely unscathed, a survival which guaranteed that throughout the modern era and even now there are many whose view of their own lives and of the history and fate of society is essentially Augustinian in character. These have preserved the past almost intact with a complete indifference to the obvious facts of social and cultural growth and development. Issuing from this sturdy and blind conservative stock there have come the liberal forms of religion, half secular and half Christian, promoting the status of man in the world even at the risk of demoting God, celebrating his freedom and rationality, and encouraging the whole gamut of human social and cultural endeavors as not only of worth in themselves and as positive and valuable gains for humanity, but even as new assets for the universe and for God. And then, of course, there has been the growing tradition of a full and conscious secularism that has refused to resist the onslaught of modernity and has abandoned the belief in God and divine providence and all forms of cosmic teleology, yet takes its stand firmly on the favorable estimate of man and on sanguine hopes for his future.

The Renaissance is the symbol of the beginning of the new age, an age of critical intelligence deeply tinctured with the ideal of individual freedom and committed increasingly to the amelioration of the human condition. The era immediately prior to the First World War was the culmination of what the Renaissance began, and it was the eighteenth and nineteenth centuries that saw the clear development of the idea and belief in historical progress which provided the intellectual framework for most social thought and eventually permeated both technical cosmology and the uncritical popular assumptions about the nature of the world and man's place in it.

In general, although the doctrine of creation was compromised or abandoned, as was the total eschatological framework that provided for the world's end, most eighteenth and nineteenth century philosophies of history abstained from cyclical and recurrence theories and cultivated the Hebraic–Christian linear concept of historical movement. It is this concept of a dynamic temporal process that lies at the heart of the modern historical consciousness and distinguishes it from the ahistorical attitude of Greek and Roman classicism.

On the level of social philosophy it was the product first of France, where secularism predominated, and secondarily of England, where there was an attempt by some to retain the Christian background for progress. The French Revolution became in a sense its symbol. On the levels of metaphysical speculation and historical scholarship it gathered its main support from Germany. Three major facts of contemporary history combined to encourage and verify it: the increase in scientific knowledge, the practical successes of technology, and the slow but apparently sure spread of political democracy. Not only the Enlightenment with its excessive faith in the saving power of human reason, but also Romanticism with its primary concern for the affections fed the belief in progress. Even Rousseau, who declared in the opening line of his *Social Contract* that man who was born free is everywhere in chains — the chains imposed by the human civilization that has artificially corrupted the state of nature—produced, nevertheless, in the chapters that followed, a social theory that betrayed a commitment to the belief in the possibility of social progress.

In the earlier stages of its development, as with Bacon and Descartes, the idea of progress referred primarily to the increase in human knowledge, while in the latter stages attention was directed to social improvement. But in the Abbé de Saint-Pierre in the eighteenth century there appeared clearly and for the first time the doctrine that we in our day had until so recently taken quite commonly as a fact of man and the universe, that the inevitable growth of human knowledge through the "perpetual and unlimited augmentation of reason" will yield an indefinite social progress and increase in human happiness. This is the primary form of the doctrine of progress. The influence of the idea is indicated by the fact that before the eighteenth century was over, those who fashioned descriptions of ideal states were projecting them into the future as societies to be achieved, rather than into the past or into an entirely non-historical setting.

From Hegel, under the influence of the nineteenth-century German romantic involvement in the problem of life, process, and development, there issued the monumental system of metaphysics that was to cast its spell even upon the British and the Americans and become, in inverted form, the chief basis of Marxian communism — the absolute idealism that describes not simply man and human institutions but God and the total universe as involved fundamentally in process. And finally, Darwinian evolution offered the suggestion that there is an inevitable upward movement of human culture just as there is an evolution of the species, a suggestion that unrestrained speculators such as Herbert Spencer were quick to expand into justification for a theory of evolution for the total cosmos. Thus began a trend that has enjoyed a vigorous run well into the present century.

Of course the doctrine of progress has been delivered up in a variety of forms, sometimes as progress under the dominion of divine providence — often as an entirely secular theory on human history; sometimes as an inevitable movement upward and onward that, like the Puritan's irresistible grace of God, seizes man with or without his concurrence and carries him along — often as a movement dependent upon the initiative of human effort and intelligence; but always as a trend toward an increase and consummation of human values the ultimate success of which, whatever the difficulties and handicaps, is virtually guaranteed.

In 1920 the historian J. B. Bury called the doctrine of progress "the animating and controlling idea of western civilization." "For," he said, "the earthly Progress of humanity is the general test to which social aims and theories are submitted as a matter of course." As an epilogue to his work he wrote "Will not that process of change, for which Progress is the optimistic name, compel 'Progress' too to fall from the commanding position in which it is now, with apparent security, enthroned? . . . A day will come, in the revolution of centuries, when a new idea will usurp its place as the directing idea of humanity." [7]

This talk in terms of centuries quite clearly shows the dominance of the idea of progress over Bury himself. Already, as he wrote, the curtain that would bring an end to the comedy of progress was beginning to fall. The symbol of a new era had already taken form. Eight years before, in 1912, even before the beginning of the war, Spengler had selected his title for *The Decline of the West*.

Now, it seems quite obvious that when viewed over a long period of time the human race has enjoyed certain gains and suffered major losses, that in some things it has moved ahead and in others it has been static and even regressive. The data of history do not justify a general theory of progress of the kind that so thoroughly captivated the nineteenth century. Moreover, that century's intoxication with progress was all too often a perverted passion for machinery, industry, and expanding commerce rather than enthusiasm for new knowledge, great art, and the cultivation of social democracy. It was a glorification of those very factors in the social order which were productive of dirty-city squalor, personality-destroying drudgery, and the exploitation of the native populations of non-industrialized regions. The indicators of progress were too often those very forces that destroyed the organic structure of communities and the wholeness and integration of the individual soul. The nineteenth was a century

---

[7] *The Idea of Progress* (New York: Macmillan Co., 1932).

enamored of the sensate facets of human experience and human value, a century that assessed its objects and ideas by standards of utility and cultivated a new sense of the sublime that was dominated by the ideal of economic expansion and exploitation.

It is a singular thing that today, in the last quarter of the twentieth century, when those very values which were so highly prized by our predecessors are insured to us in a degree far beyond the most optimistic dream, and when in some measure the evil by-products of industrialism and commercialism are being overcome, and when the expansion of knowledge and technological invention has achieved a pace difficult even for us to comprehend — in view of all this it is a singular thing that that inordinate faith in progress should have vanished and that we experience today a sense of utter ambiguity, a complex of hopefulness and hopelessness, of meaningfulness and meaninglessness, of faith and despair, of crisis and anxiety. Our view upon life has been chastened by two universal wars whose destruction exceeds comprehension, by economic chaos that reveals clearly the possibility of starvation amidst plenty, by political tyranny sprung from the collapse of democracy, by the failure of nations that have a common sense of impending doom to yield to compromise that might save them all. We have suffered a moral disenchantment through the knowledge that men in the enlightenment of the high culture of the twentieth century can bring the most unspeakable suffering upon their fellowmen, that even our own nation could pursue a tragic war which millions of our citizens believed to be wrong or useless. Above all is the frightening realization that both we and our enemies possess the instruments for total destruction, a knowledge that condemns us to live not in the century of faith in progress, but in the century of the malignant anxiety of annihilation.

Through all of this our generation has achieved a humane wisdom that exceeds that of all its forebears. It has a perspective on human history impossible in earlier eras, a perspective that reveals now the shallowness of the dogma of progress which failed utterly to divine the demonic character of political power. And it has a more profound insight into the structure of human personality, an insight which exposes the naiveté of the optimistic assessment of human nature that was the foundation for the progress doctrine. It knows now the limits of reason and of knowledge, that the morality of individual persons does not create moral nations, and that we are moved not so much by reason as by passion and self-interest. Perhaps more than anything else, our generation has come to realize that what was called progress may have the power to make life more pleasant for some of us, but it does not have the power to save us from the utter tragedy of our existence.

We are living in a new era whose statesmen have suffered the rude shock of learning that world politics has little to do with morality and everything to do with economic and military power; whose scientists make strange statements about having known sin; whose artists and essayists have cultivated obscurantism and irrationality; an era which has produced historians and pseudo-historians who are again fascinated by the cyclical view of history, for whom the circles are the movement of cultures which, like living things, are born, mature, decline, and die, and who in the presence of the high technical development of our civilization announce its impending death. Witness the ominous words of Pitirim Sorokin: "We are living, thinking, and acting at the end of a brilliant six-hundred-year-long Sensate day. The oblique rays of the sun still illumine the glory of the passing epoch. But the light is fading, and in the deepening shadows it becomes more and more difficult to see clearly and to orient ourselves safely in the confusions of the twilight. The night of the transitory period begins to loom before us, with its nightmares, frightening shadows, and heartrending horrors." [s]

Compare this with the hopeful statement of Walter Rauschenbusch in 1909:

> And sometimes the hot hope surges up that perhaps the long and slow climb may be ending . . . . The swiftness of evolution in our own country proves the immense latent perfectibility in human nature . . . . Perhaps these nineteen centuries of Christian influence have been a long preliminary stage of growth, and now the flower and fruit are almost here. If at this juncture we can rally sufficient religious faith and moral strength to snap the bonds of evil and turn the present unparalleled economic and intellectual

[s] *Social and Cultural Dynamics,* vol. 3, p. 535.

resources of humanity to the harmonious development of a true social life, the generations yet unborn will mark this as that great day of the Lord for which the ages waited . . . .[9]

But let us turn back to Spengler, whose erratic but penetrating prophecies should cause us some concern, and consider his account of our helplessness in the death of our own civilization as it declines from a culture of high art, science, religion, and philosophy to a civilization of big cities, commerce, power, and war.

> The dictature of money marches on, tending to its material peak, in the Faustian Civilization as in every other. . . . But . . . the last conflict is at hand in which the Civilization receives its conclusive form — the conflict *between* money and blood. . . . The coming of Caesarism breaks the dictature of money and its political weapon democracy. . . . The sword is victorious over the money, the master-will subdues again the plunderer-will. . . . Money is overthrown and abolished only by blood. . . . Before the irresistible rhythm of the generation-sequence, everything built up by the waking-consciousness in its intellectual world vanishes at the last. . . . *World-history is the world court* . . . . Always it has sacrificed truth and justice to might and race, and passed doom of death upon men and peoples in whom truth was more than deeds, and justice than power. And so the drama of a high Culture — that wondrous world of deities, arts, thoughts, battles, cities — closes with the return of the pristine facts of the blood eternal that is one and the same as the ever-circling cosmic flow . . . . For us, however, whom a Destiny has placed in this Culture and at this moment of its development — the moment when money is celebrating its last victories, and the Caesarism that is to succeed approaches with quiet, firm step — our direction, willed and obligatory at once, is set for us within narrow limits, and on any other terms life is not worth the living. We have not the freedom to reach to this or to that, but the freedom to do the necessary or to do nothing. And a task that historic necessity has set *will* be accomplished with the individual or against him.[10]

[9] *Christianity and the Social Crisis*, pp. 421f.

[10] *Decline of the West*, vol. 2 (New York: Knopf, 1928), pp. 506f.

If we turn to our theologians, we find the same abandonment of the liberal optimistic faith of a few decades past. In the threat of impending doom the orthodox celebrate the fulfillment of eschatological prophecy, and in the gross evils which the present generation has perpetrated upon itself, and with the support of the new psychology that has uncovered the irrational facets of human personality, the neo-orthodox have found new truth in the dogma of original sin. It is for them man's pride in his reason that will bring destruction upon him, his setting himself in the place of God, forgetting his own finiteness, his contingency, his creatureliness. More than anything else, man, whom Condorcet in the flush of the Age of Reason described as in all his faculties "susceptible of an indefinite improvement," is today defined by his anxieties: the anxiety of death, the threat of non-being, which, in the words of Tillich, gives to all anxieties "their ultimate seriousness"; the anxiety of meaninglessness, the loss of a "spiritual center" of life, of an "ultimate concern" in living; and the anxiety of guilt, which is man's "self-rejection or condemnation." [11] The condition of man is the condition of despair. Here there can be no meaning in progress, for the despairing soul demands not progress but the leap of faith for its redemption.

And one last word from Reinhold Niebuhr, a theologian for whom the doctrine of historical progress was a humanistic dogma of salvation invented to save men from the human predicament after they had abandoned genuine religion:

> The dominant note in modern culture is not so much confidence in reason as faith in history. The conception of a redemptive history informs the most diverse forms of modern culture . . . . The uncritical confidence in historical development as a mode of redemption may have . . . contributed to our present disaster by heightening the historical dynamism of western civilization to the point where it became a demonic fury.[12]

If we move from the theologians to our secular philosophers we find that the most aggressive and penetrating pronouncements are

[11] Paul Tillich, *The Courage To Be* (New Haven: Yale University Press, 1952).

[12] *Faith and History* (London: Nisbet & Co., 1949), pp. 3, 15.

those of the existentialists, whose criticism of liberal rational philosophy is continuous with the general trend of anti-intellectualism and is in part a critique of the optimistic history-mindedness that kept its eye on the happy development of the species while failing to grasp the tragic predicament of the existing individual. Why call us pessimistic, asks Sartre, when we are simply facing with courage the facts of the human predicament? Ours is but "an attempt to draw all the consequences of a coherent atheism." [13] The liberal humanists had announced that God is dead, but they had failed to realize that this makes a difference, and a very basic difference, for it means that man is alone in a world that does not know him.

Such is the intellectual temper of our time — in the presence of the enormous increase in the knowledge and control of nature, a new failure of faith in the historical vocation of man. Perhaps from it will come a more cautious and more profound commitment to the future. Perhaps an inclination to live less by absolutes and certainties and more by probabilities and adventure. But of this we may be quite sure, that, if our world survives, however much we may assert the autonomy over nature and over history of our individual and collective freedom, and with whatever determination we hold to a sense of destiny, our generation will not again know the sanguine hopes and promises that it enjoyed until almost yesterday.

The failure of the optimistic doctrine of progress in both its religious and secular forms has placed a massive strain upon the religion which helped to bring it into being — an increased alienation of the religion, with its theology and morals, from the corporate and individual experience of mankind. We must now question whether our culture, which has fallen into so much confusion, can reconstruct a doctrine of history upon the ideals of freedom and individualism which will give us a firm foundation upon which to build our present and future. It is a question also whether the Christian religion can reestablish its relevance to the world by a reformation in its theology that will bring God out of a timeless eternity and into the processes of history — whether Christianity can be meaningful in a world

[13] Jean Paul Sartre, *Existentialism and Humanism*, trans. Philip Mairet (London, 1948).

which must come to terms with science, technology, and political and
industrial power. It is not without cause or reason that both poets
and theologians have proclaimed the death of God. The living God
must have meaning in the living, temporal experience of man. Perhaps our theologians should take more seriously the neglected admonition of Alfred North Whitehead: "I hazard the prophecy," he said
in his *Adventures of Ideas* (1933), "that that religion will conquer
which can render clear to the popular understanding some eternal
greatness incarnate in the passage of temporal fact." [14]

[14] Chap. 3, sec. 4, p. 41.

6

Religion and the Denial of History

It is commonly assumed that the secular trend of our culture during recent centuries has resulted mainly from the impact of science upon society generally and, more particularly, upon religion. No doubt there is much truth in this presumption, especially if a broad and generous meaning of science is intended that does not refer simply to the findings of the special sciences but rather to a strong cultural disposition to favor such things as analysis, empirical investigation, the careful assessment of evidence, causal explanation, and a cautious construction of hypotheses.

But apparently it is more often supposed that the chief threat to religion and religious culture is simply the body of knowledge accumulated by the natural sciences, that scientific knowledge contradicts the knowledge claims of religion or the religious tradition. Accordingly, there is an opinion prevailing among us that the major academic hazard to a person's religious faith is the study of the natural sciences and that, therefore, to run this course unscathed merits high moral approbation for the victor.

Now it should be entirely obvious on a little reflection that there is no justification for this view, even though the knowledge claims of science and religion often conflict. For while the natural sciences tell us a great deal about planetary motions, the structure of atoms, the nature of protoplasm, or the function of glands, they tell us nothing about God or an ultimate meaning of life, and very little of religious importance about human beings. There is a serious question, therefore, of what if anything they have to do with religion. Those who devote themselves quite exclusively to the scientific disciplines are not, by these studies at least, brought to the most exciting or crucial discussions of religion; and although they sometimes regard themselves as the center of the dispute, they are often quite unaware of the great issues that seriously challenge religious faith. This may well account for the apparently high incidence of orthodoxy among natural scientists, rather than, as is sometimes supposed, the possession by that species of a special endowment of piety or some peculiar immunity to intellectual perversion.

It is quite true, of course, that the natural sciences have produced major disturbances in religion, as in the Copernican discovery that man may not be situated at the spatial center of the universe, or the Darwinian intimation of strong arboreal proclivities among some of our more remote relatives. But insofar as matters such as these relate importantly to religion, they do not belong simply to science but rather are the common property of all literate persons. Besides, the relation of religion to science is a philosophic issue rather than a scientific or religious one, and philosophy, as everyone knows, belongs to all of us, especially where religion is at issue.

At any rate, there seem to be obvious grounds for the view that it is the study of human beings, their ideas, and their behavior that really brings us face-to-face with the crucial problems of religion, and therefore the humane disciplines and arts rather than the natural sciences are religion's chief intellectual challenge. But more than that, and this is the crux of the matter, it is the study of religion itself that occasions the most difficult and discomposing questions. It is when religion is studied and discussed seriously by rational, informed persons with open minds and honest intentions that it encounters its most severe testing.

To say that religion is its own most persistent antagonist is not to regard it as something that can be considered in isolation, abstracted from its concrete involvement in the total life of the individual and of society. When religion looks seriously at itself it can never be as an appraisal of something ideal though nonexistent. It is pleasant to talk about ideal religion and ideal science, which combined possess all truth and lie down together like the lion and the lamb. But the only real science is the groping, unfinished science produced by live scientists, and the only real religion, the imperfect religion that we encounter about us and in which we ourselves are participants. Unlike science, religion is not a set of ideas to be treated abstractly; it is a living faith, a sentiment of commitment, a personal and even social experience that is intricately woven into the whole fabric of value. But it is inextricably tied to a massive cluster of beliefs, symbols, myths — and to its own history.

It is because it is a dynamic, living affair fully implicated in the social milieu that to be understood and appraised religion must be apprehended not only in its historical setting, but also as a central factor in the historical process. Those who have not taken a close look at religion as a historical and history-making phenomenon must be pitied for having missed an exciting intellectual experience and censured for being to an appreciable degree culturally illiterate.

But there is something even more important about this matter. It is the liberalizing power of the study of history. There is no intellectual pursuit more calculated to make a free person of an ordinary person, to free him from his own cultural bondage, and no history is more liberating than the history of religion. It is the study of history profoundly, in its depth and breadth, which provides insight into the predicaments that we are in and how we came to be in them. The most genuine and humane sophistication attaches to a person who is aware of history, for he has had his vision freed from the blinders imposed by his own place and time and therefore knows more of himself and his own world by knowing more of others and their worlds.

Now this sort of thing can produce a severe problem for religion, because one who is truly conversant with the history of religion has had more than a glimpse of the development of something that a large segment of the faithful suppose to be basically free from historical change. He knows that many of the things which religious leaders typically induce their followers to believe are probably not true, that all too often the religious tradition is not faithful to the facts, and that religion can be and often is the motive for the intentional distortion of history, especially of its own history.

It is interesting that some religions generate an acute historical consciousness while others do not, and certain facets of their character are a function of their sense of history. There is, for instance, less historical awareness in oriental religions than in occidental, a fact that reflects a basic distinction between Eastern and Western culture. There is more sensitivity to history in Judaism than in Christianity generally, and in some ways probably more in Catholicism than in typical Protestantism. Historical concern has been at a minimum in Brahmanism, where an amorphous body of scripture fails utterly to articulate a living connection with the past, or in most sectarian Shinto, where a simple communion with nature is indifferent to what has gone before or lies ahead. But in Islam, the hegira of the prophet has served always to focus the faith upon its history. And in Judaism, which anciently nourished the pattern of historical thought that more than any other has informed the meaning of history in Western culture, a sense of temporal movement affected the whole character of prophetic religion and eventually produced the apocalyptic religion that paradoxically expected the end of human history and was the foundation of Christianity. The literature of the Old Testament has a historical quality that is seen not only in the statement of basically reliable history to a remarkably early date — marking the Bible as the most important of all ancient historical documents — but as well in the very pattern of the prophetic message that moves from the warnings of impending national disaster to the frequent reminder that "you also were a stranger in the land of Egypt."

The causes of a religion's concern for history must be various and complex and are most certainly difficult to identify. No doubt geography, climate, migration, political and military involvement, great leaders, literature, natural catastrophe, cultural contacts, and the indiscernible minor accidents that somehow affect the course of major events are all involved, and much more.

If we ask what issues from historical consciousness in religion, the story is again utterly complex, and in part, at least, indecipherable; but there is no limit to the evidence that the consequences are considerable. In the first place, there are the interesting cases of the uses of history, where a definite end is intended: the nineteenth-century revival of ancient Zoroastrianism among the Parsis of western India by a deliberate introduction of the study of the religion's history; the establishment of the state Shinto cult under the Meiji in Japan as an instrument of political imperialism and effected in part by the fabrication of history; the recent and present effort of India to develop a national consciousness in part by creating a sense of religio-cultural history, an effort that apparently succeeds as the Hindus moderate their traditional bondage to the thought and language of the eternal and appropriate the temporal categories of their adopted English language.

The uses of the past are many, such as the employment of history or an imagined history as an instrument of moral instruction and inspiration, as in the instance of the Daniel stories produced by the Jews to strengthen the faith against the impact of Graeco-Syrian culture, or where history is employed as an instrument of political policy and power in the style of the reconstruction of recent history by the so-called pragmatists of the present ruling faction in communist China. It is probably true that no segment of any society has found history to be more useful, or, indeed, abused it more than has organized religion.

But there is a quite different and more important impact of history upon religion, or religion upon history — that involving historical theory rather than simply events or imagined events of the past: the Catholic doctrine of the nature of the church and its relation to the temporal, secular world, formulated in the writings of St. Augustine as a philosophy of history, which contributed effectively to the creation of the Christian church out of the ruins of antique civilization; or the historical theory of apostolic succession that contributes so much to the lasting powers of the Roman Catholic church, the most lasting of all human organizations; or, as a supreme instance, consider the power of the tragic conception of history conceived in Deutero-Isaiah to subtly inspire the life of the Jews, long ago proscribed for extinction, and strengthen them to endure the most unspeakable human suffering.

The point of this is both simple and obvious: that most occidental religion is, in one way or another, heavily involved in a concern for history, a concern for its *own* cultural and institutional history, and its place in world history — and in many ways its character is determined in part by its treatment of history, especially its *own* history, and by its *own* theories about its *own* history. When we consider, therefore, that to look quite seriously at religion means to look at its history, and when we realize that in general the study of history is the most liberating and enlightening of all intellectual disciplines, the question is raised: What impact does the competent study of the history of religion from reliable sources have on the typical religious believer?

The answer to this question is that for the most part the history of religion gives the believers a rather rough time. In fact, it divides the believers into two kinds, those who can honestly face religious history and those who cannot. There is, of course, the third category of those who abandon their religious beliefs because of the intellectual or moral disillusionment experienced as a consequence of their encountering historical facts which they cannot accommodate to their faith. Of course, that a person may dissolve his attachment to a particular body of religious ideas or attitudes or to a particular faith or religious institution does not at all mean that he has abandoned religion. The experience of coming face-to-face with the past of his religion may radically change his religious views and commitments, but in the process his faith in God may become even stronger and his religious ideas more profound and more meaningful.

History can plague religion with a variety of difficulties. In the first place, there is the common embarrassment that all must be prepared to face whenever they take even a cursory glance at their antecedents. In religion this embarrassment is prompted by a scripture that may be fraudulent, or the discovery of honored believers who were really irresponsible fanatics, the pious who murdered their fellowmen at the stake, the prophet who turns out to be a charlatan, the saint a sinner, or the priest who, by the time he is discovered in his heresy or transgressions, has left behind an accumulation of sacramental ministrations. The Catholic church, the most sophisticated of all human institutions and no novice in handling ecclesiastical prob-

lems, long ago overcame this latter difficulty by defining the priesthood as a universal reality that is independent of and unaffected by
the particular priest. Here Plato's metaphysics came to the rescue.

A second order of difficulties that cannot be so easily disposed
of as those that reside simply in the moral infirmities of men stem
from the fact that cultured religion without exception has had rude
and uncultured beginnings. The acceptance or rejection of the fact
of primitive origins sometimes determines whether a person aban-
dons religion, and quite surely it is a common and decisive factor in
separating the orthodox from the unorthodox, for it is a crucial index
to the interpretation of both the nature and value of religion.

It is not a comforting thing for religionists reared in the framework of the traditional faith to discover, for instance, that among
such ancient worthies as Abraham, Isaac, and Jacob, whose historicity
is itself not beyond doubt, are to be found the typical primitivisms
that define the childhood of religion and morals: polytheism, magic,
polygamy, wife purchase, human sacrifice, casuistry, and the making
of religion a profitable bargaining with God.

Or it is disappointing to those accustomed to the simple, naïve
narrative on the history of their church to discover the compromising
complexities of religious origins — that Christianity, for instance,
arose in a world familiar with dying and rising savior gods, or that
much of its precious liturgy is taken from the unwashed heathen and
some of its basic philosophy and theology from unchurched pagan
philosophers.

To discover the overwhelming multitude of such things, the com-
plications of what seemed so simple, the meanness of what seemed
so high, the gradual development of what had been believed to be
already complete: this is rather rough on the orthodox. And because
it is rough, the orthodox usually fail to make the discovery, and,
failing to make it, never really come to grips with the central problem that plagues religion when it genuinely examines itself and how
it came to be what it is.

Here I am referring to the general masses of believers in the
churches, those who read their scriptures devoutly but too often unknowingly. There is a class of churchmen who do know about these
things, the better informed rationalizing theologians and apologetic

scholars, a class who have never wanted for worldly sophistication or for the means to accomplish their own ends. What they know is that the faith will never be the same if they admit that religion has genuinely had a history, that not only has it had a past but things really happened during that past. They are entirely right in supposing that to admit history would produce a different kind of religion, a kind which they do not like, that often makes people less amenable to authoritarianism and churchly control. So as protectors of the faith, wherever possible such theologians seize control of the writing of history and its interpretation. They disguise themselves as historians, make history an appendage to theology, and write theology which the trusting readers believe is history. They celebrate the past and enjoy every ounce of support they can wring from it. But they are deniers of history, because they hold that in some strange way what is with us today was always with us in the past and that nothing genuinely important for religion or morals has really happened in time. Mankind, they insist, has enjoyed only an occasional glimpse of what was already laid up in eternity.

There is a kind of contradiction involved in all of this. The non-historical orthodox are often outraged at the suggestion that Jesus, for instance, may have taught nothing essentially new. But they are equally unhappy with the idea that the whole history of biblical religion is generally a coming to something that *is* new, and not only new, but often better. They roll the names of the prophets resoundingly from both their pens and pulpits, but they never admit the true greatness of those whom they honor — Moses, Amos, Isaiah, Jeremiah, or Jesus — because their greatness lies in their genius as creators of religion who have moved it upward, slowly but surely, from its crude beginnings toward its present high moral and spiritual estate. For the history-denying orthodox, religion does not have human beginnings or a development in human culture. It simply always was what it now is. In religion, the prophets make history and the theologians destroy it.

Consider as a single instance only the fate of the higher biblical criticism at the hands of many fundamentalists. More than anything else the "higher criticism" is a serious, persistent effort to look with scientific intelligence at the Bible, to read it neither for devotional nor apologetic purposes but rather in an effort to determine what it means by what it says. But this has resulted in seeing those meanings in their historical context, and in the unfortunate discovery that some of the writers of the book did not say what some users of it twenty-five hundred years later want them to have said. So the Bible scholars, who wear out their lives in a devoted search for truth, are not only condemned as wrong, but sometimes as vicious purveyors of falsehood set on destroying truth, morals, and religious faith.

The real crux of the problem lies in the fact that since by its very nature orthodox religion in its traditional occidental form considers itself the revelation of the mind and will of God, it treats its current beliefs and moral values and sometimes its institutional behavior as absolutes. Now, there are absolute truths, and it is at least conceivable that there are absolute moral values, but just how one goes about determining that he has apprehended absolutes is something of a problem, whether he be prophet, seer, or scientist. It is common for scientists to regard their knowledge, apart from mathematics and logic, as probable rather than certain, but the traditional religion thrives only on certainties. It often confuses psychological certitude, the feeling of being certain, with logical certainty. This involves numerous and interesting questions that cannot be discussed here, but this much can be said, that the purveyors of absolutes cannot afford to be caught taking history seriously. For whatever is involved in the context of history is conditioned by the circumstances of its involvement, and whatever is conditioned is not absolute. So the traditional religionists who are appointed to protect the absolutes and are committed to their task at any cost do well to practice the denial of history — to censor when it becomes necessary, mutilate the documents, and control the writing of history by carefully selecting if not distorting the facts, reading the present into the past and interpreting the past under the domination of theories that rule out a priori the possibility of religious and moral development, that, in reality, deny the possibility of genuine religious history.

Not the least effective technique employed by those whose theology and religious commitments make it impossible for them to face history honestly is to discredit the historians as questionable characters who desire to celebrate the secular and destroy the sacred, and/or to insist on theoretical as well as practical grounds that reliable historical knowledge is impossible. This is supposed to put an end to the entire discussion. But those who are conversant with the canons of evidence and the methods of knowledge, or are simply sincere and honest in a common-sense search for truth, are not likely to be impressed by such attempts to avoid facing the facts. They may resent, moreover, the emasculation of living religion by the denial of historical knowledge, especially if their own religious convictions are partially grounded in historic events.

Of course, not all history-denying is motivated by institutional interests, or prompted by the ultraconservatism and reaction of orthodoxy, or implicated in intellectual skulduggery. Its occasion is sometimes more profound and far less reprehensible. The escape from time is an escape from human contingency and finitude. The illusion of nontemporality ministers to the anxiety that arises from the human predicament, the predicament of contingency and temporariness, of the constant threat of non-being. And insofar as religion is essentially identified with the numinous in experience, as I believe it should be, it is in a sense non-historical and nontemporal in character, although even religious experience cannot escape the cultural and psychological conditioning of history.

Nor is the denial of history to be found only among theologians and mystics. It appears in many places: in pantheists, monistic metaphysicians, and sometimes even in mathematicians and politicians. But our concern here is with the common religious variety that is occasioned not by a yearning for union with God but more often by commitment to the status quo, the defense of which so frequently entails the support of the otherwise outmoded hypotheses of our remote ancestors. Here success depends in part on how well history is both used and abused. Today we are faced with a new abuser. The old orthodoxy often unintentionally and naïvely confused history with legend and myth. But for several decades past there has been a new orthodoxy that does not scruple at confusing them intentionally, and it compounds its crime by dressing up the entire result in ambiguous language to guarantee that no one will discover what has been done. This new orthodoxy shows up in strange and unexpected places, not only in the churches but sometimes even in the universities. It is a subtle handler of history, equipped with sophisticated theories of symbol and myth, ready to substitute philology for philosophy, intoxicated slightly by the new psychology, sensitive to the failures of the present, and erudite in the affairs of the past. It bids religion to come to terms once again with eschatology and rides the crest of popular reaction against the doctrine of progress. It betrays history because it must betray history to discredit the liberal thought against which it has so vigorously set itself.

Finally, the most important consideration of all — the orthodox denial of history is ultimately guaranteed by the absolutistic theology that lifts God out of time and the historical process and describes him as an eternal or timeless being for whom every event in the temporal plane of ongoing history is contained in a single simultaneous present. God is eternal. He is not in time, and for him there can be no history. So history cannot be really real. It is a kind of deception imposed by human finitude.

This dogma of the timeless nature of God, established in Christian theology largely on foundations of Greek metaphysics — a product of the quest for an absolutely changeless reality — dominates the whole structure of traditional Christian religion, both Catholic and Protestant, and its subtle implications affect every facet of religious doctrine. Even some of those who had returned to the biblical temporalistic conception of God, like Israel in the wilderness longing for the dubious security of Egypt, find it easy to forsake their prophets and yield to the temptations of the time-denying absolute. The minds of men are often enslaved by the attraction of emotive words. It takes a rugged churchman to resist the pulpit resonance of words like "infinite," "eternal," "changeless," "timeless," and the multitude of "omni's." But the failure to resist is an invitation to determinism, divine election, predestination, and the implicit doctrine that human moral effort does not really count because our future, whether good or bad, is already established in God's eternal present, a doctrine that dulls the edge of moral discrimination and may even encourage moral indifference and despair.

So religion faces its most persistent and difficult test when human intelligence is focused not so much upon such things as molecules and the stars as upon religion itself. To understand religion means to see it in its historical character and to recognize that it is in countless ways involved in the processes of history. But here lies the great difficulty, because to take religion seriously as a historical phenomenon is to implicate it genuinely in the relativities of human circumstance. This compromises religion by denying its precious absoluteness, thereby threatening the commitments of orthodoxy. As a consequence, the defenders of traditional religion frequently distort or deny history as a means of avoiding its implications, and on metaphysical grounds they may even deny the ultimate reality of time itself to insure that process and change are in some strange way illusory.

On the other hand, there are those who, when confronted by history, abandon and condemn religion out of hand, because with a biased and partial vision they see the story of its past only as an exposure of crude falsehood and human failure. They cannot face the fact of human imperfection; they are without a sense of humor.

But there are still others who take history seriously and yet find it possible to accept religion. They know that if something is good, its origins cannot make it bad, and that if it is true that there is a God, nothing discoverable in human history can make it false. They may even believe that nowhere is God more in evidence than in the processes of history. Such persons are liberated from the ideology of a fixed and finished universe and are captured by a vision of things genuinely to be done, because they know what every person of common sense should know, that historical development is real, and that in the long past of the human race many things of value have been achieved. Their world is not a place where all things are ordained from the beginning, and where nothing that happens really counts. It is a place where men are free, and where they play for keeps; where the stakes are high, the risks are real, the losses and gains are an affair of life and death, and where victory is not guaranteed. In such a world they see the history of religion for what it really is — the dramatic, heroic, and tragic upward struggling of the human spirit.

7

The Personal and Impersonal in Metaphysics and Theology

The predominant impersonalism of Indian metaphysics is in part a product of the tolerant inclusiveness which has characterized the general disposition of the people of India in religious practice and philosophical thought, while the strong personalistic tradition of the Occident, which is rooted especially in the biblical religion, is in some degree a consequence of a powerful attitude of intolerant exclusivism. I have no desire to comment here on the justification or merits of either of the cultural attitudes which I shall describe, or on the theological and metaphysical ideas to which they contributed. Rather, I am interested in simply calling attention to these dispositional factors, which seem to me to be important agents in affecting the character of Eastern and occidental religious thought and belief.

My argument is based on a broad view of the character of the two cultures and of their religious and intellectual history: for India, from the polytheism of the Vedic hymns to the culmination of the monistic trend in the sophisticated systems of the Vedānta, and extending even to the present; for the Occident, from the primitive Semitic polytheism and tribal henotheism to the achievement of the prophetic monotheism and its eventual union with the impersonalistic hellenistic metaphysics, and including the subsequent character of Western theism.

It is beyond practical possibility that the countless and intricately complex causal relationships that obtain among the elements of a culture can be fully identified. But the understanding of a culture and even a rudimentary comprehension of the differences that distinguish cultures require the pursuit of this task, a task that at best is speculative and is precarious with the likelihood of error, and which can proceed only by committing every kind of social and historical abstraction and by indulgence in gross oversimplification. It is an interesting one, nevertheless, and sometimes yields quite unexpected results.

There are at least three kinds of factors which may be causal determinants within or among cultures: *ideational, material,* and *dispositional.* These may not be entirely discrete or independent. Such material factors as climate or geography, for instance, quite certainly may affect the disposition of a people, causing them to be excessively passive or active. Or such a material element as economic or political success may profoundly influence religious ideas regarding the human predicament. But the causal relationships which obtain within a culture are often reciprocal, and metaphysical or theological ideas may have a far-reaching impact on political action or economic conditions. And there is always the possibility, of course, that of two things, where one appears to be caused by the other, both may result from a third. The whole picture is utterly complex and not a little confused, and every attempt to explain cultural phenomena must be regarded critically and with considerable reserve.

A basic difference between the cultures of Hindu–Jain–Buddhist India and the Jewish–Christian–Islamic Occident, when these are seen in a general perspective, a difference that has large and interesting practical as well as theoretic implications, is found in one aspect of the major conceptions of ultimate reality which have obtained historically in religious thought. In India the description of that reality has been in predominantly impersonal terms, while in the Occident it has been to a large degree personal. I refer here to the occidental conception of God as a person — which is for the most part, though not exclusively, a derivative of the biblical religion — and to the impact of this conception on both theology and metaphysics. And I have in mind, of course, the strong and quite general tendency in Indian thought for sophisticated metaphysics to transcend not only the personal gods of the pantheon but even the God of Hindu personalistic theism.

Among the ideas that have affected Western culture and moved Western civilization, certainly none has been more important than the biblical idea that there is a living God who is a person, and the very concept of personality has been integral to, and indeed partially shaped by, the idea of God's being. This is not to say that the Occident, even since the beginning of Christianity, has not generated impersonal conceptions of God, or that the dominant ideas of God do not involve numerous descriptions which were fashioned for impersonal reality. Consider here, in the first instance, the views of some of the more radical mystics or extreme rationalists, and in the second instance, the large hellenic component of Christian theology where the Platonic and Aristotelian descriptions of an essentially impersonal reality become properties of the living God of biblical revelation. And I do not mean to disregard the dominance in recent years of nontheistic impersonalistic metaphysics or the strength of the modern positivistic tradition, or even the doctrine that is not foreign to Christian metaphysics and theology that defines God more or less impersonally as "being" rather than "a being." My point is simply that since the confluence of ancient cultures in the Roman Empire, the chief informing idea of Western religious culture, however involved in contradictions it may have been, however much confusion it may have produced, and however much it is now disclaimed, has been the concept of God as a living person.

Central to my thesis is the idea that not only is God conceived as personal, but that in the dominant religious tradition there is no reality which is ontologically or cosmologically prior to or superior to God, nothing in the substance or structure of the universe to which he is subject. Although because of his transcendence of the world God in the traditional occidental theism is not a full-fledged metaphysical absolute, he is described nevertheless in absolutistic terms and his ultimacy is guaranteed by the dogma of *ex nihilo* creation.

Consider, in contrast, the tendency of Indian metaphysics to transcend the gods — not necessarily to deny their existence, or in many instances even their religious efficacy, but to reach beyond the anthropomorphic categories of personality in the attempt to provide a rational description of the ultimately real. I do not mean to ignore the great variety in Indian thought and the impressive diversity that is found within the several Hindu schools themselves. And it would be inexcusable to disregard the notable instances in Indian philosophy of personalistic theism where God as a person is the highest reality. Here I have in mind, for instance, such cases as the Viśishtā-dvaita Vedānta of Rāmānuja or the Dvaita Vedānta of Madhva. Rāmānuja's theism, which rejects the extreme monism of Advaita by a critical reading of the monistic passages in the Upanishadic literature, is a near Indian counterpart to classical occidental theism. I think, however, that it has inescapable pantheistic overtones. But the work of Madhva is a highly sophisticated attempt to preserve a genuine theism, yet reconcile it with absolutism — probably a more successful effort to cope with this problem than can be found anywhere among Western theologians.

It is significant for my thesis that even Rāmānuja and Madhva and their disciples, who held strong personalistic views, were deeply involved in the task of preserving the reality of the world and a personal God against the overwhelming monistic and absolutistic thrust of Advaita Vedānta, and that despite their best efforts that monism was often successful in transcending the personal in the final description of reality. The case at issue does not center on monism but rather on the strong tendency in Indian philosophical religion toward impersonalism. The importance of monism here is simply that in Indian thought it has been a powerful instrument in the cultivation of impersonalism in the concept of the ultimate reality. Some kind of dualism or pluralism seems essential to the meaning of personality. There probably is not a better exemplification of this problem than in the metaphysics of S. Radhakrishnan, certainly the most celebrated recent Indian exponent of idealism and defender of the theistic tradition. Radhakrishnan, whose metaphysics stems especially from the *Svetāśvatara Upanishad* and the *Bhagavadgītā*, has denied that Īśvara, the Supreme Person, is *māyā*, phenomenal, but he holds nevertheless to the non-dualistic position that Brahman as the transcendent Absolute is non-personal. Perhaps more than any other Hindu thinker, Radhakrishnan has faced the criticism of occidental philosophers that the monism of Advaita Vedānta negates its theism by relegating its personal God to what is at best a secondary reality. His reply that the Supreme Reality need not be conceived categorically as either personal or impersonal may provide a firm ground for theism, but it clearly falls short of the attempt at unequivocal personalism that characterizes Rāmānuja, Madhva, or the classical Christian theologians.

Turning to the dispositional factors of my thesis, I refer to what I will simply call the "inclusiveness" of the Orient and the "exclusiveness" of the Occident in matters pertaining to religion and to religious and philosophical discussion. My reference here includes the religious syncretism so common among the Chinese and Japanese as well as among the indigenous faiths of India, but it is directed especially to the remarkable attitude of tolerance that characterizes India in matters of religion and philosophic thought. I understand this tolerance to be not a matter of intellectual or moral charity, but rather a deep-seated conviction of the unity of all things and of the incompleteness of every attempted account or explanation of them. I certainly do not mean to ascribe an absolutistic metaphysic to Indian philosophy generally, but absolutism, where it does appear, which is not infrequent, is compatible with this tolerance of disposition, for it conforms nicely to the idea that the supremely real transcends every facet of reality that can be known and experienced. As Radhakrishnan has so effectively put it, "The absoluteness of truth implies the relativity of all formulations of it. . . . Truth wears many vestures and speaks in many tongues."

The inclusiveness, however, is by no means confined to sophisticated thought and discussion, but seems to characterize the culture even in its more primitive aspects, both today and in the distant past. It is exhibited in the peaceful relations that have generally obtained among Brahmanism, Jainism, and Buddhism, in the mutual accommodation of the sects that has often cut across linguistic and ethnic lines, in numerous political actions of historic import condoning and encouraging an ecumenical commitment, in the well-established practice of regarding the *shadh-darśanas*, the six schools, as in a sense orthodox, and especially in the tendency to regard the heterodox and orthodox schools as in some ways complementary rather than conflicting. Allowing for important exceptions, the inclusiveness and toleration seem to have characterized Indian thought generally through its length and breadth, from the early Vedic nature religion to the sophisticated and advanced metaphysical and epistemological systems.

But, returning to the occidental religion, with its predominantly Semitic roots, the picture is radically different. It is the story of an exclusivism that has only rarely yielded to compromise even though the religion has in some ways achieved a quite genuine universality and has had, as at present, its moments of ecumenicity. This exclusivism has well-known symbols in Judaism, Christianity, and Islam — "I am the Lord thy God, thou shalt have no other Gods before me"; "I the Lord thy God am a jealous God"; "There is no other name under heaven by which men can be saved"; and "There is only one God, Allah." There are, of course, numerous features of occidental religion that are in some ways at variance with this exclusivism and that even oppose it in principle: the absence of rigorous creedal requirements in Judaism, the missionary zeal of Christianity and Islam, or the doctrine of the invisible church in Catholicism. But these do not affect the basic exclusive character of these religions that distinguishes them so radically from the oriental faiths: that there is one and only one true God, one and only one body of true doctrine, one and only one law or true church, one and only one way to salvation.[1]

I will not argue this point further, as it appears entirely obvious and the facts on both Orient and Occident are well known. Nor will I hazard an attempt to account for this inclusiveness and exclusiveness. Their causes are no doubt both multiple and subtle. Conceivably they could range all the way from geographic to socio-psychological factors and involve such matters as migration, commerce, war and

---

[1] However, there is an important compromise in this exclusivism, in my opinion, in the Christian doctrine of the Trinity as set forth, for instance, in the Nicene Creed of 325, as well as in the occasional instances of tritheism in Christian theology. Moreover, it is obvious that in matters pertaining to "church" exclusiveness, Judaism differs widely from Christian or even Islamic sectarianism.

peace, diet, and sunshine. But that these cultural characteristics have importantly affected the structure of both religion and metaphysics appears obvious when the development of the ideas of God and ultimate reality is seen historically.

Consider, for instance, the gods of the Vedic hymns in comparison with the conception of Yahweh in the early biblical period. The great Vedic gods of India are the personifications of natural functions; they still exist today because no one of them has driven the others from the field, and because the religious culture of the masses is in that borderland that nourishes polytheism in the presence of high intellectual sophistication. But this does not mean that India has not had or does not now have a genuine feeling for monism, for quite the opposite is true. Nowhere has the inclination toward unity been more pronounced, or its impact on the metaphysics been more effective. But this is just the point. The generosity of Indian inclusiveness has let the gods dwell happily with one another, while the monism passed them by. It is found in the sages and philosophers, expressed in impersonalistic descriptions of an ultimate reality. In the Brahman-Atman doctrine of Advaita Vedānta, the most notable of the Indian monistic philosophies, it is identification with this Absolute that releases the self from the finite limitations of selfhood, the achievement of the Nirvana that is a transcending of particular personality.

The case of Brahman, incidentally, is highly instructive. Brahman today is the impersonal Absolute, the totality of reality in a sense as viewed externally. But back in the Vedic age Brahma was a personal deity who eventually rose, in the Hindu Trimurti in association with Vishnu and Shiva, to the status of creator, the all-powerful God of the universe. In this position he absorbed numerous local deities, and innumerable temples for his worship were erected. But this was, in a rather strange way, his undoing, for, although he contested with his colleagues for power and status, he did not contest their reality and did not eliminate them, but rather came to terms with them. The powerful monistic thrust of Hindu culture, therefore, changing even the gender of his name, converted him into a neutral impersonal Absolute whose reality was over and above that of the personal gods, who became thereby subordinate and convenient expressions of the

Absolute. With a few negligible exceptions the temples to Brahma disappeared and his religion was disestablished. He was received by the philosophers, whose impersonal absolutes transcend the personalistic formulations of sectarianism.

If the Vedic theology is to be regarded as henotheistic rather than polytheistic, as both Max Müller and S. Dasgupta have argued, it is still a henotheism which differs radically from that of the Pentateuch, for the hymns extolling the greatness of a Vedic god, and glorifying his powers and virtues, are apparent efforts to honor and flatter the deity but not to assert his sole importance. The very nature of the gods as representations or manifestations of natural phenomena precluded their being set against one another as competitors for sole reality. Nature is not at war with itself. It is true that this habit of describing the gods eventually produced a form of monotheism in Prajāpati, the Lord of Beings, the creator of the gods. But this was more than anything else simply a monotheistic tendency, for this early conception of the oneness of God lacked both vigor and integrity. Indian monotheism generally has been characterized by a high degree of indeterminateness.

The vagueness of this monotheism derives, it seems to me, from the indefiniteness in the conception and description of the individual gods, who often seem to have been either indistinguishable or interchangeable. Although they are to a considerable degree treated anthropomorphically, their personal character is often in some doubt and their individuality does not clearly shine through the hymns and prayers or stamp itself firmly on the later philosophical discussions. As a facet of my thesis, I am willing to argue that if the Aryan–Hindu mind had been less tolerant and generous in its attitude of inclusiveness, the individual gods would have shaped up more clearly and their personal qualities would have become more distinct. The competition which would then have developed among them would inevitably have strengthened the survivors. The Greek deities, though they too were often expressions of natural phenomena, were more vivid in their individual characters than the gods of the Vedas, perhaps in part because of the extreme anthropomorphism reflected in their often less than admirable indulgence in human practices — an indulgence which at times set them squarely against one another.

In the Hebrew religion, on the other hand, from the earliest time Yahweh was set in the sharpest contrast to the other gods. Indeed, as C. J. Labuschagne has so effectively pointed out in his monograph *The Incomparability of Yahweh in the Old Testament*, even in the Mosaic era the uniqueness of Yahweh resided in his distinctiveness, his incomparability, and the fact of his incomparability was basic to his character. Over and over again in various forms appears the question or assertion "Who is like thee, O Lord, among the gods?" (Ex. 15:11). "There is none holy like the Lord, there is none besides thee; there is no rock like our God" (I Sam. 2:2). Such references are quite unlike the Vedic hymns, which praise the god, even with exaggeration, and focus attention exclusively upon him, but do not declare his total ascendancy above all others. The god who is the object of worship is elevated to supreme status, but this honor is shared with others and is not exclusive. "Indra is sovran lord of Earth and Heaven, Indra is lord of waters and of mountains. Indra is lord of prosperers and sages: Indra must be invoked in rest and effort" (*Rig Veda* X.89). As the object of praise in the hymn, Indra is the greatest of the gods. But the other gods are equally real and when their turn comes they, too, are the greatest.

The achievement of a genuine monotheism in the biblical religion — as found, for instance, in Jeremiah, where the other gods are "worthless, a work of delusion" (10:15), "But the Lord is the true God; he is the living God and the everlasting King" (10:10), and in the Second Isaiah, "I am the Lord, that is my name; my glory I give to no other, nor my praise to graven images" (42:8) — was the climax of a long and arduous struggle of Yahweh with the gods who contended against him. In the Second Isaiah, the prophetic idea of a God of justice and mercy was identified with the popular God of Israel, who had evolved from the tribal desert deity, and with the transcendent cosmic God of Job, who created and rules the world.[2]

---

[2] Here I am following the conjecture of Robert H. Pfeiffer and some others that Job may have been written as early as 600 B.C. by a contemporary of Jeremiah. It is quite possible, of course, that the date of Job's composition was as late as 400. See Pfeiffer's *Introduction to the Old Testament*, part 5, chap. 3, pp. 675–78, for his view that Job was earlier than Deutero-Isaiah, which was presumably written during the latter part of the Exile.

The result was a pure monotheism of the universal God, the creator in whom is every power and every virtue.

It seems to me that the strength of this monotheism issued in considerable degree from the fact of struggle, often desperate struggle, between Yahweh and the national baalim, or Yahweh and the gods of the local fertility cults, a struggle which could very well have been lost, considering the radical cultural transition involved in the change from a desert nomadic culture to a walled-city–land-ownership culture. But the struggle was fought and won, the baalim proving to be powerless, as in the legend of Elijah at Mt. Carmel, and eventually becoming figments of the imagination, as in Jeremiah. And in the struggle Yahweh not only appropriated every power of his adversaries and, breaking through the bonds of parochialism, achieved a remarkable universality, but he became as well a genuinely personal living God whose character was clearly distinguished by his holiness, his power, his purpose, and the absoluteness of his moral will.

Even though the Greek deities were somewhat more distinct and articulate as personalities than the Hindu gods, Zeus, as he became the bearer of an incipient monotheism in the tragedies of Aeschylus, for instance, was no match for Yahweh either as a symbol of the ultimately real or as the embodiment of creative and moral power. For Hesiod he had been the greatest of all the gods and the embodiment of moral justice, but he was a tolerant God whose attitude toward his fellow gods was live and let live. Yahweh's was a magnificent solitude on Sinai, and he fought against every threat to his integrity and every attempt to compromise the uniqueness of his being. But Zeus was a liberal, not given to solitude, and too much involved with pantheonic society. His mountain was cluttered with a motley crowd of divinities who indeed conspired and fought among themselves in a series of in-family bouts, but he did not take a decisive stand against them and seriously challenge their power and their existence until it was too late.

It was too late because the thrust toward unity and monism, with no god capable of completely commanding the field and eliminating all contenders, simply bypassed all the gods and became the work of the philosophers and the philosophical poets. These often showed deference to the gods, employing them as religious symbols or literary devices, but they did not rescue any one of them from the impending oblivion.

Here is the crux of the matter, for both Greece and India. The philosophers, often with the monistic impulses of the rationalists and mystics, constructed their conceptions of the ultimately real with at least a partial and sometimes a complete indifference to the gods, whose easy complacency had betrayed them into forfeiting their hold upon reality. And this meant, in a sense, that the categories essential to the fact of personality were not fully admitted into the description of the highest reality. The philosophers were rarely, if ever, creators of a genuine personalistic theism. More often they were the producers of impersonalism, even when, as with Plato and Aristotle, they sometimes employed the language and sentiments of theology or adopted the form of a finitistic theism, as in the *Timaeus*. Plato and the Platonists were moved by a strong monistic persuasion, but their quest for ultimate reality and ultimate value transcended every consideration of personal deities and produced the impersonal, absolute universals that largely dominated the metaphysics of late classical antiquity. The gods faded into literary allusions, and the conceptions of supreme reality, avoiding the obvious pitfalls of anthropomorphism, were at most only partially personal or pseudo-personal.

The biblical god triumphed over the philosophers, at least for a time, because in the syncretistic culture of the hellenistic world he stood out alone as a living personal God whose strength was fed by his opposition to every challenger. The philosophers from Philo on through the Christian fathers attached their concepts of reality to him and he became the Supreme, the ultimately real, the World Ground. His victory was in a sense a victory of the moral imperative and moral action as against the calm issues of philosophic thought and intellectualized mystic insight. For Plotinus, the One was not personal, because even before he wrote his *Enneads* the gods of Greece and Rome had declined and died to sophisticated thought and religion. There was no deity in the Roman pantheon who had gained enough cosmic stature to be genuinely useful to the philosophers of his day, and the monism of Plotinus' system was in principle inimical to theism. But the Judaeo-Christian personalism thrived.

It was the triumph of a dogmatic, intolerant, and unrelenting faith in the God of time and history, who intervenes with his purpose and power in the course of human events — as against the timeless, motionless object of reason and intuition which serves admirably in metaphysical explanation and with which a mystical experience of unity may perhaps be achieved, but which makes no command to duty and action. It was the victory of the transcendent, living, personal, moral God who did not evolve from the primitive polytheism by easy and peaceful stages of development but who issued instead from the powerful thrust of the intolerant, competitive, and dogmatic exclusivism of the Mosaic and prophetic religion.

I am aware that in these last sentences I may appear to distort both the Greek and Indian theisms, ignoring the personal, activistic, and moral qualities of the gods. But my point, again, is that for most Greek and Indian philosophy, those personal qualities do not describe the ultimately real. In Indian thought especially, the ultimate is more often than not the Brahman taken not as Īśvara, but as the Absolute. The typical position taken by occidental theism, it seems to me, is that which is set forth by Aquinas when he argues in the *Summa Theologica* that God is not in a genus but is the "principle of all being" (ques. 3, art. 5), even though he held, of course, that God should be called a person (ques. 29, art. 3).

Why did the monotheisms and near-monotheisms that appeared among the philosophers not succeed as bearers of the religious and philosophical tradition? Take the Greek philosopher Xenophanes, for example, perhaps a more definite instance than any to be found in Indian literature. Strictly speaking, his theology was neither monotheistic nor polytheistic, for he did not deny the reality of gods other than his One God, nor did he conceive them to be simply natural phenomena. But his was the clearest Greek instance of the celebration of One God as the unity of the divine where the God was clearly a living, conscious, personal being and not simply a metaphysical principle or natural force with some person-like properties. Despite his powerful polemic against anthropomorphism in the description of the divine, Xenophanes' God is easily as personal as any deity to be found in Greek literature.

The answer to this question, it seems to me, is not difficult to find. It is simply that the gods of philosophers have no genuine "lasting power." Gods are like religions, of which they are the foundation. They issue from the folkways and from the living experience of the people. They are the work of the religious practitioners, the priests, the prophets, the saviors. They come from instinctive, intuitive, and dogmatic revelation — not from the pale and quiet reasonings of philosophers. Not, that is, if they are going to last and make a difference. The failure of the Egyptian solar monotheism of Ikhnaton is perhaps the classic example of the lack of strength in a religion that is imposed upon the people as against one that issues from their living experience. Some philosophers, such as the American personalistic idealists, have reared impressively argued metaphysical structures to underwrite the reality of a personal God, or, more properly, the personal character of the World Ground. Usually, however, they have not been the creators of their own personalism but are rather the rationalizers of the personalism of dogmatic religion. Which brings me to my final point.

The strength of the personalistic metaphysics in the occidental intellectual tradition has depended very much on the traditional subservience of philosophy to religion, a religion which was grounded in faith in the Supreme Person. For some time, however, this picture has been changing, for over the past three centuries Western philosophic thought has become progressively independent of religion until now its full autonomy is well established. The strength of impersonalism in Indian metaphysics has resulted in considerable measure from the non-subservience of philosophy to religion, due perhaps to the fact that in India there has been an intimate tie and partial identity of philosophy with religion. In the Occident, at any rate, in the real showdown the philosophers have rarely made the final decision on the religious view of life and the world.

8

Theses on the Idea that God Is a Person

On God as Philosophical Explanation

The question of whether God is a person requires a consideration of the meaning of "person" and of the several contexts in which the concept of God functions. The meaning of "person," as that term is commonly employed in contemporary discourse, should be examined historically, as the roots of the concept of person can be found in at least Greek, Hebrew, and Roman usage.[1] For the limited purposes of this essay, I will simply stipulate the minimum meaning that is now quite commonly accepted among religious scholars, theologians, and philosophers, and which has wide currency in ordinary discourse, that a person is a living being that is self-conscious and has the capacities for thought and volition, a being that thinks and wills. This leaves open the question of whether to be personal a living being must be capable of passion—of being affected or acted upon—

---

[1] See esp. Gordon W. Allport, *Personality: A Psychological Interpretation* (New York, 1937), chap. 2, for an analysis of competing philological and etymological interpretations of the origin of the term "person" and the historical development of the meaning of personality.

[159]

and makes no initial judgment on such issues as whether to be personal an entity must have an environment or be or "possess" a material body. It also leaves for later consideration such matters as whether a person must be an individual or can be a collective whole, whether genuine personality necessarily entails freedom, whether there can be a personal Absolute, and the question of the relation of personality to space and time. The problem of defining "person" is difficult and complex, but a full technical definition is not required for the elementary purposes of this essay.[2]

There are at least three basic contexts in which the idea of God is found: (1) the idea of God employed as a metaphysical explanation of the world of our experience; (2) God conceived as the sanction of value; and (3) God as the supreme object of religious devotion and worship. In typical theistic philosophy, of course, all of these are identified and an argument for one is usually taken as an argument for all. It is assumed that if there is a God whose existence and nature in some way explain the existence of the world, he is also the ground of moral and other value and the object of religious worship. St. Thomas Aquinas, at the close of his famous argument for the existence of God as the first cause of all motion, concludes, "Therefore it is necessary to arrive at a first mover, moved by no other; and this everyone understands to be God."[3]

Now it seems to me that if St. Thomas means by "everyone" theologians and metaphysicians like himself, his statement may be justified. But if "everyone" is really everyone, the rank and file of believers in God, they do not all understand that he is a First Mover, or a First Efficient Cause, or even Necessary Being. They understand that he is a just and compassionate Father who rejoices in their joys and suffers in their sufferings, in whom they place their hope and trust and who is the refuge of their souls.

---

[2] See esp. Edgar Sheffield Brightman's discussion of "The Problem of Human Personality," chap. 11 of *A Philosophy of Religion* (New York, 1940).

[3] *The Summa Theologica*, English Dominican trans. rev. by Anton C. Pegis, in *Basic Writings of Saint Thomas Aquinas*, ed. Anton C. Pegis, 2 vols. (New York: Random House, 1945), I, q. 2, a. 3.

My thesis is a very simple one: That the philosopher's God, who is the explanation of the world, need not be a person; and the sanction of moral virtue need not be a personal God; but that the God of religion is a person; that, if there is a personal God, religion as it has been known to us in Western culture is true. But if not, to borrow the words of Professor William Peppercll Montague, "the voice of God which has so often been heard" is nothing more than "man's own cry mockingly echoed back to him by the encompassing void." [4]

The most impressive early attempt in occidental thought to provide a philosophical explanation for the processes of the natural world was the metaphysics of Aristotle. God is the eternal, immutable, and necessarily existent first and final cause, the unmoved mover of the world. "We say," said Aristotle, "that God is a living being, eternal, most good, so that life and duration continuous and eternal belong to God; for this *is* God." [5] But Aristotle's God, though real being and not simply ideal or an abstraction, falls considerably short of being a person. He is thinking being; indeed he is pure thought — but pure thought thinking only itself. He is final cause, but is not conscious of any purpose. He is pure act, but is active only as contemplation. He moves the world, but only because it is attracted to him. He sustains the processes of the world, but he does not know that the world exists. You and I are dependent upon him for our existence, but he is not aware of us. He is without concern and without compassion. He knows nothing of human history or human tragedy. He is unaware of our hopes or aspirations and hears no cries of pain or suffering. No prayers can reach him, no devotion or worship touch him. For Aristotle God is not a person. Indeed, in Aristotle's culture the very concept of person which is fundamental in modern occidental theism was still in a rudimentary state. His is the classic form of impersonalistic theology. It is with good reason that Whitehead said of Aristotle's metaphysics: "It did

[4] *Belief Unbound* (New Haven: Yale University Press, 1930), p. 7.

[5] *Metaphysica*, book 12, chap. 7, 10721b, trans. W. D. Ross, *The Works of Aristotle*, J. A. Smith and W. D. Ross, eds. (Oxford: Clarendon Press, 1912).

not lead him very far towards the production of a God available for religious purposes." [6]

Now if we cast about in modern thought for a metaphysic that undertakes to accomplish the task which Aristotle set for himself, to provide an explanation for the world, and that in doing so describes ultimate being in its essential nature as personal, the most interesting examples are found in the German-born idealism of the last century, especially as it infected British and more particularly American philosophy into the present century. Indeed, the American forms of personalistic idealism, developed within the general framework of Protestant religious culture and set forth especially by Josiah Royce and Borden Parker Bowne and their students, are the most effective attempt since Aquinas in the thirteenth century to reconcile the classical metaphysics to personalistic theology. Despite their intentions and pretensions, however, there was little about the metaphysical systems of the idealists that suggested anything like the traditional theology beyond the idea that the foundations of reality are personal and are therefore not incompatible with that theology. The theologians will find little comfort in the work of the major idealists if they are searching for support for the typical dogmas of orthodoxy.

Since idealistic metaphysics describes reality essentially in terms of mind and the product of mind, although it is not necessarily theistic in character, the possibility of its establishing favorable alliances with theistic religion is entirely obvious. Royce's religious interests contributed to his absolutistic metaphysics where he is concerned with the interpretation of experience and knowledge and the meaning of self. His Absolute, despite its German antecedents, has a distinctively American "pluralistic" flavor, for, as the very title of his Gifford Lectures suggests, *The World and the Individual*, he employed his uncommon talents in an effort to preserve the reality of the individual self in the very structure of an absolute God. His argument closes with a summary:

> Despite God's absolute unity, we, as individuals, preserve and attain our unique lives and meanings, and are not lost in the very

[6] *Science and the Modern World* (New York: Macmillan Co., 1926), p. 249.

life that sustains us, and that needs us as its own expression. This life is real through us all; and we are real through our union with that life. Close is our touch with the eternal. Boundless is the meaning of our nature. Its mysteries baffle our present science, and escape our present experience; but they need not blind our eyes to the central unity of Being, nor make us feel lost in a realm where all the wanderings of time mean the process whereby is discovered the homeland of Eternity." [7]

Royce was determined to provide a metaphysical foundation for religion, which required, he believed, not only the ontological integrity of the individual self, but as well the reality of the community of selves. The Absolute is a personal God who guarantees, according to Royce, the individual and the community. In his last important work, *The Problem of Christianity*, Royce directed his efforts to the metaphysical support for what he considered to be the threefold basis of Christianity as a religion of redemption: the Beloved Community (the Church), the burden of morality (sin), and the atonement.[8] Here, of course, Royce's Absolute is clearly a personal God, the God of Christian theism. His idealism appeared somewhat more defensible as a possible basis for religion when he argued his position independently of the case for Christianity, for the attempt to tie it to specific Christian principles — even on an undogmatic and carefully reasoned and argued basis — has about it an air of rationalization.

Bowne's metaphysics typically sets the idealistic conception of reality in clear opposition to both materialism and mechanism as these were widely argued at the close of the nineteenth century, claiming the support of both the physical and biological sciences. Of course to deny mechanistic materialism does not in itself establish the case for religion, but Bowne developed an impressive argument from logic, metaphysics, the theory of knowledge, and value theory that the World Ground, the ground of all being, is personal, insisting that on any other terms it is impossible to account for the paradoxical facts that the world is both a unity and a multiplicity and is both identical with itself and in process. Intelligent person-

[7] *The World and the Individual*, vol. 2 (New York, 1901), p. 452.

[8] New York, 1918, passim.

ality, he held, is the only possible key to the nature of reality in all its diversity of fact and value. "Being, causality, unity, identity," he says in his *Metaphysics*, turn out to be "unintelligible and impossible apart from intelligence. . . . Living, acting intelligence is the source of all truth and reality, and is its own and only standard." [9]

Metaphysical idealism has been served up in a variety of forms. The British philosopher J. M. E. McTaggart's very rigorous idealism, although it advanced the idea, uncommon in occidental philosophy, that the human soul or self is uncreated and eternal, is basically atheistic. And whereas Royce is an absolutist, the conception of God in the metaphysics of the American idealist George H. Howison is finitistic. For Howison God is a person in a community of persons who, like God, are self-existent and uncreated. [10] Ralph Tyler Flewelling and Edgar Sheffield Brightman, both in the tradition of Bowne, had difficulties with the Absolute because of the problem of accounting for evil within an absolutistic theism. Flewelling compromises the Absolute by holding that the Absolute imposes limiting conditions upon itself, or rather himself, and Brightman's Absolute is in its very being infected with an "irrational given" which is the source of evil. Neither Flewelling nor Brightman was willing to abandon absolutism for a Jamesian type of pluralism which accounts for evil by a reality that exists independently of God's being and creative power. [11]

I have mentioned Aristotle's metaphysics and American personalistic idealism, not because of any conviction that either is in principle a true description of reality, but rather because here are two systems of metaphysics similar in intent and purpose and not entirely unlike

[9] *Metaphysics* (rev. ed.; New York: American Book Company, 1910), pp. 422, 425.

[10] See McTaggart's *The Nature of Existence*, 2 vols.; vol. 1, Cambridge, 1921; vol. 2, Cambridge, 1927. The best source for Howison is J. W. Buckham and G. W. Stratton, *George Holmes Howison, Philosopher and Teacher* (Berkeley, 1934). This volume includes Howison's only published book, *The Limits of Evolution and Other Essays* (1901).

[11] See esp. Flewelling's *Creative Personality* (New York, 1926), and *The Person* (Los Angeles, 1952); cf. Brightman's *A Philosophy of Religion* (New York, 1940).

in substance, where one settles for an essentially impersonal conception of the ground of the world and the other insists that the very nature even of impersonal reality is unthinkable unless personality lies at its foundation. It can be argued, of course, and I think somewhat justifiably, that Royce, Bowne, and others among the idealists, or outside the framework of idealism for that matter, were engaged in a subtle and sophisticated, but not-too-well-disguised rationalization of the personal conception of God inherited by Christianity from the Hebrew biblical religion. The fact remains, however, that their position is not defended dogmatically, but is argued, and argued brilliantly.

The problem which we face is whether there is any reliable method for assessing the adequacy and truth of a thesis in metaphysics, whether we can choose between Aristotle and the idealists Royce or Bowne at the point in issue, or for that matter decide for any basic philosophical claim. The problem of personalism versus impersonalism is complicated by many factors, as exhibited for instance in the stubborn position of no less a mind than the Oxford philosopher F. H. Bradley, the foremost of the British idealists, who argued that God or the Absolute cannot be conceived as personal, but must be superpersonal. "If the term 'personal,' " says Bradley in his *Appearance and Reality*, "is to bear anything like its ordinary sense, assuredly the Absolute is not merely personal. It is not personal, because it is personal and more. It is, in a word, super-personal." [12] For God to be a person, insists Bradley, he would have to be finite. But that's another story.

With regard to the question of deciding among competent systems of metaphysics, as those of Aristotle, Bowne, and Bradley, I can only admit my own strong skeptical prejudice that is rooted in a reliance on the dictates of experience and a suspicion of speculation, however closely and ingeniously reasoned. It seems to me that we have no reliable ground on which to decide among them, and therefore if the question whether God is a person must be answered simply by resort to rational metaphysics, there is no possibility of our

[12] *Appearance and Reality* (London: Swan Sonmenschein & Co., Ltd., 1908), p. 531.

resolving it. I do not mean by this to suggest that, of several arguments, one may not be more logical, or exhibit more insight or perceptiveness, or be grounded more adequately or faithfully in fact or on acceptable scientific theory. My reservations rest rather on the conviction that, when tested by rigorous empirical criteria of meaningfulness, much of the content of metaphysics, including theology, proves to be quite meaningless, however interesting and attractive, and that the meaningful remainder, such as it may be, is so highly speculative that even if we come out of the ordeal with the truth we nevertheless have no way of knowing that it is the truth.

ON GOD AS MORAL GROUND AND SANCTION

But before turning to the issue of God as the sanction of value I must confess to another relevant bias, a predisposition to favor naturalistic explanation, which raises the question whether it is meaningful to look outside nature for explanations of things, events, or processes that are found in nature. The consequences of the naturalistic bias are positive as well as negative, for although the naturalist denies himself the luxury of such a grand speculation as that there is a supernatural personal force permeating the cosmos, he is deeply conscious of the miracle of the personality that is so obviously part and parcel of nature and than which nothing is more real and which nothing in the cosmos equals in value. Whether the question of how it got there is meaningful or not, or if meaningful whether it can be answered or not, it is clearly true that persons are not less solidly built into the structure of things than sticks and stones and the sun, moon, and stars. Naturalism, indeed, is capable of genuine piety, a piety that issues from a sensitivity to the continuity of humanity with nature, a reverence of personality, and a commitment to whatever is authentically humane.

Now when we raise the question of value and its ground and sanction, the matter is again complicated by the limits of experience, the threat of meaninglessness, and the hazards of speculation. It may very well be true that there is a personal God whose mind is the ultimate residence of value and whose will is the moral law by which we live, a God even who rewards us for our virtues and punishes us for our sins. But if it is true, there would seem to be no way by which we can through natural knowledge know that it is true. And whether there is any knowledge other than natural knowledge is itself a very large problem that raises questions which may be unanswerable. We cannot argue that there is a personal God who is the ground of value simply from the fact that we have values, that we make value judgments and value decisions, that we prize some things and despise others. For there is the theoretic possibility that values exist in the very structure of reality, not as the creations of a creator God or a facet of his being, but, as Plato held, as universal entities that are objective, eternal, and impersonal. I doubt that this is true, but it is a theory that is not to be judged lightly. Perhaps no idea has had a greater impact upon our culture than the concept of real value universals, that truth, for instance, and beauty, goodness, holiness, piety, justice, and whatever else may be judged as having worth exist in their own right as immutable absolutes that are the ground for aesthetic judgment and moral decision and action. Though occidental theism has commonly conceived these absolutes as sustained, if not created, by the mind and will of God, the doctrine of their reality was well established long before they were fastened upon by the theologians in their effort to reconcile the biblical conception of a personal God with the impersonalistic metaphysics of the hellenic culture.

But the question of value sanction is much simpler than the issue of the objective reality of values, for in a sense it can be answered from moral experience. It is obvious that in occidental culture, which has been traditionally dominated by theistic religion, the religious sanction for morality is very strong. Men act in accordance with what they take to be the will of God, or at least they believe that they should act in accordance with his will. And the religious and theological literature and church creeds describe God as a transcendent person, a moral sovereign who prescribes the moral attitudes and conduct proper for mankind.

Now we would rightly deplore the worship of a God who was not believed to be in some way an embodiment of supreme goodness and concerned for the moral quality of human life. And we would be quite justified in our contempt for any church that failed to enjoin a high morality in its adherents. But the question at issue is whether our commitment to moral values in some way or another necessarily does or should depend upon the existence of a personal moral God, or upon belief in such a being, or can be taken as evidence for his existence. It seems to me that, though morality is often made dependent upon religion so that the will of God is the sanction of moral value, such a dependence is not theoretically necessary and may be most unwise in practice, even though it is obvious that the religious motivation in moral behavior can be very powerful. For we may properly ask what should be the moral conduct of those who have no belief in God. Should they not be devoted to the good life equally with those who are believers? Or what of those whose morality is grounded in religion who abandon their religious beliefs and lose their faith in God. Does this justify their abandonment of moral virtue and logically enjoin upon them a kind of amorality and indifference to all value? Clearly this would be indefensible, for by whatever way we may rationalize our moral motives, we actually seek those things which as human beings we regard as good. We may believe, of course, that God wills them, as very well he may, but to disbelieve in God would hardly justify our failure to behave as human beings. Our very humanity is itself a command to moral behavior.

In principle, morality does not require a religious sanction even though there may be those of such depravity that their own motive for good is their concern for divine rewards and punishments. If a man is an atheist he is not for this reason bad. He may in fact be mistaken in his beliefs and the temper of his life may be deeply affected by his atheism, for the tragedy of existence may be more evident to him than to some others. But he may be not only not less but even more devoted to whatever is worthy of human endeavor than one whose reason for moral effort is grounded not so much in humane considerations as in theological beliefs.

In my opinion, such considerations as these on the theoretic possibility of objectively real but impersonal value universals in the Platonic style, and on the principle of a strictly humanistic moral sanction, indicate that the existence of a personal God is not essential to either the theoretic explanation of value or the pursuit of a genuinely moral life. It seems to me that it is no more possible to make a case for traditional personalistic theism on the basis of the argument that God is the necessary ground and sanction for values than by metaphysical speculation that attempts to explain by a theory of reality the world of our experience.

ON THE LIVING GOD OF RELIGION

But when we turn from metaphysics, theology, and morals to the question of religion itself, where God is taken as an object of devotion and worship, of wonder, reverence, and awe, rather than as a principle of rational explanation or legislator of the moral law, it is quite another matter. I do not mean that there cannot be a religion that is totally naturalistic or humanistic and dispenses entirely with the idea of God. But religion as it has been known for many centuries, especially in the Western world — the Judaic–Christian–Islamic religion that has both its history and substantive roots in the prophetic religion of the ancient Hebrews — is grounded in the belief that there is a living God who is a person and in the faith that human souls are central to his purpose. It is a religion that must be defined not simply in terms of a conception of God or of man or of human or cosmic values, but rather as an experiential relation of man to God and God to man; that is, a relation of finite persons to the divine person, of contingent beings to a divine being, to the ground of their own being, or to being itself.

In the whole of the Judaic–Christian religion nothing is quite so fundamental as the often-repeated declaration of the scripture that God is a living God, who said to Moses as he stood in dread before the burning bush, "I am who I am," or "I shall be there." This was not the conceptual God of the philosophers and theologians, but the living existential God of whom Isaiah cried "For mine eyes have seen the King, the Lord of hosts," of whom Jeremiah declared, "But the Lord is the true God, he is the living God . . . at his wrath the earth shall tremble, and the nations shall not be able to abide his indignation. . . . He hath made the earth by his power, he hath established the world by his wisdom, and hath stretched out the heavens by his discretion." He is a just God, and merciful and compassionate. But his holiness overwhelms with awe and to swear by the living God is to swear by the God of terror and dread. As it is said in Hebrews 10: 31, "It is a fearful thing to fall into the hands of the living God."

This is not the God of the philosophers, however much they may wonder on the mystery of things, for their God is a principle of rational explanation. They know of him but they cannot encounter him. It is not the God of the theologians, for the theologians lay the veneer of their life-destroying intellect over everything they touch. And it is not merely the God of the moral life, though it was the supreme achievement of the Judaic religion that the God who became the God of all mankind was invested with every moral perfection and his sovereign will became the moral law. This is, rather, the God of religion. When we ask the question of whether God is a person, it is here and only here that the crucial issue lies.

Now, that God is a person is a religious belief found throughout the world. Popular religion, of course, everywhere personifies its gods, fashioning them in varying degrees in human form, for even among the most sophisticated the play of concrete imagery commonly accentuates the anthropomorphic elements in religious worship. But personalistic theism as a clearly defined, articulate, and institution-alized position is especially a phenomenon of the living religions of Western origin. It has not been unknown in Chinese culture, espe-cially in the instance of Mohism, which flourished for a few genera-tions after the death of its founder, Mo-Tzu, in the early fourth cen-tury before Christ. The God Shang Ti appears to have been for the Mohists a supreme supernatural personal deity who enjoined a uni-versal love, peace, and civic morality. But Confucianism, of which Mohism was a severe critic and rival, more adequately expressed the humanistic, naturalistic, and pragmatic proclivities of the Chinese mind, and the impersonalistic Taoism satisfied better the Chinese mystic temper when it appeared. Shang Ti as a divine person was no match for *T'ien*, the impersonal heaven that has dominated most Chinese religion, or the Tao, the nameless eternal absolute that is the harmony of all opposites and the ground of all being.

In India, on the other hand, where personal gods have flourished in profusion, personalistic theism has been often highly developed, as found for instance in the *Bhagavadgītā*, in the worship of Krishna, the greatest of the incarnations of Vishnu, or in the philosophically sophisticated Vaishnava Vedānta schools whose foremost representa-tive, the eleventh-century philosopher Rāmānuja, described God as a divine person, immanent in the world and transcendent to it, a self-conscious being of will and purpose possessing every good quality.

But if Chinese theism was defeated by naturalism and humanism, Indian theism in all its forms has been constantly pressed from below by the ever-present nature polytheism, and from above by the metaphysical monism and absolutism that have a penchant for absorbing and obliterating personality.

Certainly there is no more interesting problem in the historical study of religion than the explanation of the defeat of the divine personality by impersonal absolutes in India, China, or ancient Greece, while it achieved such an overwhelming victory in the biblical religion, giving that religion a most remarkable vitality by which it conquered much of the world. It seems to me that the personalistic theism which lies at the foundation of occidental religion is causally associated with the *exclusivism* which so commonly characterizes that religion, and that the impersonalism that dominates much Eastern religion is related to the *inclusivism* of the oriental faith. Although I comment on this matter elsewhere in this volume, a brief reference to it may be useful here.

The occidental exclusiveness is well known as a dominant character of our religious orientation and perspective, and its impact on religious doctrine is readily evident. I refer, of course, to the common view in occidental religion that there is only one true God, one true doctrine, one true church, and one way to be saved. This exclusivism, which in various ways and degrees permeates Judaism, Christianity, and Islam, the three Western faiths, and has far-reaching implications for both theory and practice, is in marked contrast to the liberal inclusiveness so common to the Eastern cultures. The oriental ecumenical tendency is exhibited in the Chinese practice of San Chiao where the masses have often practiced a kind of eclectic faith compounded of Taoism, Confucianism, and Mahayana Buddhism, and in the religious complex not uncommon in Japan where there has been a remarkable conjunction of Shinto and Buddhism. But in India, in the great conglomerate of sects, ceremonies, languages, gods, attitudes, beliefs, and technical philosophies known to us as Hinduism, there is a most remarkable degree of mutual recognition and accommodation. The relation of this inclusiveness to the concept of the divine personality is most effectively exhibited in India and perhaps also in Greece, for in the ancient hellenic religion the gods, who of course were persons, got on famously with one another in spite of their petty jealousies and warfare. The point is that no one of the gods was raised up as the only god. No one of the gods denied the power or the very existence of the others.

There have been, unquestionably, countless interrelated and subtle factors in the life and culture of China, India, Greece, or Israel that have determined the relative strength of personalistic and impersonalistic religion and philosophic thought, but it seems to me that among these factors none could be more important than this issue of exclusiveness and inclusiveness. My thesis is simply this, that the biblical exclusiveness produced, or was identified with, the contest of Yahweh against the other deities that in various ways laid claim upon the Hebrew people, and the contest resulted not only in the triumph of Yahweh over the baalim, but in the triumph of personalistic theism over impersonalism. This was a contest, of course, in the minds of men, but it is portrayed with great dramatic force in the biblical account of the movement of the Hebrew religion from its early beginnings to the majestic theism exhibited in the pronouncements of Jeremiah and the Exilic and post-Exilic prophets. It was a contest of the desert Lord of Hosts with the Egyptian nature deities of the Hebrew past, with the local divinities of the Canaanite fertility cults, or with the imported baalim of Syria and Phoenicia. It drew its sanction and certainly much of its remarkable energy from the Exodus commandment, "Thou shalt have no other gods before me." Certainly it was inextricably involved with the economic and political issues that in various and subtle ways contribute inevitably to the theology of a people. And it is symbolized for us in the tradition of Elijah's contest with the priests of the Tyrian baal Melkart at Mt. Carmel.

Now my point is that this achievement of monotheism with its high ethical character is the story of the God of Sinai who would have no other gods before him, or for that matter beside him, who, to put it crudely, took on all comers in open contest and defeated them, establishing first that they were powerless, as in the Elijah legend, and eventually, as in Jeremiah, that they were figments of the imagination. In this way the movement of the religion in the direction of an increasing moral and intellectual refinement was a movement toward a more clearly defined personalistic conception of God, for as the personal God Yahweh eliminated his competition he was by his devotees invested with the powers of the defeated, with the result that he became, as in Job and the later theology, the God who creates and moves the universe and who legislates his purpose upon human history, the God whose status as the ultimate reality was established for occidental religion by the eventual conquest of the Western world by the biblical faith.

The personal concept of God set forth in the Hebrew scriptures is not the result of metaphysical or theological speculation or disputation. It is rather the product of a sense of living involvement with a God who more than anything else is the sovereign of the moral law and the Lord of history. Nothing could have contributed more to the conviction that God is a person, or to the strengthening of that idea and its preservation as the conceptual foundation of religion, than the remarkable and quite unparalleled consciousness of history that pervades the mentality of the Bible. It is a historical sense that deeply infects the whole character of Hebrew and Judaic culture and determines in large measure the quality of both morals and religion and can be seen on virtually every page of the scripture, whether it is poetry or prose, prophecy or wisdom. The genuine reality of history is guaranteed by the temporal nature of God, whose purposes are projected and realized in the course of world events. The world had a beginning and therefore can have an end, so there is a direction and ultimate meaning in human history. It is this meaning that binds God and his purposes so intimately to the world and prevents his loss into the abstractions of the philosophers and theologians. For the Lord of time and history is living and dynamic, with a moral purpose that invades the conscience and decisions of men, instills their hearts with remorse and fear, and impels them to justice and uprightness.

As Judaism and primitive Christianity became increasingly involved with the Graeco-Roman culture of the Mediterranean world, the biblical God triumphed quite handily over the deities of the mystery religions, perhaps more than anything because he was the living embodiment of worth and value and moral will. But the metaphysics of Platonic and Aristotelian origin that permeated hellenistic thought became a permanent threat to the concept of divine personality. Given the confluence of cultures that were brought together by the Greek and Roman empires, it was inevitable that the biblical religion and the Greek metaphysics should confront one another, and it is quite understandable that they would come to terms by producing a new culture, a new philosophy, and a new religion.

At least three factors in the metaphysics posed problems for the religion as the two combined in Christian theology, as the typical Greek conception of the ultimately real was fused with the Judaeo-Christian divine Father–God. In later centuries they similarly affected Jewish thought. First was the character of the Greek metaphysics, for the philosophers had fashioned impersonal descriptions of reality. For Plato the ultimately real was the universals — the value absolutes, such as truth, beauty, and goodness. And of all the absolutes, the Idea of the Good was the highest and the realest. Not a God who is good, but *the* Good, timeless, motionless, and impersonal. But the theologians seemed equal to the task. Following the Jewish philosopher Philo Judaeus, some made the personal God the creator of the impersonal absolutes. But for the most part Christian theology has followed St. Augustine, the greatest of the theologians, in placing the absolutes in the mind of God. They are a facet of his very nature. He eternally thinks absolute truth, beauty, goodness, justice, piety, and every value for which there is an experience, and his will conforms to his intellect. In this way, allowing for occasional variations, the theologians protected the personality of God and guaranteed its ontological superiority to every impersonal reality.

But it seems to me that the second factor was not so easily handled. As a matter of fact, though even today the theologians are quite satisfied with the situation, I am inclined to think that they are in difficulties which many of them refuse to recognize. I refer to the problem of time. The ultimately real of typical Greek metaphysics was timeless and changeless. It was the motionless source of motion, the actionless source of action — an impassive, timeless eternal in which there is neither past nor future. These and other descriptions designed originally in the context of an impersonalistic metaphysics became the materials with which the theologians described the living God. They had their reasons, good reasons, for their task was the reconciliation of the revelation of God with the established philosophic cultures. But we face the question of whether it is meaningful to say that there is a person for whom, as St. Thomas says, there is no succession in time, or for whom all things happen simultaneously. Can there be an eternal, nontemporal person? What can be the meaning of personality that is not in time? And what can be the relation to the world of a being which is not in time?

The possible import of this issue becomes more obvious when we examine the third difficulty — the difficulty of absolutism. Can there be an absolute person? Or can the absolute be a person? Now in fact the Christian God is not a genuine absolute, for an absolute in some way embraces the totality of reality. The absolute is unrelated and unconditioned. The only theism that can be genuinely absolutistic is pantheism, the identification of God with everything and everything with God. But in the Christian religion pantheism has always been a heresy. God is not the world. He is its creator. And though he is in it he transcends it, and in his being he is set over against it.

Yet the classical theologians moved the idea of God as far toward an absolutism as conscience and reason would allow, and the classical theology is in many ways absolutistic, as evidenced by both the doctrinal and popular concepts of God's infiniteness, his omnipotence, omniscience, and omnipresence. This absolutistic quality is exhibited in many of the established creeds of the Christian churches. An excellent statement is given in the *Westminster Confession of Faith of 1647.* "There is but one only living and true God, who is infinite in being and perfection, a most pure spirit, invisible, without body, parts, or passions, immutable, immense, eternal, incomprehensible, almighty, most wise, most holy, most free, most absolute . . . . God hath all life, glory, goodness, blessedness, in and of himself; and is alone in and unto himself all-sufficient . . . [H]e is the alone foundation of all being, of whom, through whom, and to whom are all things . . . his knowledge is infinite, infallible, and independent upon the creature; so as nothing is to him contingent or uncertain. . . ."

This description of God, which is more or less standard for the great majority of Christianity, is supported by the doctrine of the *ex nihilo* creation, that only God has necessary being, that the totality of the world other than himself, including space and time, is his creation from nothing, created freely and not by necessity, in accordance with his free will and purpose. The question whether it is meaningful to say that God described in these absolutistic terms is a person is, therefore, the question whether God existing as the only reality, without the world, can be conceived to be a person. For under the doctrine, before he created the world God was a person, the totality of reality.

Whether there can be an absolute person is in part, of course, the question: What is a person? The classical definition of "person," grounded in Aristotelian metaphysics, accepted by virtually all medieval philosophers, and basic to the Christian doctrine that God is a person, was given by the sixth-century Roman philosopher Boethius: "A person is an individual substance of a rational nature." [13] St. Thomas Aquinas says, "*Person* signifies what is most perfect in all nature — that is, a subsistent individual of a rational nature. Hence, since everything that is perfect must be attributed to God, forasmuch as His essence contains every perfection, this name *person* is fittingly applied to God; not, however, as it is applied to creatures, but in a more excellent way." [14]

It is generally agreed that an explication of rational nature involves self-consciousness, intellect, and will. These three, at least, are what is meant by a person, whether human or divine, a being conscious of its own being, with the capability of thought, purpose, and act. I will not here press the point of "being acted upon," for though an important consideration, this facet of personality is clearly denied by those theologians and creeds which hold, following Aristotle, that God is without passions, that is, that he is totally active and not passive, that he can affect but not be affected. The God of the theologians has no passions. But the God of religion is compassionate.

---

[13] *De Duab. Nat.*, 3, quoted by St. Thomas Aquinas, *The "Summa Theologica" of St. Thomas Aquinas*, literally trans. Fathers of the English Dominican Province (London: Burns, Oates, & Washbourne, Ltd., 1920), I, q. 29, a. 1.

[14] *Summa Theologica*, I, q. 29, a. 3.

Now competent opinion differs widely on the question of an absolute person. It was held, for instance, by the nineteenth-century German philosopher Hermann Lotze, whose arguments underlie much of the technical personalistic metaphysics of the present century, that only the Absolute can be personal in the full sense of personality — a view that should endear him to the orthodox theologians. "*Perfect* personality," said Lotze, "is reconcilable only with the conception of an Infinite Being; for finite beings only an approximation to this is attainable." [15]

But the most impressive absolutistic philosopher of the past century, the Oxford idealist F. H. Bradley, insists that it is meaningless to call the Absolute personal. It includes personality, says Bradley, as I have already pointed out, because it includes human persons, and therefore it transcends personality and is super-personal. But, to quote again from his great work *Appearance and Reality*, "The Absolute is not personal, nor is it moral, nor is it beautiful or true. And yet in these denials we may be falling into worse mistakes. For it would be far more incorrect to assert that the Absolute is either false, or ugly, or bad or is something even beneath the application of predicates such as these. And it is better to affirm personality than to call the Absolute impersonal. But neither mistake should be necessary. The Absolute stands above, and not below, its internal distinctions. It does not eject them, but it includes them as elements in its fulness" (p. 533).

For the most part, says Bradley, in a passage (pp. 532f) that all theologians should read,

> those who insist on what they call "the personality of God," are intellectually dishonest. They desire one conclusion, and, to reach it, they argue for another. . . . The Deity, which they want, is of course finite, a person much like themselves, with thoughts and feelings limited and mutable in the process of time. They desire a person in the sense of a self, amongst and over against other selves, moved by personal relations and feelings towards these others — feelings and relations which are altered by the conduct

[15] *Outlines of the Philosophy of Religion* (Boston: Ginn and Company, 1886), p. 69.

of the others. And, for their purpose, what is not this, is really nothing. . . . Of course for us to ask seriously if the Absolute can be personal in such a way, would be quite absurd. . . . What is not honest is . . . to desire the personality of the Deity in one sense, and then to contend for it in another, and to do one's best to ignore the chasm which separates the two. Once give up your finite and mutable person, and you have parted with everything which, for you, makes personality important.

Now I personally agree with Bradley. I do not agree with his own absolutistic metaphysics, but I agree with his analysis of this problem — that those whose religious faith is faith in a personal God mean by God as a person something in principle very much like human finite personality. They do not want to believe that God is finite. They want him as an infinite person, perfect, without the limitations and imperfections of finite beings. But they want him, nevertheless, to be a being that, though perfect, is a self like themselves, having all their own better qualities, though in perfection. The difficulty encountered is clearly exhibited in the theologians' contention that God is pure act, without passion. On philosophical grounds this description of absolute being is not difficult to justify. The very order of the universe as well as the perfection of God seems to demand it. But the religious worshipper cannot tolerate it. His God must be a person with those qualities that are most valued in finite persons. He must be compassionate; and the theologians' God cannot with consistency be compassionate. He has no passions. Yet for Christianity the very meaning of religion is found in the fact of compassion. A religious man may believe that there is a God who is not compassionate. He may believe in him, and fear him, and revere him. But he cannot worship him.

It should be obvious that the idea that God is a person derives from the human experience of human personality. This very fact, of course, plagues theology with the anthropomorphic, and the theologians have worked diligently, and I believe quite unsuccessfully, to preserve the meaning of personality for the divine while cleansing it of its multiple anthropomorphic associations and implications. The celebrated Protestant theologian Karl Barth, for instance, has argued that the very notion of human personality derives from the concept of divine personality, a strange and clearly forced inversion of the obvious. In this way he hopes to divest the description of God as a person of all anthropomorphisms: "If we represent to ourselves what this means, it will not occur to us to see in this personalizing of the word of God a case of anthropomorphism. The problem is not whether God is a person but whether we are. Or shall we find among us one who in the full and real sense of this concept we can call a person? But God is really a person, really a free subject." [16]

A major problem is whether it is meaningful to say that there could be a solitary person, so that God was a person without the world and without any other persons. It is commonly argued that the very meaning of personality is found only in the reciprocal relation that obtains between persons, so that the fact of personality demands the "I–Thou" relation. But in the classical theology God did not become a person by creating the world. His nature required no completion. Or is it possible that the theologians are wrong in holding that God does not actually *become* a person? The philosophers are freer than the theologians, less inhibited and more adventurous. Martin Buber, with whom we so commonly associate the idea of the "I–Thou" relationship, holds that God is the Absolute, but that an absolute personality is a paradox. Being a kinsman of the existentialists and therefore not one to wince at paradoxes, Buber holds that though one cannot say that God *is* a person, he can say that God loves as a personality, for indeed only persons are capable of love.

> God loves as a personality and . . . He wishes to be loved like a personality. And if He was not a person in Himself, He, so to speak, became one in creating Man, in order to love man and be loved by him — in order to love me and be loved by me. . . . [The Absolute], though in Himself unlimited and unconditioned, lets other beings, limited and conditional indeed, exist outside Himself. He even allows them to enter into a relation with Him such as seemingly can only exist between limited and conditional beings.

[16] *Doctrine of the Word of God*, trans. G. T. Thompson (New York: Charles Scribner's Sons, 1936), p. 157.

This relation is religion. Buber continues:

> It is indeed legitimate to speak of the person of God within the religious relation and in its language; but in so doing we are making no statement about the Absolute which reduces it to the personal. We are rather saying that it enters into the relationship as the Absolute Person whom we call God. One may understand the personality of God as His act. It is, indeed, even permissible for the believer to believe that God became a person for love of him, because in our human mode of existence the only reciprocal relation with us that exists is a personal one.[17]

This remarkably paradoxical and bold idea could come only from a person in whom are joined the unimpassioned reason of the philosopher and the impassioned faith of religious piety.

A somewhat similar position is held by the German-born American philosopher and theologian Paul Tillich, perhaps the foremost theologian of our time. The personal God of the divine–human encounter, the God of theism, must be transcended to the God above God. For the personal God is a symbol not of being but of *a* being, a being in the world among other beings, a thing among other things, an object among objects. Such a God, says Tillich, is an idol and is used by those who use idol gods in their own interest. God cannot be called a self, for God is not *a* being. Rather he is *Being*. "God is called a person," says Tillich, "but he is a person not in finite separation but in an absolute and unconditional participation in everything. . . . The symbol 'personal God' is absolutely fundamental because an existential relation is a person-to-person relation. Man cannot be ultimately concerned about anything that is less than personal. . . ."[18] But "Personal God" does not mean, he insists, that God is a person. It means, rather, "that God is the ground of everything personal and that he carries within himself the ontological power of personality. He is not a person, but he is not less than personal" (p. 245). He is not *a* being. He does not exist as a thing

---

[17] *Eclipse of God* (New York: Harper and Brothers, 1957), pp. 60, 96, 97.

[18] *Systematic Theology* (Chicago: University of Chicago Press, 1951), vol. 1, pp. 243f.

exists. He is Being, the ground of all existence. Atheism is right, says Tillich, in protesting against God conceived as a personal being who exists.

One final example of a philosopher struggling to accommodate the absolute of rational thought to the personal existential God of religious experience is S. Radhakrishnan, the foremost recent philosopher of India, formerly president of India and professor at Oxford. Radhakrishnan, who held that his metaphysics was grounded in the ancient Upanishads, is both a personalistic theist somewhat in the manner of Rāmānuja, and an absolute idealist not unlike the eighth-century philosopher Shankara, the chief figure in Vedānta absolutism. The Absolute, insists Radhakrishnan, is not personal. It is the boundless ground of being that is beyond the distinction of personal and impersonal. In the highest mystic experience there is a union with the Absolute, Brahman, a union that transcends personal relationships but does not destroy individual being. But there is another experience, the personal confrontation of the personal God of theistic religion. Against his Western critics, who have seen inconsistency and confusion in this dualism, Radhakrishnan has advanced an ingenious argument — God and the Absolute are not ". . . exclusive of each other. The Supreme in its nonrelational aspect is the Absolute; in its active aspect it is God." [19]

Now I have cited several examples of the attempt to reconcile in some way the concept of the absolutistic God with the fact of religious experience in order to exhibit the persistence with which this enterprise is engaged in theology and religious philosophy. But there is another tradition in occidental religious thought more radical, more adventurous, and far less popular — the abandonment of absolutism and the frank adoption of a finitistic theology. Where finitism has appeared in churched theology it has been readily branded as heresy. Where it has appeared in academic philosophy it has had a tenuous existence as an unstable ground between metaphysical absolutism and naturalistic humanism.

William James, of course, is the most interesting advocate of a finitistic theology. Here was the most brilliant and most ruthless

---

[19] *The Philosophy of Sarvepalli Radhakrishnan*, ed. P. A. Schilpp (New York: Tudor Publishing Co., 1952), p. 796.

enemy of absolutism in all its forms, the metaphysical absolute, absolutism in moral values, and the absolute God. For James the greatest sin was the denial of the obvious testimony of ordinary experience, to submit to the seductions of a speculative reasoning that describes reality in terms not drawn from the concrete facts of life. A conception of God that does not have genuine relevance to the religious and moral experience was for him nothing less than the perpetration of a fraud.

But James's objection to absolutism was on theoretical as well as practical grounds. He was convinced, and I fully agree with his position, that absolutism makes a genuine discrimination between good and evil an impossibility, that an absolutistic conception of God allows no possibility for a theoretical explanation of the existence of evil. Here is the most difficult theoretic problem confronted by the theologians — the reconciliation of the existence of moral and natural evil with the absolute goodness and absolute power of God. The finite conception of God provided an explanation of evil and it made of God a genuinely living person, involved, as James would put it, in the thick of the very work of the world, enhancing its good, destroying its evil in league with man, creating values in a world in which dangers are real and failures are real, but where triumphs also are real and where they make a difference, a difference not only from the perspective of man, but as well from the perspective of God.

Here there is no problem in describing God as a living person, for the materials with which to paint that description are taken from the concrete facts of the most common experience. The finite God of James's philosophy — finite only in power, to make the facts of evil, tragedy, suffering, moral effort, and moral progress meaningful to theology as they are real in experience, but infinite in goodness, if it is infinitely good to suffer in the true sufferings of mankind and rejoice in the happiness and moral achievement of men — that God, described as a genuine person, the champion of every value and filled with love and compassion for mankind, would seem to have great appeal to religion. Here at last is a philosopher who has come to terms with religion as a fact.

But James and the finitistic theologians have failed to capture religion — failed miserably. Even James, the archpluralist and finitist, confessed a mystic's longing for union with the infinite. It is clear that most religionists want an absolute to worship as much as they want a person. Their God must have the whole world in his hand, for they do not propose to take their problems to a God who has problems of his own.

I have failed even to mention mysticism as an approach to the question of whether God is a person. But here there is nothing definitive even if one were to accept as veridical the mystics' accounts of their own experiences. There is always the problem of the impact of philosophical or theological ideas on the very character of the mystic experience. In India mysticism tends toward unity or even complete identification with an impersonal absolute, although the experience of the presence of a personal God is not foreign to Indian mystics. In occidental religion the mystic experience more often is an experience of the person of God. Although this experience is usually regarded as a coming into the presence of God, the claim of union with an impersonal absolute is not entirely foreign to Western mysticism. The foremost authority on Jewish mysticism, Professor Gershom Scholem, has shown, for instance, that even in Jewish Kabbalism the issue arises of whether the ultimately real, *En-Sof*, is personal or impersonal — impersonal being that becomes personal only in the process of creation.[20]

I do not believe that we can establish by reason whether there is a God, or if there is, whether God is a person. Religion is a matter of faith and hope, or perhaps of mystic experience. It is, again to borrow the words of one of my teachers, Professor Montague, the faith that "what is highest in spirit is also deepest in nature," the faith that the things that matter most are not ultimately at the mercy of the things that matter least. It may be that there is no God, that "the existence of all that is beautiful and in any sense good is but the accidental and ineffective by-product of blindly swirling atoms," that we are alone in a world which cares nothing for us or for the values that we create and sustain — that we and they are here for a moment only, and gone, and that eventually there will be left no trace of us in the universe. As Montague says, "A man may well believe that this dreadful thing is true. But only the fool will say in his heart that he is glad that it is true." [21]

---

[20] See Gershom G. Scholem, *Major Trends in Jewish Mysticism* (Jerusalem: Schocken Publishing House, 1941), First Lecture.

[21] William Pepperell Montague, *Belief Unbound*, pp. 6, 66, 67.

9

Cause, Determinism, and the Freedom of the Will

I

In his plea to the court to avoid the death penalty for Loeb and Leopold, Mr. Darrow argued that the defendants were not responsible for the act of murder which they had committed, because that act followed from their being the kinds of persons that they were, together with the circumstance of their mutual association, and, he insisted, they surely were not responsible for being what they were. He laid that responsibility upon their biological inheritance and social environment.

Mr. Darrow hesitated to fix a definite responsibility for the crime on any thing or person in particular, but he eloquently implicated the nerves, muscles, endocrine glands, vegetative systems, parents, grandparents and great grandparents, abnormalities, emotions, lack of emotions, intellect, instincts, lack of instincts, madness, training, psychophysical machinery, governesses, tutors, money, fantasies, education, youthful lying and cheating, and the "dwarfed and twisted brains" of the defendants. Also implicated in the inevitable chain of causes of the murder were lack of love, direction, and understanding, automobiles, philosophy, the University of Chicago, the "infinite economy of nature," Friedrich Nietzsche, and the universe.

In short, Darrow declared, "Something was wrong." [1] But the wrong was in no way a responsibility of the murderers, who were themselves but the tragic victims of chance or inexorable fate. "I know," he said, "that one of two things happened to Richard Loeb; that this terrible crime was inherent in his organism, and came from some ancestor, or that it came through his education and his training after he was born." [2] And again, "Nature is strong and she is pitiless. She works in her own mysterious way, and we are her victims. We have not much to do with it ourselves. Nature takes this job in hand, and we play our parts." [3]

Now Mr. Darrow shrewdly avoided calling the judge's attention to the fact that his honor was himself equally a victim of pitiless nature, as also was Darrow in taking the case in the first place, and the judge, encouraged by Darrow's eloquence into the error of supposing that he was himself free and could make a decision, decided for the defendants and returned a judgment of life imprisonment rather than execution, for which mercy not he, but his endocrine glands, the universe, and a singularly aggressive sperm of some remote ancestor should have received the credit.

In the seventeenth century, Baruch Spinoza had already accounted for the murder, Darrow, Judge Caverly and all their ancestors by a piece of reasoning quite uncommon in its rigor. And whereas Darrow, whether out of his well-known agnosticism or a judicious piety, constrained himself against specifically naming the Almighty in his list of suspects, Spinoza, being a pantheist and therefore on somewhat more intimate terms with divinity, was without scruples in such matters and barefacedly declared that every event in the universe is necessitated by God. And not only that, but that God is the cause of these events, murders included, not by any freedom of will that is his, but rather from their following necessarily from his very nature,

---

[1] Clarence Darrow, *Plea in Defense of Richard Loeb and Nathan Leopold, Jr., on Trial for Murder*, August 22, 23, and 25, 1924.

[2] Ibid.

[3] Ibid.

as do theorems from their axioms and postulates.[4] Nor did Spinoza hesitate to face the final implicate of his argument, that the murder of Bobby Franks had to happen, and that not only Loeb and Leopold but even God himself could not have prevented it, since for it not to have happened there would have to have been a different God.[5]

Now Darrow's views were the product of his sympathy for those who face condemnation together with the new social psychology of the twenties that served a growing social conscience with a combination of bad sentimentality and good theory, while Spinoza, one of the most compassionate of men, derived his theory from an almost ascetic discipline of the emotions and an inordinate passion for mathematical demonstration which dictated that whatever happens, happens necessarily. This means that it could not have not happened, and it is futile to assert a freedom of will that in some way determines some events to be what they are, whereas they might have been otherwise.

The question of free will is old, complex, ambiguous, unanswered, and quite possibly without meaning. But meaningless or not, there is no problem since the beginning of serious thought that has been more persistent or more fundamental in the intellectual, moral, and spiritual enterprise of man. It lies at the foundation of all great religion and most great literature, is an ever-recurrent theme of both

---

[4] *The Ethics*, part one, Concerning God, proposition 29, "Nothing in the universe is contingent, but all things are conditioned to exist and operate in a particular manner by the necessity of the divine nature."

[5] Ibid., proposition 33, "Things could not have been brought into being by God in any manner or in any order different from that which has in fact obtained." And, in note 2 of the same proposition,

> Further, all the philosophers whom I have read admit that God's intellect is entirely actual, and not at all potential; as they also admit that God's intellect, and God's will, and God's essence are identical, it follows that, if God had had a different actual intellect and a different will, his essence would also have been different; and thus, as I concluded at first, if things had been brought into being by God in a different way from that which has obtained, God's intellect and will, that is (as is admitted) his essence would perforce have been different, which is absurd.

Nevertheless, God is free, for Spinoza, because he causes according to his own nature and is the cause of himself; see part one, proposition 34.

metaphysics and ethics, and invades the physical as well as the life sciences. It is an eternal story of man against his world; of freedom struggling with a universe necessitated and determined; of hope and aspiration against a life ordained and a future predestined; of the fight against fate, providence, or the cold necessity of the world machinery. And more than anything else it is the rebellion of the moral conscience against the injustice of a morally indifferent universe. It is here in the metaphysical controversy on the freedom of the will that we encounter the chief foundation of human tragedy.

It seems obvious that the primary reason for believing that we have freedom of the will is that we seem to ourselves to be free. That is, that on occasion we intentionally and perhaps with deliberation choose a course of action when we might have done otherwise. Because it would seem that this quite ordinary experience of free will is universal, being common to all men of whatever race, place, or time, and because the experience itself seems entirely persuasive as an argument, the denial of free will that has been such a persistent and pervasive factor of human culture requires some explanation. I believe that there are five fundamental forms of the denial of freedom, which may be designated *mythological, mechanical, logico-mathematical, theological,* and *metaphysical.* Separately and in combination, these have described a large measure of the world's fundamental thought and attitude.

1

The antique world was under the dominion of the dogma of *fate,* that life is lived under the rule of necessity and the freedom which men find in themselves is somehow an illusion that is banished by a more adequate perspective. The courage of the ancient poets, prophets, and philosophers may often be measured by the radicalness of their objection to this doctrine, a view somewhat dominated by an aesthetic orientation to the world which encouraged moral indifference. Aeschylus' Prometheus, suffering the ravening vulture to feast upon his heart rather than submit to the dominion of an immoral Zeus, is the supreme symbol of rebellion against the classic mythology with its implication of the bondage of fate and destiny.[6] It is quite possible that the general structure of myth which undergirds the ancient belief in fate evolved prior to the achievement of the clear consciousness of individuality presupposed by the conception of freedom and responsibility.

But the maturing of moral conscience and the rise of scientific intelligence did not readily dispel the Fates. The decline of the Olympian deities raised the myth of fate to the stature of a religious principle where it was made orthodox by time and was secured by incorporation in the official institutions. Its role even in affairs of state is indicated dramatically by the coin struck in the first decade of the fourth century by Diocletian to mark his abdication of the imperial office, a coin celebrating the "All-powerful Goddesses of Fate." And this to mark the abdication that he himself had carefully planned, dated, and announced twenty years earlier as part of a remarkable effort to save the Empire from the plague of short-tenured military rulers.[7]

2

The *mechanical* denial of free will is simply a causal determinism that dispenses with both gods and goddesses, and, caring nothing for astrology and divination by entrails, accounts for events entirely by reference to prior events which are their causes, insisting on a causal law that describes the universe totally, there being no events in nature that are not caused by other events in nature. Our friend Mr. Darrow, a champion of nature on more occasions than one, was a member of the class of accepters of this thesis. But almost twenty-five hundred years before Mr. Darrow's appearance on the scene, Democritus of Abdera, one of the foremost liberators of the human mind and the

---

[6] *Prometheus Bound*, Herbert Weir Smyth trans.

HERMES: Bend thy will, perverse fool, oh bend thy will at last to wisdom in face of thy present sufferings.

PROMETHEUS: In vain thou troublest me, as though it were a wave thou wouldst persuade. Never think that, through terror at the will of Zeus, I shall become womanish and, with hands upturned, aping woman's ways, shall importune my greatly hated foe to release me from these bonds.

[7] See, e.g., Jacob Burckhardt, *The Age of Constantine the Great*, chap. 2.

chief inventor of the idea of atoms, described the world, including the mind, its sentiments, and even the knowledge process, as a rigorously determined and purposeless machine, totally governed by the laws of mechanics.[8] Now had this atomistic mechanical conception of the world prevailed in antiquity it might very well have radically changed intellectual history, but it was not a successful competitor against the purposive conception of reality that eventually, with the triumph of Platonism and Aristotelianism, pervaded even the sciences themselves. Yet mechanism was to have its day, and from Galileo until Einstein the growing success of physical science as a technique of explanation produced an extension of causal determinism from simple mechanics to include astronomy, optics, electromagnetism, and thermodynamics resulting in a mechanical synthesis that has claimed biology as well and has attempted to capture even psychology and the social sciences.

This modern conception of a mechanistic world had a more subtle theory of atoms than that of Democritus and, unlike his, was supported by mathematics and by both a disposition and a technique for observation. But in principle, when accepted as a full account of reality, its implication for free will was the same — apparently there isn't any. Everything happens by rigorous causal necessity. Things could not be other than they are.

In ancient times the chief, but not the only, challenger of the Democritan mechanism was Epicurus, a moral philosopher who founded his metaphysics on the atomistic theory but who rejected determinism in favor of free will as a guarantee of moral responsibility. Free will for the Epicureans, as for most free-willers since their time, meant that the will is an uncaused cause, that in willing events occur which are not caused by any other events. Such freedom

[8] See H. Diels, *Fragmente der Vorsokratiker*, for the extant fragments of Democritus. English trans. Kathleen Freeman, *Ancilla to the Pre-Socratic Philosophers*. For the atomistic metaphysics, see, e.g., Aristotle, *Physics*, 3:4; 4:6, 8:1; *Metaphysics*, 1:4. Democritus' own extensive writings on atomism, causation, and mechanism are lost. A fragment from Leucippus, described by Aristotle as an associate of Democritus (ca. 430 B.C.), indicates the necessitarian character of atomism: "Nothing happens at random; everything happens out of reason and by necessity." Diels, fragment 2, Freeman trans.

is possible in the metaphysics and physics of Epicureanism because it resides in the atoms themselves, which, in falling through empty space, deviate without cause from the perpendicular and thereby upset the otherwise causal order of the world.[9]

We still have Epicureans among the modern opponents of scientific determinism. They find freedom in the subatomic particles, insisting that a fundamental indeterminism characterizes the world on the lowest level, where electrons behave in a quite unorthodox uncaused manner.[10] But the justification for this view, the quantum theory principle of uncertainty, admits of other interpretations that may be less congenial to freedom.

3

But to turn from the mechanistic to the *logico-mathematical* argument for determinism, the point is obvious. By its very nature, logic is characterized by necessity. Logical conclusions follow necessarily from their premises; they cannot possibly be other than what they are. Or consider the theorems of geometry, that they follow necessarily from their axioms and postulates. Now I am not suggesting that one committed to mathematics must be committed also to a necessitated world, but it is true that the formal structure of logic and mathematics has been a powerful support of determinism, particularly through the fundamental role of mathematics in mechanics.

[9] The Roman poet–philosopher T. Lucretius (d. 55 B.C.), in the *De Rerum Natura* (book 2, R. E. Latham trans.), is the chief ancient expositor of Epicureanism.

> If the atoms never swerve so as to originate some new movement that will snap the bonds of fate, the everlasting sequence of cause and effect — what is the source of the free will possessed by living things throughout the earth? What, I repeat, is the source of that will-power snatched from the fates, whereby we follow the path along which we are severally led by pleasure, swerving from our course at no set time or place but at the bidding of our own hearts? There is no doubt that on these occasions the will of the individual originates the movements that trickle through his limbs.

[10] See, e.g., Arthur S. Eddington, *The Nature of the Physical World*, and Hans Reichenbach, *Atom and Cosmos*.

The classic example is Laplace's calculator who, in the system of Newtonian mechanics, could calculate the total future of the universe from its present state as one deduces a theorem from its axioms, for under such a system the future is contained in the present and the present in the past as the theorems are contained in the axioms.[11] The chronological is in principle logical.

But if logico-mathematical determinism has been most effective in mechanics, it has still been a major impact as the immediate basis of deterministic metaphysics, as in the instance of Spinoza already mentioned. Spinoza's passion for mathematical models and his geometric method were derived in large measure from the mathematician René Descartes, who, with less consistency than Spinoza, had declared that the world is a deterministic machine, but only up to a point, the point where the mind or soul enters the picture. The physical world, including your body, is rigorously mechanical. Your soul is free, yet it has a physiological tie-up with your body and can affect your bodily actions.[12] But just how this can be the case and the body remain a strictly deterministic affair is a secret that Descartes never disclosed.

4

The *theological* argument against freedom has had a long and somewhat interesting career from the earliest biblical attempt to fashion an adequate concept of man's relationship to God by the simple story of Adam's fall and his expulsion from the garden, through the countless efforts to read sophisticated meanings into that

---

[11] "Given the distribution of the masses and velocities of all the material particles of the universe at any one instant of time, it is *theoretically* possible to foretell their precise arrangement at any future time." This version of the principle of Laplace is quoted from W. P. D. Wightman, *The Growth of Scientific Ideas*, p. 112.

[12] See *Meditation II*; Objections to the Second Meditation by P. Gassendi; and *Reply to Fifth Set* [Gassendi's] of *Objections to Meditation II*; *Meditation IV*; *The Passions of the Soul*, part 1, art. 30 et seq. Descartes' treatment of the nature and relation of the mind and body as totally different realities initiated the discussions of the Occasionalists (especially Geulincx and Malebranche), Spinoza, and Leibniz, and set the foundations for the main tradition of psycho-physical dualism.

narrative. The Bible moves between myth and theology in its graphic account of the achievement of the free conscience. Nowhere is man's demand for freedom more eloquent than in Adam's decision to obtain the knowledge of the gods, nor is it more dramatic than in the tragedy of Job condemning the injustice of orthodoxy's god and the tyranny of a morally indifferent universe.[13]

During the era between the Testaments there was an elementary structuring of Hebrew theology and the free will controversy became explicit. In Ecclesiasticus of the second century before Christ, Jesus ben Sira asserts an unqualified freedom of will in man's choice of sin.[14] And with more inspiration than logic he affirms that God who is almighty and the total creator of the world, and planted in man an evil impulse, is nevertheless not responsible for man's moral evil. He thus formulated the fundamental problem of theodicy, the reconciliation of divine omnipotence with the reality of evil.

In the theological controversies of the Jews under the Hasmoneans and the Romans, the Essenes denied that man has freedom of choice, affirming that everything in the life of man is determined. The Sadducees, with less humility and more pride in human achievement, preferred prudence to providence and insisted on the freedom of the will. The Pharisees, interpreters of the common religion and the chief influence on both Judaic and Christian theology, compromised somewhat paradoxically, especially in the dominant school of Hillel, giving God credit for all as a divine Providence, yet refusing to let men escape responsibility for their moral decisions.[15]

---

[13] "Therefore I will not restrain my mouth; I will speak in the anguish of my spirit; I will complain in the bitterness of my soul. . . . Behold, he will slay me; I have no hope; yet I will defend my ways to his face." Job 7:11, 13:15, RSV.

[14] E.g., chap. 15, "God created man from the beginning and placed him in the hand of his inclination."

[15] This comment on Essenes, Sadducees, and Pharisees is based primarily on Josephus. See *Antiquities of the Jews*, book 13, chap. 5, and *Wars of the Jews*, book 2, chap. 8. See also Louis Finkelstein, *The Pharisees*, vol. 1, chap. 11, and G. F. Moore, *Judaism*, vol. 1, pp. 456f.

In the second century the great Rabbi Akiba wrote in the Mishnah, "All is foreseen, but freedom is granted";[16] and in the fourth, St. Augustine insisted on the absoluteness of God's foreknowledge while still defending the freedom of the will.[17]

Now of course every alert teenager has harassed his Sunday School teacher with the insistent question, if we are *really* free to choose, how can God know our choice in advance? And the teacher, frustrated by his inability to put his hands on a satisfactory answer, has usually condemned the inquisitor for impudence. The only sure cure for those who raise such questions is to make Sunday School teachers of them. This should put an end to their questions. But such harassed teachers may at least enjoy the consolation of good company, for the greatest of the theologians, who worked out most of the problems and most of the answers, had to be satisfied with the same emotional reaction. In the *De Libero Arbitrio*, St. Augustine held that for the most part men are tormented by the question of whether God's foreknowledge is a denial of human free will "only because they do not seek with piety, and are quicker at excusing than at confessing their sins." [18]

But to worry about free will in the face of God's foreknowledge is but the beginning of the problem. For the God of the traditional theologians is eternal, by which is meant that he is timeless, without a past or a future, living in a sense in a kind of nontemporal omni-

---

[16] *Abot*, 3.16.

[17] *De Libero Arbitrio Voluntatis*, trans. C. M. Sparrow, book 3, chap. 3, "And so it comes about both that we do not deny that God foreknows all that is to be, and that notwithstanding we may will what we will. For when He foreknows our will, it will be that very will that He foreknows. It will therefore be a will, because His foreknowledge is of a will. Nor can it be a will if it is not in our power." See also *De Civitate Dei*, book 5, chap. 9–11, "For a man does not therefore sin because God foreknew that he would sin. Nay, it cannot be doubted but that it is the man himself who sins when he does sin, because He, whose foreknowledge is infallible, foreknew not that fate, or future, or something else would sin, but that the man himself would sin, who, if he wills not, sins not. But if he shall not will to sin, even this did God foreknow." From chap. 10, trans. J. J. Smith.

[18] Ibid., book 3, chap. 1.

present — a dogma developed largely on the inheritance from Greek metaphysics and mathematics. Now what is the status of free will if God not only knows what is going to happen, but is already experiencing it; if your thoughts tomorrow, or your descendant's actions a thousand generations from now are already occurring for God, together with whatever has happened in the near and distant past? This is a difficult thought, the eternalness or nontemporality of God, and we have no common term to represent it. But there is one near at hand. Those who have no qualms about the orthodox dogma that God, being nowhere in particular, is everywhere in general, should feel no hesitation in affirming that, being nowhen in particular, he is everywhen in general. Indeed, the nontemporality of God is a far more important doctrine in technical theology than is his nonspatiality; its implications are richer and more far-reaching. God is everywhere and everywhen.

The classical Christian doctrine of God's eternity was formulated by St. Augustine in the *Confessions* in one of the most brilliant of treatises on the nature of time, the eleventh book, where he discusses the nature of time and its relationship to eternity as a response to the question, "What did God do before He created the world?" Augustine's answer, of course, is that since time was created with the world, with the creation of heaven and earth, there was no "before" the world was created.

Those who say these things do not as yet understand Thee, O Thou Wisdom of God, Thou light of souls. . . . They even endeavor to comprehend things eternal; but as yet their heart flieth about in the past and future motions of things, and is still wavering. Who shall hold it and fix it, that it may rest a little, and by degrees catch the glory of that ever-standing eternity, and compare it with the times which never stand, and see . . . that in the Eternal nothing passeth away, but that the whole is present; but no time is wholly present; and let him see that all time past is forced on by the future, and that all the future follows from the past, and that all, both past and future, is created and issues from that which is always present?[19]

---

[19] *The Confessions*, book 11, chap. 11, trans. J. G. Pilkington.

In the *Institutes of the Christian Religion*, Calvin describes God's foreknowledge as being not a matter of future and past, but as meaning that "all things always were, and perpetually remain, under his eyes, so that to his knowledge there is nothing future or past, but all things are present. And they are present in such a way that he not only conceives them through ideas, as we have before us those things which our minds remember, but he truly looks upon them and discerns them as things placed before him." [20]

God's eternity is perhaps even more explicit in the more becalmed, consistent, and systematic work of St. Thomas Aquinas, who is today the dominant philosophic voice in the Catholic world. In the *Summa Theologica* Aquinas defends the definition of the sixth-century philosopher Boethius, that "Eternity is the simultaneously-whole and perfect possession of interminable life," insisting that God's eternity follows from his immutability and that he alone is eternal and that to be eternal is to have neither "before" nor "after." [21] But this does not deter Aquinas from defending the freedom of the will. On the contrary he wrote it into the fundamental structure of Catholic philosophy and theology. In the *Summa Contra Gentiles*, [22] after asserting that "God, by His providence, is the governor of all" (book 3, chap. 64), and that "it is He who causes the actions of all things" (book 3, chap. 67), he insists, in the same discourse, that "the divine providence does not impose necessity on things, by excluding contingency from them altogether" (book 3, chap. 72).

[20] *Institutes of the Christian Religion*, book 3, chap. 21, trans. Ford L. Battles.

[21] See *Summa Theologica*, I, q. 10, art. 1–3. "Further, *those things are said to be measured by time which have a beginning and an end in time* . . . because in everything which is moved there is a beginning, and there is an end. But as whatever is wholly immutable can have no succession, so it has no beginning, and no end. Thus eternity is known from two facts: first, because what is eternal is interminable — that is, has no beginning or end; secondly, because eternity itself has no succession, being simultaneously whole" (article 1). "Hence, as God is supremely immutable, it supremely belongs to Him to be eternal" (article 2).

[22] Cf. *Summa Contra Gentiles*, book 3, chap. 64–75.

Fortunately for the richness and variety of religion, our better theologians, among their other virtues, have never lacked the courage to propound inconsistencies, however great. Indeed, it would seem that today paradox and antinomy are among their chief commodities. But it is not that they are no respectors of logic, or of common sense. To condemn them on such a ground is to fail utterly to sense the profundity of their problem and the quality of their motive. For they are at one and the same moment obsessed with the moral responsibility of man as the cause of his own evil and with the omnipotence and omniscience of God, the utter absoluteness of his goodness and power, his presence, and his providence. To deny the first would be to abdicate human freedom and thereby negate the very ground of personality; to deny the second would be, for them, to commit blasphemy.

The denial of God's absoluteness has been attempted on numerous occasions as a solution to the problems of free will and moral and natural evil, the most celebrated theory belonging to our own time, the finitistic theology of liberal religion that was given a brilliant philosophical foundation in the pluralism of the American philosopher William James.[23] But with all the inroads of liberalism and finitism, whether in Islam, Judaism, Catholicism, or Protestantism, and despite all the charges of inconsistency, the absolutistic conception of God still reigns as both the pattern of orthodoxy and the general belief.

I believe it is common to suppose that the typical theologians of the major Christian traditions were deniers of free will. But this is not true. It simply appears to be the case if one notes only the obsession with providence and grace, or the persistence of the doctrines of election and predestination. But divine election to salvation and predestination are by no means necessarily incompatible with free agency and are usually propounded in company with the doctrine of freedom. And further to the contrary, there is every evidence that the theologians struggled manfully to protect freedom. But whether it was Paul, Augustine, Aquinas, Luther, Calvin, or Edwards, they refused to sacrifice to free will the foundation dogma of the Christian

[23] See his *Pragmatism, A Pluralistic Universe*, etc.

religion, that man is a dependent being and his salvation is a gift of
God through Jesus Christ. Every major symbol of the Church reflects
the divine–human tension, the theoretical conflict between grace and
human freedom with its implicate of merit. The Church has quite
persistently attempted the defense of free will, but within the limits
of the doctrine of grace, and those whose emphasis on human responsibility and merit has threatened the orthodox commitment to salvation by grace have been declared heretical. The predestinarian doctrines of Luther and Calvin resulted not from any desire to deny freedom and responsibility but from their assumption that the Augustinian formula of double predestination, that there is appointment to
both damnation and salvation, was the only alternative to a grace-
denying Pelagianism.

The position of Aquinas has already been indicated. His defense
of freedom, with its doctrine of partial merit, was justified by the
sixteenth-century Council of Trent. Among the propositions that
were there anathematized was the assertion "That man's free will
has been wholly lost and destroyed after Adam's sin." And the proposition immediately following, "That it is not in the power of man to
make his ways evil, but that evil works as well as good are wrought
by God. . . ." [24]

Adam, who was simply following his wife's urging, has taken a
severe beating in this matter. Every theologian has assured us of all
forms of desirable freedom, that in the beginning Adam had'm.
And all in all he seems to have done what he was supposed to do to
get the whole thing started off right, with plenty of evil for men to
enjoy and from which they could then be redeemed. And yet he has
had nothing but blame for it. [25] At any rate, the Augustinian formula

---

[24] Council of Trent, Canons on justification, Session VI, January 1547.

[25] Even Augustine, who under the influence of Neoplatonism defined
both the evil will and evil in negative terms of deprivation rather than as
positive and absolute, held that God would not have created man with the
capacity to will evil had he not foreseen that man as evil would better sub-
serve the ultimate end of a greater good than man without the freedom to
sin. A world of oppositions, seen in its wholeness, is good. "And the sinful
will, though it violated the order of its own nature, did not on that account
escape the laws of God, who justly orders all things for good. For as the

on Adam and original sin, which is based especially on the Epistle to
the Romans — and which, while of basic importance in Catholicism,
became the main foundation of the Protestant doctrine of salvation
and predestination — describes the first man as having free will
before the fall, possessing freedom to choose either good or evil.
But in choosing evil he lost his freedom to choose the good, while
retaining freedom to choose evil.[26] Likewise the rest of us, thanks to
the fall, are free, but free only to do evil. Our good is by the grace
of God. Now this may seem to be a questionable freedom, but it was
at least a try, and even a cursory reading of Augustine, Calvin, or
Luther will convince one that much serious thought went into its
justification.[27] Indeed, no one has discussed the problem of the
human will with more brilliance and originality than Augustine.

The sixteenth-century Augsburg Confession, the first symbol of
the Lutheran religion, while condemning Pelagianism, the most persistent and consistent form of free-will doctrine, still affirmed a
guarded freedom in the following: "They teach that human will has
some liberty in the accomplishment of civil righteousness and in the
choice of things which are subject to reason. But without the Holy
Spirit it has no power of accomplishing the righteousness of God,
or spiritual righteousness. . . ." Moreover, "although God is the

---

beauty of a picture is increased by well-managed shadows, so, to the eye that
has skill to discern it, the universe is beautified even by sinners, though, considered by themselves, their deformity is a sad blemish." *De Civitate Dei*,
book 11, chap. 23; cf. book 12, chap. 3, and *De Vera Religione*, 44.

[26] See *De Civitate Dei*, book 14, chap. 10–13, and book 22, chap. 30.
Before the fall, Adam was able not to sin — *posse non peccare* — but after
the fall, all men were unable not to sin, *non posse non peccare*. But man's
supernatural destiny, by the grace of God, is to become unable to sin, *non
posse peccare*.

[27] To the complaint of the Pelagians that without the freedom to choose
good as well as evil there is no genuinely free will, Augustine replied that
fallen man's choice of evil is free because whatever is willed is thereby freely
willed. "Why perplex a very plain subject. He is free for evil who acts with
an evil will. He is free for good who acts with a good will." *Ap. Imp.* 1:3,
c, 120.

creator and preserver of nature, yet the cause of sin is the will of evil persons. . . ." [28]

Calvin, the favorite whipping boy in matters of this kind, is the chief sinner against free will, insisting that not only does God intervene to direct men's wills but that "to carry out his judgments he directs their councils and excites their wills, in the direction which he has decided upon, through the agency of Satan, the minister of his wrath. . . ." [29] Calvin was never one to wince at involving the Almighty in the devil's work, yet he still held that although man cannot choose freely between good and evil, in the pursuit of evil he exercises his natural freedom.

But the great tradition of Calvinist religion has refused to go along with such hardhearted doctrine. The Westminster Confession[30] is typically Augustinian in its concept of free will, asserting that man in the state of innocence "had freedom and power to will and to do that which is good and well-pleasing to God," but "by his fall into a state of sin, hath wholly lost all ability of will to any spiritual good. . . ." Yet by God's grace as a converted sinner he is enabled "freely to will and to do that which is spiritually good" while also in his corruption willing evil. The Confession has suffered numerous changes since its definition in 1647, but the original of the chapter on free will is untouched and is still binding on the Presbyterian Church in the United States of America. The celebrated contemporary Reform theologian Emil Brunner has even insisted that in the Christian sense, without divine election to salvation there would be no genuine freedom.[31]

---

[28] The Confession of Augsburg (1530), 18, Of Free Choice; 19, Of the Cause of Sin. Luther's own position is believed to have changed after 1525, which marked the beginning of an orientation of his thought on salvation less in terms of the Augustinian–Pelagian intellectualized controversy and more in terms of the personalized biblical doctrine of grace, a change which softened the double predestinarianism Augustine had inspired in him.

[29] *Institutes of the Christian Religion*, book 2, chap. 4.

[30] *The Confession of Faith*, chap. 9, Of Free Will.

[31] In his defense and definition of the Christian dogma of election presented in a context of opposition to the Augustinian and Reform doctrine of double predestination, Brunner asserts that "not only do election and freedom

Now the point, again, is that the theologians and creeds that denied free will really wanted to in some way preserve and champion it, for freedom as the foundation for moral righteousness is a dominating character of cultivated occidental religion, its priority secured by the persistence of the Hebraic conception of God as essentially a moral will. But they usually failed to preserve it because of the doctrines of omnipotence, grace, and predestination.[32]

Of course there has been in the Christian religion a long tradition of heterodox opposition to the dogma of salvation by grace, at least in its extreme form, an opposition expressed in the doctrine that human freedom of the will cannot be compromised and that salvation, therefore, is a matter of merit. The norm for such doctrine, which has been the basis of liberal Christianity, was set by the fourth-century Pelagians and has been emulated with variations by the Socinians, Catholic Molinists, Arminians, American Unitarians, Baptists, Disciples, Mormons, and numerous others in the tradition of organized religion, to say nothing of the extensive amorphous body of religious liberals determined to champion humanity if necessary by the compromise of divine absoluteness.[33]

———

[defined especially with reference to the Christian decision of faith] not cancel each other out, but freedom is based upon the fact of election. Only he who knows that he is elect, who accepts his election in Jesus Christ, is truly free. . . . The only true freedom is to know that from all eternity we have been destined, through the Son, for communion with God." *Dogmatics*, vol. 1, *The Christian Doctrine of God*, p. 313.

[32] In his essay *On Grace and Free Will*, Augustine explicitly attempted a reconciliation of grace and free will, insisting that without grace it is impossible to will the good. Genuine freedom for fallen man is possible, therefore, only when his will is possessed by the divine will.

Luther held (in *De Servo Arbitrio*) that although from some perspectives man has free will, from the standpoint of divine omnipotence, grace, and predestination, there can be no freedom: "For if we believe it to be true that God foreknows and predestines all things, that he can neither be mistaken in his foreknowledge nor hindered in his predestination, and that nothing takes place but as he wills it (as reason itself is forced to admit), then on the testimony of reason itself there cannot be any free choice in man or angel or any creature."

[33] Pelagius denied the dogma of original sin and championed a doctrine of salvation by merit on the basis of his conviction that the human will is

Just as Epicurus with his denial of causality stands historically behind the argument against scientific determinism, so the theological affirmation of free will, whether in Christianity, Judaism, or even Islam, derives in principle in large measure from Philo Judaeus, the foremost Jewish philosopher of antiquity, who established at Alexandria the structural foundations of occidental philosophical theology.[34] In Philo's theory God, who had established the causal order of the world and yet interrupts it in the performance of miracles, has endowed the human will with the same power of interruption, enabling man thus to escape the bonds of determinism miraculously. Or in a modified but influential theory, Philo held that there is no causal order in the world, every separate event being occasioned by the will of God, a view which our theologians sometimes managed to find compatible with the miraculous free will of the human soul.

---

genuinely free to do good or evil. "Everything good and everything evil, in respect of which we are either worthy of praise or of blame, is *done by us*, not *born with us*. We are not born in our full development, but with a capacity for good and evil; we are begotten as well without virtue as without vice, and before the activity of our own personal will there is nothing in man but what God has stored in him." *Pro Libero Arbitrio, ap. Aug., De Peccato Originali*, 14. Those who followed the Jesuit Luis de Molina (1535–1600) held, as against the Dominicans, that grace assists but in no way coerces the will in the acceptance or rejection of salvation, although God knows in advance the course that each individual may take.

[34] Philo Judaeus, *The Unchangeableness of God*, 3.

For it is mind alone which the Father who begat it judged worthy of freedom, and loosening the fetters of necessity, suffered it to range as it listed, and of that free-will which is His most peculiar possession and most worthy of His majesty gave it such portion as it was capable of receiving. For the other living creatures in whose souls the mind, the element set apart for liberty, has no place, have been committed under yoke and bridle to the service of men, as slaves to a master. But man, possessed of a spontaneous and self-determined will, whose activities for the most part rest on deliberate choice, is with reason blamed for what he does wrong with intent, praised when he acts rightly of his own will. . . . For God hath made man free and unfettered, to employ his powers of action with voluntary and deliberate choice. . . .

See also the definitive essay on Philo's conception of free will by H. A. Wolfson in volume 1 of his work *Philo*, pp. 424–62.

5

Leaving now the *theological* opposition to the freedom of the will and turning to the *metaphysical*, the general form of the latter seems obvious. Again it is determinism occasioned by absolutism, but this time simply by the *world* as an absolute rather than by an absolutistic God as in the theologies. In our examples the determinism is identified with logic, reason, and organic process, but not with mechanism.

Roman Stoicism was the most influential instance of absolutistic metaphysics. Its universe was rigorously deterministic, a kind of living, rational machine, and the true Stoic recognized that he could change neither his environment nor his predicament. Indeed, for the Stoic, virtue was in part the recognition of one's inevitable and necessary role in the world, whether murderer or saint. Yet never did a philosophy or religion declare more eloquently that man can be free. With an engaging inconsistency the Stoics insisted that in his inner life the true Stoic achieves genuine freedom, the freedom of reason that renders him independent of the world that binds him.[35] In *The Consolation of Philosophy* the Roman–Christian–Stoic Boethius thus defined Stoic free will: "Wherefore all who have reason have also freedom of desiring and refusing in themselves." [36]

[35] Epictetus, in the *Discourses*, book 4, chap. 1, trans. P. E. Matheson.

He is free, whom none can hinder, the man who can deal with things as he wishes. But the man who can be hindered or compelled or fettered or driven into anything against his will, is a slave. And who is he whom none can hinder? The man who fixes his aim on nothing that is not his own. And what does "not his own" mean? All that it does not lie in our power to have or not to have, or to have of a particular quality or under particular conditions. The body then does not belong to us, its parts do not belong to us, our property does not belong to us. If then you set your heart on one of these as though it were your own, you will pay the penalty deserved by him who desires what does not belong to him. The road that leads to freedom, the only release from slavery is this, to be able to say with your whole soul:

Lead me, O Zeus, and lead me, Destiny,
Whither ordained is by your decree.
[Cleanthes]

[36] *The Consolation of Philosophy*, Book 5.

Spinoza, whose logically structured absolutistic determinism has already been indicated, was really a better Stoic than any Greek or Roman and in true Stoic fashion identified freedom with reason, the reason that overcomes the bondage of passion and gives men a vision of themselves and their world under the aspect of eternity, releasing them thereby from slavery to vain fears and hopes.[37]

A final type of absolutism, that of Hegel and the Hegelians, deserves mention because of its deterministic implications for history. Nowhere has the problem of freedom been formulated as a more adequate expression of a culture than in the interpretation of events by its great historians. Herodotus, for instance, was subject to the mythology of fate, while Polybius, with greater rigor as a historian, prescribed explicitly that historians analyze causes if they seek real understanding of events.

In Hegelianism the absolute is a universal, rational, historical process and the individual is caught inevitably in its grasp. History is made through him or in spite of him, but never *by* him.[38] In Hegel's metaphysics the "cunning of reason" determines the course and char-

---

[37] *The Ethics*, part five, Of Human Freedom, proposition 42, note, "Whereas the wise man, in so far as he is regarded as such, is scarcely at all disturbed in spirit, but, being conscious of himself, and of God, and of things, by a certain eternal necessity, never ceases to be, but always possesses true acquiescence of his spirit." See also *A Political Treatise*, pt. 2, "And so I am altogether for calling a man so far free, as he is led by reason; because so far he is determined to action by such causes, as can be adequately understood by his unassisted nature, although by these causes he be necessarily determined to action."

[38] For Hegel, human history is the development of absolute spirit, determined internally by the laws of the dialectic. It is progress in the consciousness of freedom, but only the Absolute as a whole is genuinely free, as being self-determined, for all else is externally determined as part of the Absolute. "The principle of development implies further that it is based on an inner principle, a presupposed potentiality, which brings itself into existence. This formal determination is essentially the spirit of which the scene, property, and sphere of realization is world history. It does not flounder about in the external play of accidents. On the very contrary, it is absolutely determined and firm against them. It uses them for its own purposes and dominates them." *The Philosophy of History*, The Course of World History, "The Principle of Development."

acter of large events; in the Marxian inversion of Hegelianism the social process is determined by an inevitable dialectic, while the ideational and spiritual facets of the culture are a function of economics;[39] and in the Hegelian-oriented theory of Spengler, all cultures, including our own, decline inevitably like dying organisms, and nothing that men can do can alter the form of their disintegration or foreclose their death.

Yet even in these systems, the idea of freedom, however perverted, is not entirely abandoned. In Hegelianism freedom is the acceptance of nature and one's place in it, the realization of inevitable destiny, and conformity to the whole of which one is a part —a doctrine that served admirably as a foundation for Nazi social philosophy. Marx, however, objected to this very feature of Hegel's universe and softened his own economic determinism with the argument that the mechanical processes of society are in some way amenable to human intelligence, and that with collective action at the proper place and moment men can achieve a mastery of their fate.[40] Although classes rather than individuals are the makers of history, history is not totally determined. In particular, the revolution, though inevitable, is the product of conscious purpose.

[39] Karl Marx, from the introduction to *Critique of Political Economy*, In the social production of their subsistence men enter into determined and necessary relations with each other which are independent of their wills — production-relations which correspond to a definite stage of development of their material productive forces. The sum of these production-relations forms the economic structure of society, the real basis upon which a juridical and political superstructure arises, and to which definite social forms of consciousness correspond. The mode of production of the material subsistence, conditions the social, political and spiritual life-process in general. It is not the consciousness of men which determines their existence, but on the contrary it is their social existence which determines their consciousness.

[40] It is paradoxical that the Hegelian and Marxian determinisms were descended metaphysically from the Kantian conception of the noumenal or transcendental self as unconditionally free (in contrast to the empirical self, which is subject to the causal determinism of phenomenal reality). Fichte, the chief creator of German objective idealism, elaborated upon Kant's thesis in an excessive effort to glorify freedom by defining reality primarily as free will, with the result that an absolute will absorbed the individual, whose free-

Today the major issue of historical methodology is clearly a formulation of the ancient free will problem: are there general laws of history which permit in principle causal explanations and scientific predictions of historical events? Are such laws formulable if there is genuine free will and if the events that constitute history are affected by human volition?

In brief, the history of our culture, to say nothing of the Near East and the Orient, at the point of the free will problem, is the story of a long and determined intellectual struggle to defend both determinism and freedom, the absoluteness of God and nature and the creativity and responsibility of men.[41]

II

Almost a century ago, William James declared that psychology, being a science, must necessarily indulge in deterministic formulations and it therefore proceeds as if there were no free will even though our moral sense justly demands that we believe that freedom is real and that we act on that reality.[42] James apparently intended that science, which decides all matters of fact, must, for methodologi-

---

dom thereby was lost in the life of the whole, individual choices being determined by the internal processes of the absolute — an absolute that was described as ideational and spiritual by the Hegelians, and as material and social by the Marxists.

[41] It is not irrelevant here that Existentialism — a latecomer in contemporary philosophical types — which defines man in terms of his own freedom, indeed in a sense as his own creator, arose in opposition to the mathematically dominated rationalism that supported determinism.

[42] *Principles of Psychology*, Shorter Course, chap. 26:

The fact is that the question of free-will is insoluble on strictly psychologic grounds. . . . She [a scientific psychology] must deal with the *general laws* of volition exclusively; with the impulsive and inhibitory character of ideas; with the nature of their appeals to the attention; with the conditions under which effort may arise, etc.; but not with the precise amounts of effort, for these, if our wills be free, are impossible to compute. She thus abstracts from free-will, without necessarily denying its existence. Practically, however, such abstraction is not distinguished from rejection; and most actual psychologists have no hesitation in denying that free-will exists. . . . For ourselves, we can hand the free-will controversy over to metaphysics.

cal purposes, assume this one rather than decide it. But it does not seem right to hold one view within the context of scientific analysis, and defend its contradiction on extrascientific grounds. It is encouraging, therefore, that we have some justification today for holding that if we could properly formulate the problem of free will science might sometime give us the answer we seek. On such an interesting subject as free will, however, we cannot just stand by and wait for the scientists to reach a verdict that may never come and which, if it does come, will not be beyond controversy. We can, of course, while waiting for the verdict of science, engage with the theologians and metaphysicians in soul-satisfying speculation in the matter, but such speculation, though it may be world stirring and may accidentally bring us to the truth, gives us no way of knowing whether we have the truth and for that reason is an intellectual pastime that must be indulged in with much caution. Moreover, the habit of moralists, in the manner of Immanuel Kant, of postulating freedom to give meaning to moral oughtness is at best a dignified begging of the question.[43] To employ a proposition as a postulate neither confers truth on it nor contributes to our determination of its truth or falsity, and there must be a grand metaphysical presumption to enable us to deduce the fact of freedom from our sense of moral obliga-

---

[43] In the *Critique of Pure Reason*, Transcendental Dialectic, book 2, chap. 2, sec. 2, Kant described the conflict of freedom and determinism as his third antinomy, i.e., a relationship of antithetical propositions where neither assertion "can establish superiority" over the other. "*Thesis*: Causality in accordance with laws of nature is not the only causality from which the appearances of the world can one and all be derived. To explain these appearances it is necessary to assume that there is also another causality, that of freedom. *Antithesis*: There is no freedom; everything in the world takes place solely in accordance with laws of nature." Norman Kemp Smith trans.

But whereas Kant held that on the ground of pure reason alone the reality of the metaphysical freedom of the will cannot be established, in the *Critique of Practical Reason* he insisted that freedom was demanded as a postulate of the practical reason, one of the "suppositions practically necessary" to give meaning to moral experience in a rational creature. The postulate of freedom results from "the necessary supposition of independence from the sensible world, and of the faculty of determining one's will according to the law of an intelligible world, that is, of freedom." Book 2, chap. 2, sec. 6, Of the Postulates of Pure Practical Reason in General, T. K. Abbott trans.

tion. There is, nevertheless, an activity that is proper to philosophy and is appropriate here, that of *definition* and *analysis*, and this may prove useful toward a more adequate formulation of the issue.

It has long been recognized in the philosophic profession that when you are confronted by a difficult situation such as this one, the thing to do is to make a distinction. This is always a convenient intellectual stall and it has the great value both of distracting the listener's or reader's attention from the weaknesses of one's arguments and giving the impression of insight and profundity. And sometimes it even helps to clarify matters. Accordingly, I shall here and after make not one, but several distinctions.

In the first place, the freedom of the will must not be confused with the usual freedoms that are intended by the ordinary usage of the term "freedom": political, social, academic freedom; freedom to think, believe, or worship as one pleases. In short, the freedom of the will is not a freedom of the kind that can be deprived simply by ordinary coercion from other human beings. If it is real it is a natural property of the human soul or personality in its fundamental being and is essential to the very definition of a person, so that to the degree that such freedom is destroyed, personality itself is importantly affected. For this reason, among others, it is ordinarily technically distinguished by the designation *metaphysical freedom of the will*. Presumably the freedom of the will could be destroyed by a mental breakdown or disorganization of the individual, because this would be a deterioration or destruction of personality itself. But free agency of the type that concerns us here would not be interfered with by a denial of the right to vote or a proscription on religious worship. It would still remain to make possible the objections that might be raised against such denial. The metaphysical freedom of the will, as has already been seen, is a problem not between man and man,[44] but between men and God or men and the universe.

Now at this point I must mention again the possibility that the question whether there is freedom of the will is a meaningless one.

---

[44] An exception, of course, might be the destruction of freedom through a systematic breaking down of the decision-making powers of the individual through the process of so-called brain-washing, but this involves the partial or full destruction of personality.

It seems to me that there are two grounds on which it may be meaningless. The first is *pragmatic* and the second *positivistic*.

The *pragmatic* criterion of meaningfulness may be stated as follows: of two propositions, they are not different in meaning unless they make a practical difference. Now the question arises, does the proposition "I have free will" produce practical consequences different from those that follow from the assertion "I do not have free will." Or in other words, does a free-willer behave in a particular relevant situation differently from a non-free-willer.[45] It would seem not. Those who believe there is no freedom of choice go right ahead and make choices just like the rest of us. They simply interpret the causal factor in the choices differently. It is not possible to act as if there were no freedom of the will, even though it may be possible to construct a consistent and persuasive theory that there is none. Accordingly, we must at least conclude that although it is of great theoretical interest, the free will problem, except for the impact that a belief may have on men's emotions and attitudes, has no genuine practical importance for human action.

The *positivistic* criterion of meaningfulness requires that a proposition be capable in principle of either direct or indirect confirmation or disconfirmation.[46] This means that it must be possible in prin-

---

[45] William James advanced a somewhat loose pragmatic conception of meaning on foundations laid especially by C. S. Peirce. "The pragmatic method . . . is to try to interpret each notion by tracing its respective practical consequences. What difference would it practically make to any one if this notion rather than that notion were true. If no practical difference whatever can be traced, then the alternatives mean practically the same thing, and all dispute is idle. Whenever a dispute is serious, we ought to be able to show some practical difference that must follow from one side or the other's being right." *Pragmatism*, pp. 45f. For Peirce's historic formulation of his pragmatic principle of meaning, see *Collected Papers of Charles Sanders Peirce*, edited by Charles Hartshorne and Paul Weiss, vol. 5, pp. 388–410. Peirce's interpretation of the principle, as well as that of John Dewey (see, e.g., *Logic: The Theory of Inquiry*, pp. 112f.), relates especially to the context of scientific investigation and approaches the positivistic concept of meaning found among logical empiricists.

[46] For analyses of the positivistic concept of cognitive meaning, see, e.g., Rudolf Carnap, *Philosophy and Logical Syntax*, passim, and *The Logical*

ciple to bring scientific evidence to bear on the probability of the truth or falsity of the assertion under consideration. The "in principle" qualification means that if you cannot actually obtain such factual evidence, at least you must be able to tell what such evidence would be like, and this in operational or experiential terms.[47]

Now I do not mean to insist that the proposition "There is freedom of the will" is meaningless by this criterion, but rather that its meaning depends on the operational definitions of the terms employed in it, and that under some formulations or interpretations it has quite surely been without meaning and that therefore much of the discussion of the problem heretofore has been abortive. To construct the proposition meaningfully, if this can be done at all, is a task in philosophy and logic, but the determination of its truth or falsity is an enterprise that belongs to science.[48]

The crux of the problem here is whether there is any genuine difference between what is meant when one says "I will freely" and what would be meant if he were to say simply "I will." How, for instance, would it be possible to will unfreely. To will under duress, as in the case of a threat of physical harm, would not constitute the absence of free will because here one wills freely in conformity to the condition of duress. The freedom lost thereby is not the freedom of the will. But if we cannot designate an instance of unfree will at least we must be able to describe what such an instance would be like

---

Syntax of Language, part 5; A. J. Ayer, *Language, Truth, and Logic*, 2d ed.; Bertrand Russell, *An Inquiry into Meaning and Truth*, passim.

   [47] For the operational factor, important in the pragmatic and positivistic concepts of meaning, see esp. P. W. Bridgman, *The Logic of Modern Physics*, chap. 1; *The Nature of Physical Theory*, chap. 2; and A. C. Benjamin, *Operationism* (1955), passim.

   [48] The positivistic view, with its physicalistic bias, is expressed by Philipp Frank in his monograph *Foundations of Physics* (International Encyclopedia of Unified Science, vol. 1, no. 7, p. 56): "Quite a few philosophers and scientists have claimed that the 'Indeterminacy Relation' gives a support to the philosophical doctrine of 'Free Will.' However, no statement can be supported by physical theories which cannot be formulated in terms of physical operations. The statement 'the will is free' has, certainly, no operational meaning. It is a purely metaphysical statement and cannot be supported by any physical theory."

if there were one. Otherwise, there is not a theoretical possibility of deciding the issue and to say "free will" is the equivalent of saying simply "will." But thereby, of course, the issue at hand proves to be a meaningless one. I have been unable to ascertain a meaning for "unfree will," which appears to be a contradictory term, and I strongly suspect, therefore, that to say "free will" is redundant and that the free will problem is factually meaningless. However, this may not be so and I shall accordingly proceed on the presumption that it is *not* so.

Of the sciences, it would appear that psychology is the most responsible for this project of answering the free will question. But the sciences are not mutually exclusive and these days they become much involved with one another, and if the free will question is genuinely meaningful and is resolved scientifically, as it must be if it is to be a matter of reliable knowledge, physiology, chemistry, and physics will no doubt have their say in the matter. I have omitted the social sciences with intention, because, as has already been indicated, it is the distinguishing feature of free will as compared to other human freedoms that it is not a sociological phenomenon.

It should be entirely apparent that the historical discussions of free will described above, though sometimes definitional or logical, have been essentially metaphysical and therefore speculative in character and as such, though they have been interesting and have had value because of their broad cultural implications, they have not yielded anything like genuine factual knowledge on the question at hand. Today it appears that the question, if, indeed, it can be meaningfully stated, may be immensely complicated by new knowledge — knowledge relating, for instance, to such matters as the age-old problem of the mechanics of physiological processes, the chemical and physiological ground of mental operations, and the derivation of biological from physical laws, to say nothing of more adequate use of probability statistics and more sensitive techniques for quantifying psychological data. The entire question of the nature of causation and further of the relevance of causation to determinism, fundamental to the whole issue, is still unsettled, and the current successes in the field of electronics together with the implications of quantum theory may well produce a new conception of mechanics in terms of indeterminate and even telic factors.[49] At any rate it is not unlikely that the future may bring a scientific answer to our question, and the answer may indicate that important structural similarities obtain between organisms and the most complex machines.

Meanwhile, assuming that it *is* meaningful, what is meant when we say that the will is free? It seems to me that this question can be formulated *objectively*, with reference to the structure of the world, and *subjectively*, with reference primarily to our own disposition. Interpreted objectively, the problem of free will is twofold: Is it possible to predict human actions and is human volition the consequence of external compulsion? This has to do, of course, with causality and determinism and occasions three more questions: Is the world described totally by a causal order? If so, are its events determined? And do causation and determinism support or deny freedom?

Without becoming involved in the interminable discussion on the nature of causation, it may be recognized that although the causal structure of the world is generally assumed and is often regarded as a necessary presupposition of science, whether causation obtains with respect to all events is a factual matter that must be decided by empirical considerations. The problem here is whether human choices and actions are caused. That some at least of our choices are caused is known from the fact that with a low degree of precision it is nevertheless possible to predict human actions. That some actions are predictable does not establish that all actions are caused, but as Bertrand Russell has pointed out, the empirical evidence of general causality in the physical world is simply the predictability of some events. It is the weakest defense of free will defined as the absence of causation to argue that although many choices are caused, freedom depends only on occasional uncaused choices, and to hold further, by an argument from ignorance, that such choices may be taken as uncaused simply because we do not know their causes.

The question of cause immediately involves the problem of determinism. The deterministic view of the world in modern times has

---

[49] For a description of computing machines as analogous to neuro-processes, see Norbert Wiener, *Cybernetics*. For a treatment of biological processes in terms of classical mechanics, see E. Schroedinger, *What Is Life?*

had its chief support from the classical mechanics identified historically with the extension of Newtonian physics. But the interpretation of causal laws as statistical laws[50] and particularly the Heisenberg principle of uncertainty in contemporary quantum theory have threatened this determinism.

The uncertainty principle, which asserts that the path of electrons cannot be predicted due to the impossibility in principle of establishing, beyond a minimal point, concurrently and with accuracy both their position and momentum, has been interpreted by Eddington, Reichenbach, and others as a principle of indeterminacy,[51] indicating that in its fundamental structure the universe is undetermined in the sense that the behavior of electronic particles is uncaused.[52] This

---

[50] H. Reichenbach, himself an indeterminist, holds that the principle of indeterminacy antedates the development of quantum theory, appearing in principle at least in Boltzmann's statistical interpretation of the second law of thermodynamics, which describes the law in terms of probability only. See, e.g., Reichenbach's *Philosophic Foundations of Quantum Mechanics* (1944), part 1, sec. 1, 3, and *The Rise of Scientific Philosophy* (1951), esp. chap. 10.

[51] See Arthur S. Eddington, *The Nature of the Physical World*; Hans Reichenbach, *Atom and Cosmos*, *Philosophic Foundations of Quantum Mechanics*, *Experience and Prediction*; James Jeans, *The Mysterious Universe*; Arthur H. Compton, *The Freedom of Man*, etc.

[52] Indeterminists have commonly held that under the circumstances indicated it is meaningless to assign simultaneously both an exact position and an exact momentum to an electron, and further have interpreted this to mean that the behavior of the electron is uncaused. The uncertainty principle was advanced in the nineteen-twenties especially by the German physicist Werner Heisenberg. Reichenbach thus describes the argument for indeterminism independently of but inclusive of the principle of uncertainty.

The idea of determinism, i.e., of strict causal laws governing the elementary phenomena of nature, was recognized as an extrapolation inferred from the causal regularities of the macrocosm. The validity of this extrapolation was questioned as soon as it turned out that macrocosmic regularity is equally compatible with irregularity in the microcosmic domain, since the law of great numbers will transform the probability character of the elementary phenomena into the practical certainty of statistical laws. Observations in the macrocosmic domain will never furnish any evidence for causality of atomic occurrences so long as only effects of great numbers of atomic particles are considered.

prospect of a disorderly world has given some theologians a new lease on life, under the assumption that causation had adequately disposed of both the necessity and possibility of the divine will, and has provided the advocates of free will an apparent foothold in the formerly impenetrable physical world. But the principle of uncertainty, the interpretation of which has divided both experts and laymen, may mean, as it probably does, not that the world is objectively free and indeterminate, but rather that its determinateness simply is not known. Besides, even if the insisters on indeterminacy are correct, that the mechanical character of physical phenomena above the atomic level is a matter of gross statistics on a world whose basic particles are free, it is difficult to see where any definite gain has been made for freedom of the will. After all, the will just doesn't happen to be an electron. Or at least if it is, there is no way of knowing that it is.

Of course, if the world is genuinely and objectively indeterminate it may be argued that whatever else the will may be, if it is an uncaused cause and its reality is tied to the unpredictability of the future, the world is the kind of place that can accommodate it. But even then there remain two difficulties. In the first place, the world of gross matter, in which the free will must produce its effects, is as determined under quantum physics as it was in classical mechanics. The apparently deterministic laws of physics have not been abandoned and are in principle derivable from indeterministic foundations by probability logic. Laws described as statistical probabilities are not less laws of nature. And secondly, the interpretation of indeterminism as the absence of causality is itself questionable. It may be, as some physicists have insisted, that causality, however related to it, is not properly defined in terms of determinism,[53] and that quantum mechanics, even if indeterminate, is yet causal in a strict

---

Philosophic Foundations of Quantum Mechanics, p. 1. For Heisenberg's discussion of indeterminism and the uncertainty principle, see his *Physics and Philosophy* (1958), passim. An earlier, more technical work by Heisenberg is *The Physical Principles of Quantum Theory* (1930).

[53] E.g., the physicist Max Born. "The concept of causality is closely linked with that of determinism, yet they seem to me not identical." *Natural Philosophy of Cause and Chance*, p. 5.

sense, a sense that would interfere with the argument for free will as uncaused cause. More important still is the possibility that physics will arrive at a new determinism through the revision of its present theory.[54]

In the absence of anything like a conclusive decision in this controversy, I shall rule for this discussion that determinism, in the sense of universal causation, has the best of the argument and I shall pursue the free will problem under the assumption that every event is caused, including human choices and actions. If, contrary to this assumption, the world, both physical and mental, is not determined, then at least the will is probably not less free than it would be in a deterministic system. But whether under such circumstances there would be meaning to moral responsibility becomes a question.

[54] Einstein, who contributed to the foundations of quantum theory, was a defender of determinism. In a letter of Nov. 7, 1944, published by Max Born in *Natural Philosophy of Cause and Chance*, he asserted, "You believe in the dice playing god, but I in the perfect rule of law in a world of something objectively existing which I try to catch in a wildly speculative way. . . . The great initial success of quantum theory cannot convert me to believe in that fundamental game of dice."

It is not without interest that Max Planck, the chief creator of quantum theory, refused to accept the indeterministic interpretations of Eddington and others, and, while admitting that among physicists the indeterminists are in the majority, held out for the eventual vindication of determinism. "We see then that there is fully as rigid a determinism in the world image of quantum physics as in that of classical physics. The only difference is that different symbols are employed and that different rules of operating obtain." *The Philosophy of Physics*, p. 65.

Einstein gave Planck full support in his determinism. "I am entirely in agreement with our friend Planck in regard to the stand which he has taken on this principle. He admits the impossibility of applying the causal principle to the inner processes of atomic physics under the present state of affairs; but he has set himself definitely against the thesis that from this *Unbrauchbarkeit* or inapplicability we are to conclude that the process of causation does not exist in external reality." Max Planck, *Where Is Science Going?*, p. 210.

But whereas Planck held that determinism is compatible with free will, which is properly a matter of subjective feeling, Einstein asserted, in conjunction with the statement above, "And when you mention people who speak of such a thing as free will in nature it is difficult for me to find a suitable reply. . . . Honestly I cannot understand what people mean when they talk about freedom of the human will."

The crucial problem is, assuming a universal reign of causality and therefore a determinism that in principle appears to be compatible with predictability, must the will be regarded as not free?

Now, still considering the matter objectively, the position that the will is not free must mean that the will is coerced by forces or influences external to it. But to say that an action is caused is quite surely not to say that it is coerced, for no acceptable scientific meaning of cause even approaches the notion of coercion. It is a vulgar view that compares causation to the human volition that is the norm of coercion. Science long ago abandoned such anthropomorphisms, including the idea that causes *produce* their effects, in favor of more subtle notions of causation that have to do primarily simply with an invariant relation of events.[55] To be determined in the sense of being within the structure of a determined system means simply to be in conformity to immutable general rules or descriptions, that say, in effect, that every instance of "a" is accompanied by an instance of "b." Without being concerned further with the various interpretations of the cause–effect relationship, this much can be said with definiteness, that causes in nature neither compel nor coerce their effects. Therefore, if freedom is defined simply as the absence of coercion, as I believe it should be, it cannot be held that if human choices and actions are caused they are *therefore* not free.

It may be objected, of course, that I have overlooked the possibility that there is a soul, spirit, or mind active in every instance of free will and that although the mind can be a cause of a bodily event, it is itself uncaused. But, ignoring the difficult problem of the relationship of such a mind to the body, I can see no reason for supposing that minds or souls, however free they may be, are uncaused.

---

[55] See, e.g., Victor F. Lenzen, *Causality in Natural Science*, p. 54:

Primitive thought interpreted nature as constituted of living things akin to man. This animistic conception of nature was given its most picturesque formulation in the personification of natural forces. Thus the original model for explanation of natural phenomena was the activity of life. In the modern era, however, scientific method as exemplified by physical science has worked to purge the concept of causality of its animistic element. Causality has become functional relationship which is most adequately expressed by the differential equation.

On the contrary, insofar as the mind is made an object of psychological study, such study is in terms of causal relationships, and theological speculation on souls, even the souls in heaven, indicates that they are subject to causation. On other grounds, such stories as the declension of the angels under Lucifer could have no meaning. Without cause and effect, one soul could not influence another. We must conclude, therefore, that whether or not the self is identified with a soul or mind separable from the body has no bearing on the problem of whether human choices are caused.

Or if it is objected that the ideals or anticipated ends that determine our choices and actions are of a supernatural source or are in any way nonnatural in character and therefore not subject to causation, it may again be insisted that if there is such a supernatural or nonnatural realm, there is not the slightest reason for holding that its events are chaotic rather than ordered. More appropriately, it must be argued that whatever their justification, human ideals and purposes, insofar as they relate importantly to human choices, are as clearly a part of nature as anything else. The crude identification of nature totally and exclusively with the physical or material has no place in serious philosophic discussion.

Now it seems obvious that our primary interest in free will arises from our desire to justify the common assumption of moral responsibility upon which rests our chief dignity as human beings, and that the argument that our choices are uncaused is intended as a defense, therefore, of our character as genuine moral beings. It is quite commonly supposed that only if in some way we are uncaused free-floating causes are we responsible for our actions. This view, sometimes aptly called *libertarianism*, is the naïve doctrine of free will that is most frequently employed against determinism.

But it is difficult to see how such an uncaused will could be genuinely moral in the sense that its apologetes suppose it would be. For a person of good moral character is one who has been affected by his experience, whose will, for instance, is the product of innumerable influences that are judged to be good. If this were not so there would be no occasion for moral or character education, for such education presupposes educability, the possibility that a person can be influenced by ideas, attitudes, and actions, and that thereafter those influences may determine his moral choices. But this means that his choices will be caused.

The libertarian, who insists on moral responsibility only in the presumed instances of conscious volition that is uncaused, crosses himself if he condones punishment for an immoral act. For the ethical justification of punishment is that it will have some effect on the will of the offender, but under libertarianism this is in principle not possible.

Now if we approach this matter from the standpoint of prediction, we must arrive at the same conclusion. It is not true that we cannot predict moral choices of the type that are usually regarded as free. Such predictions are common and frequent, and their possibility implies causality in human choice. By them we trust some persons and distrust others, confide in some and refuse confidence to others. Of course our predictions are far from exact, but the same is true of many scientific predictions, as for instance in meteorology. Nevertheless, they have enough accuracy for ordinary practice and, indeed, the moral structure of social conduct depends upon them. Important for our problem is that these predictions indicate that human choices are caused and that we can in a measure ascertain their causes.

Finally, if our choices were uncaused, they would be totally a matter of random chance, without order or continuity, and morality, which involves responsible action, would be a complete impossibility. Conduct would be nothing but chaos.

It cannot be argued that although the will is uncaused it is nevertheless subject to various influences, for this is a contradiction. These influences are the very causes that we are considering.[56] The defender

---

[56] It is not an adequate defense of the libertarian doctrine to plead ignorance of the causes of volition. It is impossible to establish an affirmative position by an argument from ignorance. Of course, this principle is a two-edged sword, and it does not prove that the will is caused to establish that it is impossible to prove that it is uncaused. Spinoza, who opposed libertarianism, held that "men think themselves free, inasmuch as they are conscious of their volitions and desires, and never even dream, in their ignorance, of the causes which have disposed them to wish and desire." *The Ethics*, part one, Appendix. And further: "In the mind there is no absolute or free will; but the mind is determined to wish this or that by a cause, which has also been deter-

of libertarianism usually recognizes that there are numerous factors in experience which affect the volition, and for this reason he often bases his case for uncaused freedom on the argument that granted the presence of various causes, both known and unknown, there is still an "area" or "moment" of free decision which makes of the will an uncaused cause. But he is always unable either to explicitly locate or define operationally the fact which he asserts and therefore he is unable to adduce empirical evidence to support his thesis. Indeed, on any self-respecting concept of factual meaning he appears to be unable to establish that the thesis is genuinely meaningful. I have promised, however, that I would not press this embarrassing point.

But of course the problem seems to be still with us: if our choices are caused, how can they be called free? The answer to this again is that to be caused is not to be coerced, and we are free if our wills are self-determined, that is, if they are directed by our own desires and interests and are not compelled by external forces.[57] We are

---

mined by another cause, and this last by another cause, and so on to infinity." Ibid., part two, proposition 48.

[57] There is much to be learned from the Puritan theologian Jonathan Edwards, whose essay *On the Freedom of the Will*, the most famous American philosophical piece, combines Calvinistic determinism and Newtonian mechanics for the glory of God. Edwards did not, as is commonly held by the libertarians, deny the freedom of the will. He defended it, but within the framework of causal determinism. A man is free to do as he pleases, insisted Edwards; but of course he is not free to please as he pleases. Careful reflection on the matter should reveal that Edwards had a point, and a very fundamental one.

Immanuel Kant, than whom there is no more vigorous defender of the freedom of the will as the foundation of moral responsibility, did not hesitate to assert the compatibility of that freedom with causality. In the *Critique of Practical Reason* he asserted, "It may therefore be admitted that if it were possible to have so profound an insight into a man's mental character as shown by internal as well as external actions, as to know all its motives, even the smallest, and likewise all the external occasions that can influence them, we could calculate a man's conduct for the future with as great certainty as a lunar or solar eclipse; and nevertheless we may maintain that the man is free." Book 1, The Analytic of Pure Practical Reason, chap. 3. It must be recognized, however, that for Kant the causal world is an appearance, being *phenomenal*, while the self has both a phenomenal and a noumenal nature, being

confronted here, therefore, with the fundamental question, what is the self? For our problem, the self is not an entity that has a will and yet can be abstracted from the interests and desires which it is commonly said to possess. On the contrary, the self is, among other things, those very interests and desires that determine its volitions, as also its volitions, and because this is the case, the causes of our actions are not external to us, but rather internal, indeed, are identified with us, and the description of them is a description of ourselves. However much we may be the product of our inheritance and our environment, we are free because we are the causes of our own choices; they proceed from our natures, from what we are.

Aristotle pointed out long ago that our actions directed to the achievement of certain ends follow from our states of character for which, he held, we are at least partly responsible.[58] And to say that we act according to our characters is to say that we act as we desire to act and therefore that we are free, without regard for the causes that account for our characters. The assertion that a person's volitions follow from his character is in a sense tautologous because the

---

in the latter instance independent of the causal order of nature and therefore possessing the freedom of uncaused willing. (See, e.g., the *Critique of Practical Reason*, book 2, chap. 2, sec. 2, Critical Solution of the Antinomy of Practical Reason.) Elsewhere Kant asserts that,

> Every rational being reckons himself *qua* intelligence as belonging to the world of understanding, and it is simply as an efficient cause belonging to that world that he calls his causality a *will*. On the other side he is also conscious of himself as a part of the world of sense in which his actions which are mere appearances [phenomena] of that causality are displayed; we cannot however discern how they are possible from this causality which we do not know; but instead of that, these actions as belonging to the sensible world must be viewed as determined by other phenomena, namely, desires and inclinations. If therefore I were only a member of the world of understanding, then all my actions would perfectly conform to the principle of autonomy of the pure will; If I were only a part of the world of sense they would necessarily be assumed to conform wholly to the natural law of desires and inclinations, in other words, to the heteronomy of nature.

Fundamental Principles of the Metaphysic of Morals, sec. 3, How Is a Categorical Imperative Possible. The foregoing passages from Kant trans. T. K. Abbott.

    [58] *Nicomachean Ethics*, book 3, chap. 5, 1114b–1115a, 1–5.

full description of his character is possible only if there is a knowledge of all his voluntary acts. This fact precludes the possibility of a complete and exact prediction of a person's future voluntary behavior. This means, of course, that the future must remain unknown even to a being who knows the total present and past.[59]

To the objection that what we are is determined by a multiplicity of causes, it must be replied that the human self is a complex composite and is not to be described or explained in terms of any of the particular factors which produced it or entered into its composition, and that it is this very fact of identity in multiplicity which indicates its uniqueness and makes it a free center of causation.

Now does this mean that we are simply cogs in a great machine and that the high dignity that we have been accustomed to regard in the creative personality is an illusion? I think not. Whatever the mechanical side of our nature may be, we are infinitely complex organisms which are the recipients of untold numbers of influences, the centers of their redistribution and transformations and the creators thereby of new causal sequences. And if the unfathomable mystery of the human personality lies in this inexpressible complication of psycho-neuro-bio-physical elements, the human soul, whether it comes from God or from nature, is not for that reason less responsible, and quite certainly it is not therefore less real or less precious.

Or does the thesis that the will is caused mean that the world is finished; that its history throughout, including even our own lives, our loves, our tragedies, our moral losses and our moral gains, is all wrapped up in one motionless, lifeless present, and that there is no real creation and no genuine achievement? I believe not. Only if the whole were encompassed by a single mind could this be true. But the future is yet unknown and unlived, even by God, and whatever it

[59] This argument disposes of Laplace's calculator and would apply to God if his omniscience were of the predictive variety, but not if he is conceived as genuinely eternal in the sense that reduces the temporal future to his ever-present experience. It is of interest that Werner Heisenberg, who enunciated the uncertainty principle, held that "The question whether from a complete knowledge of the past we can predict the future, does not arise because a complete knowledge of the past involves a self-contradiction." Quoted by Eddington in *The Nature of the Physical World*, pp. 228f.

holds will be in part our creation and will be new and filled with surprise, variety, and adventure.

In the *Purgatory*, the poet Statius describes for Dante and Virgil the release of a soul as it leaps upward on the mount to approach or even to enter the presence of God:

> But when some spirit, feeling purged and sound,
> Leaps up or moves to seek a loftier station,
> The whole mount quakes and the great shouts resound.
>
> The will itself attests its own purgation;
> Amazed, the soul that's free to change its inn
> Finds its mere will suffice for liberation . . . .[60]

There has not been a more dramatic indication that the soul is free which feels itself to be free. In our experience of willing freely we do not have an argument for the freedom of the will. We have a knowledge of that freedom, and we thereby establish it subjectively. Whatever may be otherwise true of the world as a whole or in any of its other parts, this reality cannot be denied, for the experience of free will is the experience that affirms our very selfhood. It is the chief ground on which we assert our own existence as independent beings.

To the question, therefore, is there freedom of the will, I answer, "No," if by freedom is meant that the human will is an uncaused cause. But I answer "Yes," if to be free means simply that we will in accordance with our own interests, inclinations, desires, and purposes; that is, if freedom means that our will is genuinely our own.

So Mr. Darrow was entirely right in describing the complex causes of the tragic murder, both inherited and environmental. But his defense of the murderers was a complete denial of all individual responsibility. Fortunately for the moral dignity and high value of the human soul, what he said on this subject is probably not true.

---

[60] Canto XXI, 58–63, translated by Dorothy L. Sayers.

10

Comments on the Meaning of Immortality

This statement is restricted to a discussion of two facets of the problem of the meaning of immortality. In the first part of the paper I will bring attention to the important fact that the meaning of a concept of immortality is to be found in part in its relationship to other ideas and attitudes basic to the culture in which the concept is generated. In the second part, I will call attention to some implications for the concept of immortality that issue from a consideration of logical and empirical criteria of meaning.

I

It seems entirely obvious that beliefs respecting immortality — whether there is immortality, what it is that is immortal, what is the condition of the immortal, whether the assertion of immortality is to be taken factually or symbolically — are to a high degree functions of the cultures in which they are found. The determinants of a culture are many and various and their causal connections, together with the historical processes in which they are involved, are usually so subtle that to identify them with any reliability is quite impossible. But to attempt to locate them is at least instructive. Of course the truth value of any claim is quite irrelevant to the causal factors which may produce that claim, but its meaning and certainly its symbolic value are associated with those factors and are in part determined by them.

It appears, for instance, that initially the belief in the resurrection in ancient Judaism was essentially an eschatological doctrine referring to the end of history and the renewal of the Jewish state and that it only later became basic to the concern for the eventual fate of the individual. Clearly a full explanation of this development would engage a broad spectrum of political, economic, and socio-psychological factors that relate to social solidarity, the sense of historical continuity, or the emergence of individual consciousness and commitment to the individual as the supreme value. It will not do to simply say that the idea of the resurrection appeared when a sufficient degree of individualism was present, for that idea was a part of the individualism as it developed especially in the pharisaic tradition.

Or to take a more dramatic case, compare the traditional Judaeo-Christian bent toward personal individual immortality with the determination of much Hinduism and of Hinayana Buddhism to annihilate the ground of particular individual being by the conquest of the karma that generates and sustains the individual life and maintains the cycle of rebirth. Countless economic, social, physical, and intellectual factors affecting the quality and satisfaction of life must have produced and continue to produce those attitudes and their associated beliefs, but their subtlety and complexity make it quite impossible to gain more than a general and precariously speculative understanding of them. Nevertheless, such matters are a part of any thorough consideration of the meanings of immortality even though they are not relevant to its truth or falsity. They are not relevant to its truth value unless, of course, we are to adopt the bizarre notion that thinking or believing or hoping might make a proposition come true.

The factors in the intellectual culture that affect the idea of immortality can be large or small, conspicuous or inconspicuous. It is instructive to examine comparative examples of intellectual determinants among basically diverse cultures to observe their impact on the immortality idea. It is well known, for instance, that the basic metaphysical and moral assumptions of traditional Chinese thought are

predominantly naturalistic and humanistic and that this naturalistic
humanism is reflected clearly in the traditional Chinese treatment of
immortality. Neither the generality of men nor philosophers in China
have been greatly concerned with the condition of man after death
apart from guaranteeing the amenities of the ancestral cult. The
concept of personal immortality is by no means unknown in China,
as in the *Lao-Tzu* or *Chuang-Tzu*, but even these give little attention
to detail in this matter. Rather, the typical view has been that death
is a necessity to be accepted as inevitably following birth; as Yang
Hsiun (d. A.D. 18) said quite matter-of-factly, "Those who were born
will surely die. It is a natural principle that things which have a
beginning will have an end."

Now, if we attempt to find an explanation for this naturalistic
and humanistic character of Chinese thought, we are obviously caught
in a circle of reciprocally interacting cultural elements which in a
sense define one another without giving us a firm ground for distinguishing causes from effects — a practicality and concreteness, for
instance, that favors ethics over metaphysics and yields a perceptually
grounded knowledge which is concerned with particulars rather than
universals; a grammar without copulas which makes grammatical and
logical attribution and predication difficult; an intensely social disposition which shows clearly even through the growth of individualism;
an exasperating cultural syncretism that insists on harmonizing even
the disharmonious. All these factors and many more, both indigenous and imported, have a bearing on the traditional Chinese views
regarding death and immortality. Yet what produces what is quite
impossible to say, and where the ultimate causes may lie, as in such
mundane places as diet, climate, commerce, diction, ideography, or
conceivably even in genetics or physiology, must always remain
undecided.

But whatever the conditions and causes, and I believe there are
causes for everything, including ideas on immortality, the Chinese
typically have found immortality in "influence," in "virtue, achievement, and words." Influence is immortal, and in a man's influence
he becomes immortal. He is dead, but immortal. In the sixth century B.C., Mu-shu, when asked whether an unbroken heritage is the
meaning of immortality, replied: "According to what I have heard,

this is called hereditary rank and emolument, not immortality. There was a former great officer of Lu by the name of Tsang Wen-chung. After his death his words remained established. This is what the ancient saying means. I have heard that the best course is to establish virtue. The next best is to establish achievement, and still the next best is to establish words. When these are not abandoned with time, it may be called immortality" (*Tso chuan*, Tso's Commentary on the *Spring and Autumn Annals*, Duke Hsiang, 24th year). The similarity of this position to common views in contemporary American naturalistic humanism is entirely obvious.

An interesting and significant difference in the cultural backdrop for immortality appears when we compare the naturalism of China with its metaphysical counterparts in India and Greece. Unlike the case of China, in India and classical Greece the idea of the immortality of the soul was common and its basis was, and in India is to this day, a set of metaphysical presuppositions which may appear to us at first sight to possess the flavor of supernaturalism, but which are not at all supernaturalistic within the contexts of the Indian and Greek cultures. They are naturalistic in the sense that immortality, to put it simply, comes naturally. This point is immediately evident if we consider that in Judaeo-Christianity immortality, whether as the immortality of the soul or the resurrection of the body, is considered to be in a sense the result of God's miraculous intervention. Without that intervention the nation would die and the souls as well as the bodies of individual men would die — and stay dead. Unless the creative power of God cuts through the bonds of nature or the eternal God intersects the course of time and history, there is no miracle of life that overcomes death. Here it is because God is the creator of the world that he can thus interfere with its natural processes. Yet it is interference nevertheless.

But for the generality of Hindu and Greek thought the world is not created and there is no creator; there is no miracle, no intervention, and the soul's immortality, however much it may seem to us to involve otherworldliness or the supernatural, follows simply and inevitably from the nature of reality taken together with the nature of the soul itself. The Katha Upanishad (I ii 18) says forthrightly, "The knowing Self is not born; it does not die. It has not sprung from anything; nothing has sprung from it. Birthless, eternal, everlasting and ancient, it is not killed when the body is killed" (Nikhilananda trans.). This is not supernaturalism; it is naturalism.

But even more, whereas in classical Christian thought the miracle of immortality is by the grace of God, with little (Catholic) or no (Protestant) possibility of the subject's improving his lot through the accrual of merit, in Hinduism the individual can determine his own future state. The Taittiriya Upanishad (I ix 1), for instance, in keeping with the dominant trend of Hindu thought, describes the disciplines which can move the soul toward immortality in the bliss of Brahman — rightness, truth, self-control, tranquility, penance, the learning of the Veda, the performance of social and ritual duties. Here the soul faces its future on terms that are set not by a divine will but by the eternal structure of an impersonal reality, terms on which the soul itself can proceed to determine its own destiny. Indeed, if we take the example of orthodox Buddhism, where the ideal is not the achievement of an immortal felicity but rather the annihilation of the self — which is the center of attachment and desire and therefore of suffering — the way to salvation is a kind of scientifically designed, almost clinical, prescription relating to mind, emotion, and will. Salvation, the destruction of the impersonal force of the karma which produces rebirth, and the consequent achievement of Nirvana, follows from a knowledge of the truth concerning man's nature and his condition in the world. Salvation here is not a gift, nor is it earned; it is negotiated with the world on objectively established terms in a context of fixed physical and moral law. In the *Samyutta-Nikāya* (XI.62) the Buddha addressed the priests by saying, in part, "Perceiving this, O priests, the learned and noble disciple conceives an aversion for contact, . . . for sensation, . . . for perception, . . . for the predispositions, . . . for consciousness. And in conceiving this aversion he becomes divested of passion, and by the absence of passion he becomes free, and when he is free he becomes aware that he is free; and he knows that rebirth is exhausted, that he has lived the holy life, that he has done what it behooved him to do, and that he is no more for this world" (Warren trans.).

Something like this was common among the classical Greeks, that is, that immortality follows simply from the nature of the soul and natural events. In Plato's *Phaedo*, Socrates concludes his discourse on the immortality of the soul by saying of death, perhaps not dogmatically but hopefully and in a matter-of-fact way: "The venture is a glorious one . . . . Wherefore, I say, let a man be of good cheer about his soul, who having cast away the pleasures and ornaments of the body as alien to him and working harm rather than good, has sought after the pleasures of knowledge; and has arrayed the soul, not in some foreign attire, but in her own proper jewels, temperance, and justice, and courage, and nobility, and truth — in these adorned she is ready to go on her journey to the world below, when her hour comes" (Jowett trans.).

Here immortality belongs to the natural order — not the order of *material* nature, for the Socratic–Platonic soul belonged ultimately to the world of the intellect and the spirit, but to the world which is simply there, uncreated, unquestioned, neither friendly nor unfriendly, a world not made for man but also not made against him. In the *Apology*, addressing the judges who had condemned him to death, Socrates had said, "Wherefore, O judges, be of good cheer about death, and know of a certainty, that no evil can happen to a good man, either in life or after death." Here, perhaps, was the highest achievement of the religious spirit of the Greeks. But it was a religious spirit free from the elements of supernaturalism which are so familiar to us.

A similar attitude toward death and immortality is found among the hellenistic and Roman Stoics who, perhaps more than any others, grounded their treatment of human issues in the integral continuity of man with the natural world. " 'But now'," says Epictetus in the *Discourses* (chap. VII), " 'the time is come to die'. What do you mean by 'die' . . . . Now is the time for your material part to be restored to the elements of which it was composed. What is there dreadful in that? What loss to the universe will this mean, what strange or irrational event? . . . [N]o one has authority over me. God has set me free, I have learnt to understand his commands, no one can make a slave of me any more . . . ." And in his *Meditations* (IX), the Stoic Emperor Marcus Aurelius Antoninus said, "Do not despise death, but be well content with it, since this too is one of those things which nature wills."

Now in contrast to this naturalism which sees life and death and immortality as simply "built-in" features of the world, to be more or less taken for granted as the way the world is and the way it behaves, in the Judaeo-Christian religion, to repeat my main point, the issue of life, death, and the resurrection has been the issue of God the creator set over against the world and the individual, his creation. "There is no greater sense of distance," says the Protestant theologian Emil Brunner, "than that which lies in the words Creator–Creation. Now this is the first and the fundamental thing which can be said about man: He is a creature, and as such, he is separated by an abyss from the Divine Manner of being. The greatest dissimilarity between two things which we can express at all — more dissimilar than light and darkness, death and life, good and evil — is that between the Creator and that which is created" (*Man in Revolt*, p. 90).

Here the abyss of creation separates man from God. But however wide and deep the abyss, the absoluteness of God — the totality of his creative power, his overwhelming and omniscient purpose — seizes man and holds him in its awful and unrelenting grasp. God's holiness overwhelms with awe, and to swear by the living God is to swear by the God of terror and dread. As it is said in Hebrews (10:31): "It is a fearful thing to fall into the hands of the living God." Man's life, his death, his salvation — all are at the mercy of a God who creates freely, who could have created something else, who might not have created man at all, who created him from nothing — a nothing to which he will return if the creative act ceases. A man's life is totally precarious — precarious in the finitude of his creatureliness, doomed to endure the finite and yet to long for the infinite, elected to salvation or damnation, impotent to determine its own destiny, hovering every moment over the abyss of death, waiting for the hour of judgment, engulfed in the anguish of annihilation. If this is not the whole of the Christian picture of man, it is at least a part, and a very important part, of both the classical and neo-orthodox doctrine — man at the mercy of a divine and omnipotent personal will; man singled out and numbered as a distinct individual, burdened with the responsibilities of reason, knowledge, and moral action; man an unwilling victim of a God who has created and can destroy him and of a world which is indifferent to him and to whatever is precious to him.

Professor Oscar Cullmann of the Sorbonne, in tying the Christian belief in immortality to the death and resurrection of Christ, argues that Jesus had a deep and overwhelming fear of death because he had no belief in the immortality of the soul, a fear that shows through his last actions and words and through his dread of being forsaken on the cross — a dread arising from the expectation of death as annihilation.[1] In contrast, Cullmann describes Socrates' positive serenity and composure as he discourses on the immortality of the soul moments before his execution. On the contrary, insists Professor H. A. Wolfson, late of Harvard University, Jesus went to his death "amazedly, sorrowfully, and with strong crying and tears" because he did, in fact, believe that his soul was immortal and that he "would have to face the inscrutable judgment of the Lord his God, the Most High." [2]

Now, whatever may be the merits of these two arguments, it seems to me that Cullmann and Wolfson both fail to rise to the crucial point, the point which I have been laboring, that the cosmologies and the intellectual and spiritual cultures of Socrates and Buddha made man at home in the world, however much he might desire to escape from it, and not simply the world in which he bodily lives, but also the world of his soul, both here and hereafter, and a world with which both his moral will and his contemplative intellect could come to terms; while the world and culture of Jesus, a world separated from its creator, was a world where man, both body and soul, existed only by the grace of a transcendent and divine power from whom alienation was both real and dreadful, an alienation which could be overcome only by a miracle and divine initiative.

In considering the nature of the cultural determinants and concomitants of the idea of immortality, it is of more than passing interest that essentially the same argument that is employed in Greek metaphysics to support immortality is employed in Hinayana Buddhism to prove that the self is not immortal. I refer to the Platonic argument from the simplicity of the soul, which became and remains

[1] *Immortality of the Soul or Resurrection of the Dead,* The Ingersoll Lecture for 1955.

[2] *Immortality and Resurrection in the Philosophy of the Church Fathers,* The Ingersoll Lecture for 1956.

to this day a more-or-less standard argument for immortality in Christian theology. As any reader of the *Phaedo* is aware, Plato was well stocked with arguments for the immortality of the soul, no one of which seems especially compelling, but which taken together provide fairly good coverage of the whole field of speculative or logical proofs for immortality. In his discourse on immortality, Socrates moves in a variety of directions, ranging from the simplicity argument, with its similarities to the treatment of the structure of compounds by the Greek atomists, to the genuinely Platonic argument that the soul as an entity of pure reason belongs to the world of the absolutes, the forms, "the region of piety, and eternity, and immortality, and unchangeableness" (79b), the intelligible world that is known to the intuitive reason, though not at all to the senses.

The argument from simplicity holds that since the soul is a simple entity and not a compound of parts it cannot disintegrate and therefore cannot perish or die. Though a spiritual rather than material entity, the soul can be regarded very much as if it were one of Democritus' material atoms — uncuttable, unsplitable, indestructible. "I cannot get rid of the feeling," said Simmias, ". . . that when the man dies the soul will be dispersed, and that this may be the extinction of her." But "Must we not," said Socrates, "ask ourselves what that is which, as we imagine, is liable to be scattered, and about which we fear? and what again is that about which we have no fear? And then we may proceed further to enquire whether that which suffers dispersion is or is not of the nature of soul — our hopes and fears as to our own souls will turn upon the answers to these questions. . . . Now the compound or composite may be supposed to be naturally capable, as of being compounded, so also of being dissolved; but that which is uncompounded, and that only, must be, if anything is, indissoluble . . . . And the uncompounded may be assumed to be the same and unchanging, whereas the compound is always changing and never the same" (*Phaedo*, 77–78). Here incidentally is the chief origin of the article in the Christian creeds that God is a being without parts. His indestructibility depends in principle upon his uncompounded simplicity.

But the Buddhists, who preferred that the individual self, as the seat of desire and suffering, be destroyed rather than preserved, found the soul, or self, to be a compounded aggregate rather than a simple entity and to be, therefore, subject to dissolution and annihilation. The goal of life is to produce that dissolution through the conquest of the demonic creative power of the karma and thereby to destroy the cycle of rebirth and to effect the achievement of Nirvana. The parts of the Buddhist self are quite unlike Democritan atoms, though not totally unlike the parts of the soul described by Aristotle, the active intellect, the passive intellect, etc. What are the elements of the Buddhist soul? In the *Visuddhi-Magga* (chap. XIV, Warren trans.), the Buddha instructed the priests in the five elements, which are called the five groups: "All form whatsoever, O priests, past, future, or present, be it subjective or existing outside, gross or subtile, mean or exalted, far or near, belongs to the form-group. All sensation whatsoever, . . . all perception whatsoever, . . . all predispositions whatsoever, . . . all consciousness whatsoever, past, future, or present, be it subjective or existing outside, gross or subtile, mean or exalted, far or near, belongs to the consciousness-group." These elements form the basis for the "figment of an Ego," for by "attachment" to these, through "engrossment" in them, "the persuasion arises, 'This is mine; this am I; this is my Ego' " (*Visuddhi-Magga*, XIV). The Self is an illusory reality, an illusion produced by the attachment and desire which hold the elements together. When attachment and desire are destroyed by moral and intellectual discipline the elements are released and the Self is destroyed, rebirth is exhausted, and Nirvana is achieved. "It is the complete absence of passion, the cessation, giving up, relinquishment, forsaking, and non-adoption of desire." It "is called the laying down of the burden" (*Samyutta-Nikāya*, XXii 22).

I can see no reason for supposing either that the ancient Greeks were more competent in these matters than the ancient Buddhists or that the Buddhists were more competent than the Greeks, that either possessed more capacity in logic, reason, or insight or were more sensitive in observation. Certainly neither won the argument on formal grounds, and neither adduced empirical evidence on the continued existence or non-existence of the soul, or even on its existence or non-existence in the first place. Here, with each employing essentially the same argument with contradictory results, is an excellent example of what can happen when matters of presumed factual import are placed at the mercy of speculative reason with no reliable access to any concrete experience that is relevant to the resolution of the issue. It is appropriate to ask whether under such circumstances the issue is genuinely factual. Leaving this question aside for the present, however, it is obvious that the outcome of the argument depends on the correctness of the reasoning and the factual reliability of the premises.

Different cultures, of course, may produce and employ different logics and even different rules of evidence, considering especially the relation of these to language rules and usage, and such differences do in fact obtain between Greek and Buddhist logic. But the main issue is what the culture feeds into the premises, inputs that reflect philosophical assumptions, personal and social values, scientific or non-scientific dispositions, or moral and artistic attitudes, all related in various ways to those basic economic, social, and political factors which define and distinguish the satisfactions and dissatisfactions of life. Here, it seems to me, is a situation that we cannot overcome when we face such a question as immortality, that belief or disbelief in immortality is tied to almost everything except genuinely reliable evidence that will support cogent and responsible argument. This predicament does not inconvenience those wishful thinkers who are accustomed to take as evidence the pious and dogmatic pronouncements of others who equally have no evidence, but for some of us this kind of consolation, whether we like or dislike the prospect of immortality, is something less than morally and intellectually acceptable.

As a last example of the cultural context of a belief on immortality, I refer to the doctrine of the resurrection of the body. Here is the supreme expression of the Judaeo-Christian affirmation of the world, of the high value which the biblical and rabbinical and early Patristic religions placed on God's physical creation. The first great struggle of the Christian Church was against the Gnosticism which denied the reality of matter and made it the seat and source of evil. The doctrine of the resurrection was crucial to that struggle. The resurrection was both the symbol and promise not only of the victory over death and thereby over sin, but as well the victory of the creator God and his world over meaningless and purposeless natural process.

Here was the assurance that the true self, the self that might achieve immortality, is not a disembodied soul that belongs to a world totally unknown, not a half-self that comes from a split between body and soul, but a whole unitary self of body, mind, and soul, a union that God created and found good.

The Gnostic attack on matter was destructive of the biblical tradition's high evaluation of the physical as God's creation. Equally destructive centuries later was the Cartesian split between the mind and body that destroyed the unity of the self for much modern thought and religion, a unity which modern psychology is only now slowly restoring. But for the Christian the resurrection represents much more than a psycho-physical theory, however attractive it may be. The resurrection is the word of hope, of life, the answer to the persistent threat and terror of death which constantly engulfs man. It is the overcoming of the dominion of sin and death and the rising in the glory of God. The resurrection idea could have no meaningful place in Greek philosophic thought, but it is very much at home in the Judaeo-Christian religion, for in a sense it is a summary of the basic meaning of that religion.

II

The question of the meaning of immortality requires a consideration of two matters — what it is that is held to be immortal, and what it means for something to be immortal. It can then be asked whether the claim of immortality is a genuinely meaningful assertion, and if meaningful, whether there is a theoretic or practical possibility for its verification.

In this context, consider again the idea of resurrection. I refer, of course, to "resurrection" taken in the literal and non-symbolic sense as the resurrection of the body, the restoration to life of the body of flesh that was laid in the grave, as this was quite certainly taught in the pharisaic religion and by the early Christians, and is even today widely believed among literalists and fundamentalists of the biblical faith. Surely this belief must severely tax the credulity of all but the most naïve among the faithful, whether Jews, Christians, or Muslims. It is a vestige of a different world, a different culture. It has about it an air of miracle, magic, mystery, and myth, if not just plain nonsense, that clearly does not fit the patterns and criteria of thought to which we are accustomed. It would hardly be believed at all in twentieth-century America if it had not been so firmly built into the foundations of religion in a much earlier age, a religion which produced a remarkably persistent mixture of piety and hope that at this point was shaped into one of the dogmas of orthodoxy.

In some respects the first century was a time of high culture and sophistication, but at least in the matter of the criteria of meaningfulness and truth, in the question of what constitutes reliable knowledge or knowledge claims of high probability, our own century has exceeded all others. Here our sophistication, whatever skepticism or agnosticism or disenchantment or even despair it may generate, is more authentic. That our commitment to more rigorous criteria of knowledge and truth denies to most of us the solace of some of the most cherished beliefs of our cultural ancestors may be a measure of our heresy, but it is also a mark of our intellectual integrity.

This brings me to my main point, that belief in the resurrection of the body would seem to have the quite important virtue of being meaningful. I mean "meaningful" in the sense of satisfying the basic criteria of meaningfulness which modern logic and scientific and philosophical analysis have generated in the attempt to construct adequate theories of knowledge and truth. It is unfortunate for a proposition when it is false rather than true. But if you are a proposition, it is far better to be false than to be neither true nor false, for this would be to be meaningless, not to be a genuine proposition at all — to appear, perhaps because of grammatical structure and the felicitous employment of symbols, to express a fact, but indeed not to be a statement of fact at all because of the failure to satisfy minimal semantic and syntactic requirements. My point is the simple one of holding that when we say "On the morning of the resurrection the body will rise from the grave and become alive," our statement is cognitively meaningful because when it is taken literally it is possible for us to designate in empirical or operational terms the kinds of events which would be necessary to establish its probability or truth values. Whether these events could or would take place is quite irrelevant to the point, as the issue which I am raising here is not the truth or falsity of the proposition, but rather its meaningfulness.

It is a serious question whether the typical claims to the immortality of the soul, which have so widely replaced the idea of the resurrection, are thus genuinely meaningful. Because at the least they seem to be instances of metaphysics of a quite speculative and therefore dubious sort, and they suffer therefore the criticism which the empirically- and positivistically-oriented mind of our era has leveled against all metaphysics — that in its better forms it may be a satisfying and highly cultivated art, but it is not a science and may not be, except in appearance, an authentic venture in knowledge. I have no desire here to press this point, although I will refer to it later, but I simply point out that the idea of the resurrection, at least on the "body" side, seems to be able to survive the empirical and positivistic criticism of meaning because in a sense it is physics, at least a kind of magical physics, rather than metaphysics. Leaving aside some of its more detailed adornment, resurrection has to do with physical processes. I can understand the modern and even the ancient "liberal" wanting to settle for the immortality of the soul rather than the resurrection of the body, because, whereas resurrection appears to be patently false as a literal claim, the immortality of the soul appears to be safe from any likelihood that it can be shown to be false. If it cannot be shown to be true, it also cannot be shown to be false. There is no possible empirical evidence that can be used against it. But the price paid for its security may well be the price of being consoled by a belief that is not capable of being established as false because it is meaningless. There is no evidence against it because evidence is not relevant to it at all.

The immortality of the soul depends on the reality of an entity separable from the body which can survive the death and disintegration of the body. The soul might be composed of a special kind of matter and therefore not subject to dissolution under the same conditions as the death of the body, a view sometimes though infrequently held, or it may be, as is usually held, an immaterial substance not subject to the conditions affecting materiality. At any rate, the question of the reality of "substance" apart from the phenomenal reality known through the bodily senses is crucial to the whole issue. It is here that earlier metaphysics and psychology, often serving the interests of religion and theology, seemed secure in supporting the immortality claim, because the theory of substance, grounded especially in the metaphysics of Aristotle, seemed to be beyond doubt. And it is here also that modern psychology and empirical and positivistic methodology, and we might say even common sense, have severely undercut the belief in immortality.

In its simplest form, the basic issue is whether the intellectual or mental life of the person, the mind, is simply a function of the body — whether when the body ceases to function, the mind, which is identified with the soul, ceases to exist. Here again the theory of orthodox Buddhism is unequivocal. In the *Visuddhi-Magga* (XVIII) we learn that, "Just as the word 'chariot' is but a mode of expression for axle, wheels, chariot-body, pole and other constituent members, placed in a certain relation to each other, but when we come to examine the members one by one, we discover that in the absolute sense there is no chariot; . . . and just as the word 'fist' is but a mode of expression for the fingers, the thumb, etc., in a certain relation; in exactly the same way the words 'living entity' and 'Ego' are but a mode of expression for the presence of the five attachment groups, . . . (and) we discover that in the absolute sense there is no living entity there to form a basis for such figments as 'I am' or 'I'; in other words, that in the absolute sense there is only name and form" (Warren trans.).

Despite its simplicity and naïveté, this view has much in common with the modern pragmatically-based functional theory of the mind. In the theory that mind is function, as with John Dewey, for instance, the functions are basically organic functions; they are functions in the interest of life. But they achieve a distinctively mental level as the symbolic functioning of natural events which in themselves are not mental. Mind is genuinely mind, but it is nonetheless a mode of behavior and is in no way a so-called mental "substance." The same may be said for most other modern theories of mind and consciousness — that there is no consciousness in the sense of a conscious substance that can persist independently of the body, that there is no mind in the form of a mental substance, no immaterial substance which is the soul. A landmark in this discussion, of course, was the famous essay of William James, "Does Consciousness Exist?" Yes, he said, consciousness exists, but not in the way that is commonly supposed. "Let me then immediately explain that I mean only to deny that the word stands for an entity, but to insist most emphatically that it does stand for a function. There is, I mean, no aboriginal stuff or quality of being, contrasted with that of which material objects are made, out of which our thoughts of them are made . . . thoughts in the concrete are made of the same stuff as things are" — not made of matter but, like material things, of neutral experience.

Modern philosophy and psychology, of course, have produced a variety of theories on the nature of the mind and its relation to the body. And combinations and refinements of those theories may be expected in the future and no doubt there will be genuinely original thought in these matters that will be empirically grounded in laboratory and clinical work. It seems to me, nevertheless, that it is highly probable that the basis for such theories will continue to be ideas of mind or soul as substance or quasi-substantive, as the function of material organism, as relations among entities that are intrinsically non-mental, or as some kind of symbolic function that is at once bodily and organic as well as mental. It is not likely that totally new approaches to the nature of mind will be forthcoming.

The concept of substance, though frequently under fire and now largely abandoned in non-Catholic philosophy, has had a long and somewhat favorable life. Its chief foundations in Western thought are found in Aristotle's metaphysics, where "substance" refers to the essential being of a concrete reality, that which makes a thing what it is, the subject of which predications or attributions are made in declarative discourse. The problem of verifying the existence of substance conceived in this way has always been that whatever can be experienced of a thing turns out to be its attributes rather than the thing itself, the substance. What is experienced is always the whiteness, sweetness, swiftness, smoothness, location, or motion of the thing. But the thing itself is not its whiteness nor its smoothness; it is presumably something which is white and smooth. In brief, it — the substance — is always the subject, and what we experience of or about it is always the predicate. How, then, can we ever find the substance in itself if whatever we can experience is simply its attributes or predicates? The verdict of many has been that there is no substance, that a thing is simply the conglomeration of its attributes taken in certain relations, as Hinayana Buddhism held in the case of the chariot or the fist. This, indeed, is the position of most contemporary philosophy. It is a position which is entirely consonant with the empirical and positivistic temper of modern thought. Hume's argument that nothing of the nature of self can be found in experience is perhaps extreme, but he set the stage for an effective onslaught upon both the whole theory of substance and the doctrine of the soul as a separable entity.

Aristotle, whose temperament was empirically inclined and whose metaphysics favored the concrete and particular, argued that the soul of the individual is not separable from the body but is the form of the body. Yet when his argument was all in he held that the distinctive soul which informs the body, the passive intellect, is only part of the story and that the active, creative intellect is immortal and survives the death of the body and the passive intellect. But the active intellect freed from the body is not individual; it is identical with the divine intellect, and although it is immortal its immortality is not in any way experienced as an individual soul.

In the thirteenth century, Thomas Aquinas argued for the Aristotelian principle that the soul is complete only with the body and is the form of the body, a position strong even today in the Roman Catholic Church. St. Augustine, following Plato, had defined man essentially as a soul, an immaterial substance, who possessed and used a body. Aquinas, however, insisted that man is not a soul which has a body but rather is soul and body, that soul alone does not define man's whole nature even though it is an immaterial spiritual substance.

Needless to say, St. Thomas had difficulties with this concept, just as Plato and the Platonists had trouble with their doctrine. What is the state, for instance, of the soul after death and before the resurrection? — the same question faced by the early Christians. His solution was not entirely satisfactory but nevertheless it preserved his doctrine of man as a unity of soul and body — the soul can exist without the body, though not the body without the soul, but the soul is not complete man without the body; the body is in the soul rather than the soul in the body. There follows from this, of course, the prime importance of the resurrection.

It was Descartes who more than any other upset this ideal of unity. Though he considered himself a good Catholic, in this matter

Descartes set the stage for much later Protestantism in clearly and unequivocally championing the ontological separation of mind and matter. He says, in his *Discourse on Method* (part IV), "From that I knew that I was a substance the whole essence or nature of which is to think, and that for its existence there is no need of any place, nor does it depend on any material thing; so that this 'me', that is to say, the soul by which I am what I am, is entirely distinct from body . . . and even if body were not, the soul would not cease to be what it is." Here is the classical dichotomy of body and soul, connected but ontologically independent and exclusive: extended substance, the matter which occupies space, and thinking substance, the immaterial nonspatial entity that is the immortal soul.

What Descartes took apart, modern psychology is putting back together, but the whole process has produced severe pain for religion. For the distinct separation of mind and body seemed to make it possible for the liberals to abandon the miracle of resurrection yet keep the immortality of the soul, something which they were quick to do. It seemed like a nice case of having one's cake and eating it too. And the definition of the soul as conscious, thinking, immaterial nonspatial substance put the case for immortality beyond the possibility of serious refutation, for how could anyone even investigate the claim of immortality by examining such an immaterial substance, let alone disconfirm that claim on factual evidence. But factual evidence was really not much in demand, for most metaphysics and philosophical theology proceeded on essentially rationalistic rather than empirical grounds at least into this century. Moreover, to the great delight of much theology, until well into this century, the idealists gained and held the center of the metaphysical stage, the Idealism which held that ultimately reality is mind and the function and product of mind, while matter depends upon mind for its existence. It is true that in Idealism the mind or soul was often thought to be process or act rather than substance, but mind as process was not only not less real, it was for the idealists the clue to all reality and all existence. Here in Idealism the supremacy of mind joined the supremacy of human values to guarantee the truth of religion, that whatever has ultimate worth will eventually prevail. Those who championed idealism in one or another of its countless forms were the great names in metaphysics: Kant, Schelling, Hegel, Bradley, Bosanquet, Gentile, and Royce, to mention only an obvious few. They represented varying degrees of heresy from the religious tradition, but they seemed to hold, nevertheless, a proprietorship over religious philosophy, and when their citadel of logic and reason, mind and idea, came under the attack of empiricism in its many forms, pragmatic, realistic, and positivistic, the philosophical foundations of theology appeared to be doomed — doomed until it was recognized that the idealists were not the sole proprietors of religion and that realistic or pragmatic or possibly even existentialist foundations might support its intellectual edifice.

As I have already indicated, the question of the meaningfulness of the concept of immortality is the question whether the statement "there is an immortal soul" can satisfy the criteria of factual meaningfulness. The most rigorous criteria of meaning were established a few decades ago by the logical positivists, first as involving the actual processes of empirical verification. In the process of criticizing and refining these criteria, however, the positivists moved away from verification of a sentence as true or false to its confirmation or disconfirmation with some degree of probability or improbability, and to confirmability in principle rather than in fact. This meant, in effect, that a sentence has genuine factual cognitive meaning, that is, that it is in fact "true or false," if it is possible to designate what kinds of experiences would in principle be relevant to the determination of its probability value.

In recent years positivism has subjected itself to continued criticism and the meaning of factual meaning is still a matter unsettled, due largely to intricate logical and linguistic issues; but it seems to me that we can at least hold that to establish that a sentence is factually meaningful we must be able to describe what would be the case if it were true as compared to what would be the case if it were false. For us to hold that the sentence "there is an immortal soul" is meaningful, we must be able to tell what it means at least to the extent of saying in what way the state of there being an immortal soul is different from the state of there not being an immortal soul.

Now I believe that the person who says that immortality consists of the continuation or renewal of life on the order in which he now finds it clearly makes a meaningful claim — that is, his claim is in fact true or false, because it is possible for him to tell what would be the case if it were true or if it were false. Whether it is "true" or is "false" is another matter. We know what he means because we know what life here and now is like and he means that immortality is essentially more of the same — a body and mind, for instance, that are associated with thought, disposition, and action, and that endure through time. And, of course, memory, the crucial factor that maintains the identity of the person — memory which establishes the continuity of the present person with the person who persists after death, or after what appears to be death.

But meaningfulness here is established primarily by the idea that the future life will be essentially like the present life, where the crucial factors seem to be the bodily functions and temporality. These are the factors, of course, which recommend belief in the resurrection and which account for the fact that immortality by resurrection seems to make cognitive sense and, except for the sophisticated, to be desirable. But what sense or meaning can we make of the more abstruse idea of immortality where the claim involves an eternal, immaterial soul — but no body and no time?

Here we seem to be up against two kinds of difficulties. In the first place it is a question whether it is possible to describe what such a condition, the state of an eternal, immaterial soul, would be like. To use these words in an acceptable syntax is not enough; they must have some semantic reference, and it must be a reference which provides some communicable experiential meaning. But how can we, whose experiences are all temporal, give anything but negative clues to the meaning of eternal. Have we had eternal or timeless experiences that enable us to describe the state of an eternal being — not establish that there *is* an eternal being, but simply to give some indication of what an eternal being would be like if there were one? And what experiences have we had which enable us to describe what an immaterial being would be like if there were one? Not an immaterial concept or idea or ontological universal or something like that, an object simply of thought, but an immaterial, concrete, particular, living being.

The second difficulty is a logical one. It is obvious that if a proposition cannot survive logical analysis it is not a serious candidate for factual analysis. The logical problem here seems to be that the typical case of holding that there is an immortal, eternal, immaterial soul is a case also of describing that soul by employing bodily and temporal experiences. There seem to be no other experiences to employ in describing a living thing.[3] We are caught in a predicament something like that of Schopenhauer, who said that when it comes to describing hell we have an abundance of experience from which to draw our descriptions, but for the description of heaven we have little or nothing to go on. But if this is the case, and at least it seems to be the case, we may become caught in a contradiction — a disembodied, immaterial, timeless soul which can be described only by those properties which belong to temporal, materially embodied minds. At least this is a problem which cannot be ignored.

If we attempt to get around this difficulty by employing nonexperiential criteria of meaningfulness, so that, for instance, we are willing to talk about an eternal entity although we have never experienced one or have never had in any way a nontemporal experience, we still face the valuational problem, insofar at least as the claim to immortality is tied to religion or morals and is not simply a matter of intellectual curiosity. This is the problem of whether there should be any interest in the soul's immortality if in immortality it bears no resemblances to its condition in mortality, and if, therefore, it is a hollow and somewhat trivial claim to say that it is a continuation of the same soul or the same person. This is a large problem and it gets at the roots of religion. I will not press it further other than to indicate its possible bearing on the meaningfulness of immortality claims.

Although it is obvious that materiality is not a necessary condition for all reality and although the claim of an immaterial immortal soul is commonplace, I frankly believe that any claim to a disembodied existence of a living entity is probably meaningless. This depends, of course, on the criteria of meaningfulness which we are willing to settle for and such criteria are no doubt to a degree culturally determined. But critical thought has done much to support

---

[3] I will raise a serious question on this point later in this essay by reference to the possible nontemporal element in mystic experience.

the empirical criteria toward which our culture inclines and which are, indeed, among its defining properties. We may not be willing to settle for strict empirical criteria of meaning, but at least we must come to some kind of terms with empiricism.

To hold to the possibility of mental processes apart from a material brain is not logically contradictory even though it may be false — provided, of course, that the mental processes have no relevance to bodily functions. Here, of course, we are dealing with atypical cases of immortality claims, claims describing conditions where there can be no functions such as seeing, hearing, talking, moving — in short, the kinds of experiences most people apparently hope to have in the hereafter. There can only be experiences such as thought, which may in fact require a physical brain but which may conceivably and logically require no brain. At any rate, I believe that while most claims to immortality are probably illogical and the remainder are not factually meaningful, it may well be possible in principle to construct claims that are both logical and factual. The meaninglessness of the common claims results partly from their being generated within the context of religion and theology where they have been constructed to conform more to human hope and aspiration than to the requirements imposed by logical and empirical criticism.

But one final item relating to the problem of meaningfulness — the idea of eternity. Just what can eternity mean? and can the word "eternal" be meaningfully employed as a predicate in a factual sentence? The historical consciousness and the ordinary concept of time that are common with us are largely a product of our biblical heritage, both nourished and defended by the occidental religions and religious philosophies. The Greeks, however, had inclined strongly toward the idea of the eternal, holding that the ultimately real is timeless; that it is being free from all becoming, from motion, change, or process, and is therefore free from time. In hellenic and hellenistic culture, even the temporal processes of history were often seen against the backdrop of eternity, and the movement of historic time therefore, as observed for instance in the changing character of social institutions, was a cyclical passage where time proceeded in circles — a fact which seemed to obliterate the ultimacy of past and future and to approximate the ideal changelessness and timelessness of whatever is in the highest sense really real.

At least something like this dominated the thought of those Greek thinkers who were eventually to have the largest impact on the world's thought, Parmenides, Plato, and Aristotle, and seems also to have in some degree infused the Greek mind generally. Here there was no clear conception of creation nor of linear historic movement; the world was without beginning or end; and whatever change might be real in the world that is observed, perfection consisted in the fixedness and stability and motionlessness — and therefore timelessness — of the intelligible world that can be thought but cannot be known by sensory experience.

In Judaism, Christianity, and Islam there was an uncomfortable but quite permanent marriage of the Greek eternity with the Semitic time-consciousness which was rooted in the biblical faith that God is the Lord of History, that his purposes are fulfilled in a temporal world which has a beginning in time and will have an end. For classical Christianity, the personal temporal living God of the Bible was given descriptions designed for the impersonal, eternal, motionless absolute of Platonic–Aristotelian metaphysics, and Christian theology ever since has wrestled with the contradiction of eternity and time. In Christ the eternal God entered into time and thereby gave meaning to history; because of this, by a divine miracle the soul of man, created and enduring in time, will enter into eternity.

The crux of the meaning of eternity in metaphysics and theology is "timelessness" — not an endless time as in popular discourse, but the absence of time, a state free from the distinctions of past, present, and future, a state only exceptionally if ever simulated in human experience and difficult if not entirely impossible to describe with our temporally conditioned language. This is the problem in discussing immortality. It is one thing for the believer to assert his faith in immortality and mean by that a continued existence in time. He may, of course, say that his soul will exist in "eternity," but he usually means some kind of continuing existence which involves an endless future. But it is quite another thing for the theologian to discourse on the eternal nature of the soul, where life beyond death has a timeless quality, not timeless in the poetic and common sense of a never-ending time, but timeless in the technical sense of eternity, that is, without the past, present, and future distinctions of time. How can this have any meaning for us? Where is the experience that enables us to say what would be the case if something were eternal? And, getting again at the valuation facet of the problem, what would be the value of being an eternal rather than a temporal self? For one who knows only temporality, what point would there be in becoming eternal?

We seem to encounter "eternity" on at least five occasions: in the timeless quality of "intelligible" entities such as the Platonic forms or other universals; in the dogmatic pronouncements of religion that God is eternal; in the speculative rationalizations of philosophers that the world is eternal; in such assertions of the theologians as that in Christ the eternal God entered into time and established thereby the center and meaning of history; and in the mystic's experience of the timeless quality of his rapture in the moment of his encounter with God or the Absolute. If it is in fact the case that the mystics do have an authentic experience of eternity, it is perhaps probable that most of us at some time or another have experiences that at least approach the eternal. Certainly we must recognize that in what we often call psychological time, or what may be called the individual consciousness of time, there is great variety, as when we say the time has passed rapidly or slowly, and it may be that there is some form of intuition of time "standing still," as is sometimes claimed. I am aware also that impressive arguments have been advanced, as for instance by Josiah Royce, that the human experience of timelessness is not uncommon, as in the grasp of a musical sequence in the mind's "specious present." I fail to see, however, that those experiences which gather up the immediate past and immediate future into a present are experiences of the eternal. Their very nature is dependent on the temporality of their object.

Nevertheless, I think we should not rule out of consideration the expansion of the meaning of empirical to include the mystic experience even with respect to the claims of empirical knowledge, even though this is a distortion of common usage. My point, of course, is that even while we insist on empirical criteria of factual meaningfulness, there may be some basis for holding that a claim involving eternity may be meaningful if we include such experiences as the mystic experience within the meaning of empiricism as a way of knowing or of justifying knowledge claims.

There is a difficulty here, of course, in the fact that mystics have quite commonly held that their experience is ineffable, which would presumably remove it from the context of knowledge in the ordinary sense of discursive knowledge, which must be communicable. But for the present purpose this difficulty should be overlooked, as even those mystics who claim that their experience is incommunicable often manage to communicate a great deal about it, as for instance that it is immediate or intuitive and that it is timeless and its object a total unity or absolute.

I mention mysticism because it may give a clue to an experiential meaning for "eternity" and because I think that to some extent the creedal conceptions of immortality may have something in common with the mystic experience — as for instance that in the official Christian heaven or paradise nothing seems to be going on except a kind of timeless adoration of God. If heaven is eternal there isn't any time there during which anything can happen. Yet it seems to me that the so-called "true" mystics have little or no interest in immortality, and the common believer has little or no interest in an immortality that would consist of mystic-type experience. The mystic seems to achieve his bliss in an eternity that is, paradoxically, here and now, and the true believer seeks his bliss in an immortality that is, paradoxically, a kind of temporal existence in God's eternal presence.

The consideration of mysticism brings to attention another problem already mentioned in reference to Aristotle's distinction of active and passive intellect — the issue of the immortality of the particular, individual self or soul versus some kind of non-particular or general immortality. It seems to me that here there are claims of two types: the immortality of what is sometimes called the social mind, where a collective social mind is taken as a real entity somewhat independent of particular minds, and the immortality of a universal mind or soul which is taken as a reality over and above particular minds or souls which may be considered to be its manifestations or to in some way depend upon it for their apparent being. I will pass over the problem of the social mind, which though interesting is probably

of less concern to most, and will give attention only to the matter of
the individual versus the universal mind or soul.

It seems obvious that in our culture most believers in immortality
mean that the particular individual soul is immortal and that as it
survives death it also retains its numerical identity—a position which,
as I have mentioned, would seem to entail continuity through memory — so that in effect the soul after death could claim identity with
a particular soul that existed before death and not simply some kind
of karmaic continuity with another soul. But the immortality or indestructibility of only the universal soul has been widespread as a
belief among the philosophically sophisticated, as also among the
mystics. Unlike Plato, Aristotle did not believe in the immortality
of the individual soul. As I have indicated, he did believe that the
creative intellect of the individual is immortal, but its immortality is
its identity with the universal active intellect in which there is no
individuality, no particularity. Advaita Vedānta, currently the most
popular school of Indian thought, holds that the soul's immortality
is its identity with the Absolute. Here the end of life is to achieve
the experience of the identity of the self — Atman — with the Absolute — Brahman. Shankara, even though a theist, held on grounds
set forth in the Upanishads, that the search for the true nature of the
self yields the Brahman, the impersonal Absolute. Shankara was a
vigorous critic of Buddhism's denial of a permanent soul. He argued
that consciousness is not a compound of elements and is not caused
or produced and therefore is eternal and infinite. The self is pure
consciousness, but as pure consciousness it is impersonal, an impersonal reality that manifests itself as God or *Isvara*, or as *jiva* or individual souls, depending on conditioning factors. But the self as
impersonal Brahman–Atman is the only and ultimately true reality.

Something like this is found in the Christian mystic Eckhart. At
least Eckhart approaches the Absolute by searching the depths of the
individual soul. Indeed, he appears to identify the soul totally with
God, to say that the soul *is* God, as that Atman *is* Brahman. It is not
that the Atman unites with Brahman, but that the Atman *is* Brahman.
And yet, to follow the analysis of Rudolf Otto, "the self is God"
and "the Atman is Brahman" is the union of two subjects. The "is"
is an "is" of synthesis, not of genuine identity. It is the theism of

both Shankara and Eckhart which prevents that identity. In some final sense God must be differentiated from the self even when the self is taken in its ultimate nature.

One final point: although mysticism may well be involved in concepts that are cognitively meaningless, it may also be the key to the meaning of self-transcendence, that supreme quality of experience which today's theologian sometimes offers as a replacement for old-style salvation in immortality. It is the achievement of eternity here and now; the rising above the conditioned existence of finite created being; the overcoming of the anxiety of death and annihilation. It is the entering into eternity in the similitude of those who intersect the eternal through the sublimity of the arts, or of mathematics, or of love and compassion. This may be the real salvation, the real immortality that we can hope for — and not only hope for, but possibly achieve.

It is not inconceivable that eventually meanings and methods will be reached which will permit the empirical investigation of the immortality of the soul. But it is a fair assumption that immortality conceived in the high terms that have issued from religion and religious philosophy may never be an object of knowledge, but always a matter of hope and faith. I do not say this in support of those who prefer faith to knowledge as a ground for religious beliefs, because I hold that reliable knowledge is essential to religion. I say it only because in my opinion there is little evidence in the question of the immortality of the soul that reliable knowledge is a viable probability.

11

Evolution, Religion, and Human Hope

In 1909, in the distinguished Cambridge essays celebrating the centenary of the birth of Darwin and the fiftieth anniversary of *The Origin of Species*, P. N. Waggett wrote confidently:

> The object of this paper is first to point out certain elements of the Darwinian influences upon religious thought, and then to show reason for the conclusion that it has been, from a Christian point of view, satisfactory. I shall not proceed further to urge that the Christian apologetic in relation to biology has been successful. A variety of opinions may be held on this question, without disturbing the conclusion that the movements of readjustment have been beneficial to those who remain Christians, and this by making them more Christian and not only more liberal.[1]

This sanguine testimony to the compatibility of science and religion expressed the liberal spirit of the early decades of this century. The liberal religion is now severely weakened, pressed from one side by the resurgence of orthodoxy and biblical literalism and from the other by the reasonableness of naturalistic humanism. As before,

[1] A. C. Seward, ed., *Darwin and Modern Science* (1909).

the central issue is the implications of science for religion, and, today, long after the question of organic evolution has been in principle settled by science, the argument against evolution is gaining strength, not as a scientific inquiry, but as a social movement that sets ancient literature and primitive pre-scientific thought against the methods of modern science and the plentitude of relevant knowledge which these methods have generated. My primary interest here is not in the clash of evolution and fundamentalist religion, but rather in the implications of evolutionary theory for what might well be called cosmic human hope. It is the question of whether ultimately the world is on our side.

I believe that the scientific theory of organic evolution and the classical Judaeo-Christian theology are at crucial points in principle incompatible, and that therefore if the theory of the origin of species by some kind of natural selection is true, as in all probability it is, the traditional theistic religion of our culture is engrossed in basic theological difficulties. From opposite poles both the fundamentalists and the humanists have recognized this predicament, but the liberals in religion, still persistent in the effort to reconcile science and religion, have generally refused to acknowledge this contradiction and have muddied the waters of discussion by their treatments of both theology and evolution.

For our culture, cosmic human hope has been so thoroughly grounded in, and indeed virtually confined to, the classical, traditional theology that for large segments of humanity this hopeful faith, the supreme confidence, has been severely depressed if not destroyed; and all efforts to reconstruct and strengthen it have been futile. It is not that evolution by itself has discredited the traditional faith. It is rather, as John Fiske (1842–1901) — America's chief advocate of the evolutionary dogmas of Herbert Spencer — pointed out in his *Outlines of Cosmic Philosophy*, that the classical theology is disbelieved because "the belief is discordant with the mental habits induced by the general study of science." Not that the traditional theology will be disproved, but rather that there is "no sufficient warrant for maintaining it." [2]

----

[2] Vol. 2, 1874, pp. 378, 380. "It is, indeed, generally true," wrote Fiske, "that theories concerning the supernatural perish, not from extraneous vio-

The Roman Catholic position on organic evolution is not fully defined and allows some room for maneuver. *Moderate* evolution, the development of species, both plant and animal, from a limited number of types created by God, is acceptable to Catholic belief. But being devoid of reason, an animal soul is material and therefore cannot be the evolutionary base for a human soul, which is immaterial. The rational soul, of course, is declared to be a special individual creation of God. The church has made no final, formal pronouncement on the matter of the evolution of the human body exclusive of the soul except to indicate that belief in such evolution is allowed. The encyclical *Humani Generis* of Pius XII (1950) declared that "The magisterium of the Church does not forbid that the theory of evolution concerning the origin of the human body as coming from pre-existent and living matter — for the Catholic faith obliges us to hold that human souls are immediately created by God — be investigated and discussed by experts as far as the present state of human science and sacred theology allows." [3] The tendency to favor this view was encouraged in part by the omission of Darwinism from specific mention in the 1864 *Syllabus of Errors*, and today it is quite widely accredited. There have been many efforts, however, to discourage its acceptance. The *Humani Generis*, while allowing investigation, does not throw the weight of its authority behind evolution. It specifically warns that "those go too far and transgress this liberty of discussion who act as if the origin of the human body from pre-existing and living matter were already fully demonstrated . . . ." [4]

Even where Catholic authors have been careful to avoid the notion of spontaneous generation and have attributed the evolutionary process to a creative act of God, and where they have been free of

---

lence, but from inanition." Ibid., p. 378. Notwithstanding his criticism of the traditional theology, as is indicated later in this essay, Fiske held that evolution, which he defended in Spencerian form, is compatible with religion, but a higher form of religion than that expressed in the commonly accepted theology.

[3] Pius XII, encyclical *Humani Generis*, Denzinger 2327.

[4] Ibid.

involvement with a biologically-based conception of the mind that would compromise the doctrine of the special creation of the soul, their works have sometimes been subjected to severe criticism and condemnation and, in a number of celebrated cases, withdrawn. Immediately following the publication of *The Origin of Species*, the Provincial Council of Cologne, for example, issued in 1860 the following canon under approval of the Holy See: "Our first parents were created immediately by God (*Gen.* 2,7). Therefore, we declare as quite contrary to Holy Scripture and the Faith the opinion of those who dare to assert that man, in respect of his body, is derived by spontaneous transformation from an imperfect nature, which improved continually until it reached the present human state." [5]

An authoritative Roman Catholic work of the present century, Cardinal Ernesto Ruffini's *The Theory of Evolution Judged by Reason and Faith*, is a clear objection to any compromise of the traditional doctrine with evolutionary theory. Cardinal Ruffini, a conservative seminarian, closes his dissertation with the following admonition:

> . . . we cannot conceal our profound sorrow at perceiving that, while the theory of evolution and transformism is regarded with increasing distrust by persons of unquestionable scientific competence, it has found tardy supporters in men who boast of their filial devotion to the Apostolic Roman Church. We entreat Catholic anthropologists to ponder seriously the very grave responsibility which lies upon them. [Pp. 165f]

Whatever one may think of Cardinal Ruffini's position, which apparently enjoys wide though probably diminishing support in the church, there can be no argument with his refusal to tolerate the intellectually questionable tactics of some writers who seem willing to try anything that gives promise of satisfying the church while preserving the appearance of science. When in 1909 a pontifical biblical commission, for instance, decreed unequivocally that God engaged in a "particular creation of man," some Catholic evolutionists deferred to the decree by holding that God employed the body of an animal rather than dust in arranging a suitable habitation

---

[5] Decreta Concil, prov. Coloniensis an. 1860, pars. 1, cap. 14.

for the soul. A Catholic conservative is entirely justified in holding that this kind of argument makes a mockery of the church's claim of a biblical foundation of the faith and is at best a well-meaning but abortive attempt at allegiance to science. The church, however firm its determination to support both faith and reason, is right in holding, as it apparently does, that if a man is sincere in his commitment to empirical science as the final arbiter of truth in matters pertaining to the natural world, he should be prepared to abandon any literal commitment he may have to the antique biblical pronouncements on nature that lie at the foundations of traditional church doctrine. Something like the inverse of this position is clearly set forth in the *Humani Generis* when it declares that all should "be prepared to submit to the judgment of the Church to whom Christ has given the mission of interpreting authentically the Sacred Scriptures and of safe-guarding the dogmas of faith." [6] The question is whether we are to be openly honest and entirely consistent. Most of us, of course, are neither openly honest nor consistent. But it may be assumed that within the fold of the Catholic Church, as elsewhere, a large segment of the faithful have a genuine commitment to science, independent of the specific question of evolution, that manages to keep company with both a genuine biblical faith and submission to ecclesiastical authority, whether this is consistent or not.

Protestantism, which institutionally has been less concerned with science than has Catholicism, exhibits results of the Darwinian impact that are on the whole less moderate but nevertheless in principle not different as far as the orthodox position is concerned. Here the orthodox, with their determination to protect the faith at whatever intellectual cost, refused to compromise biblical revelation by any scientific tinkering that identified man with the animals or questioned the fact of a special and immediate creation. Lacking anything like the scholastic metaphysic, which through its distinctions between matter and form and nature and grace encouraged Catholic orthodoxy to cast around for some meeting-ground with science, Protestant orthodoxy was obliged to encounter evolution head on. But if established Protestant theology was short on the grace of Aristotelianism in con-

[6] Pius XII, loc. cit.

tending with evolution, science itself was not, and, for a time at least, the orthodox enjoyed a measure of comfort from the company of those scientists such as Jean Louis Agassiz (1807–1873), who from theology, metaphysics, or piety defended the fixity of species.[7]

Of course, apart from official church dogma, individual Protestant thinkers, employing especially the Aristotelian doctrine of final cause or purpose defined in terms of the end, found grounds for accepting organic evolution as set forth by Darwin while at the same time interpreting it in terms of design in nature.

The debate on evolution and its philosophical and religious implications developed in the United States especially following the publication of Darwin's *The Descent of Man* in 1871, more than ten years after the *Origin of Species.* The scientific case for evolution was argued most effectively by the botanist Asa Gray (1810–1888), but perhaps the most important early discussion of evolution and religion in the United States was a symposium published in the *North American Review* (1879). The symposium engaged Simon Newcomb, the nation's leading astronomer of that time, Noah Porter, professor of moral philosophy at Yale University, James Freeman Clarke, a leading Unitarian clergyman, and James McCosh, president of Princeton University. Newcomb argued against the existence of evidence for final cause (purpose) in the natural universe, while the others, all of whom held divinity degrees, defended both evolution and the reality of design in nature. Clarke concluded that:

> The phenomena of the universe cannot be satisfactorily explained unless by the study both of efficient causes and final causes. Routine scientists, confining themselves to the one, and routine theologians, confining themselves to the other, may suppose them

[7] In his *Contributions to the Natural History of the United States of America* (1857), part 1, Agassiz argued that,

> All organized beings exhibit in themselves all those categories of structure and of existence upon which a natural system may be founded, in such a manner that, in tracing it, the human mind is only translating into human language the Divine thoughts expressed in nature in living realities.
>
> All these beings do not exist in consequence of the continual agency of physical causes, but have made their successive appearance upon earth by the immediate intervention of the Creator.

to be in conflict. But men of larger insight, like Leibnitz, Newton, Descartes, and Bacon, easily see the harmony between them.

But this provided at best only a temporary breather, for the Aristotelian metaphysics, which had already been banished from the physical sciences, was fast losing ground even among conservative biologists while Newtonian physics, with its inherent indifference to teleology, was progressively invading the biological, psychological, and social sciences. With the discrediting of the Aristotelian component of biology — both the Linnaean system of classification, which had held the biological sciences in the grip of a kind of logical tyranny, and the doctrine of final cause, which found purpose in the development of species — the fundamentalists lost the support of science and, accordingly, retreated to their now-common stand against science and scientific intelligence. They are still holding out. Genuine fundamentalism, which, paradoxically, has a strong appeal for many scientists, continues to aggressively push biblical literalism and an antiquated theological tradition that is basically antagonistic to science.

For the past half century, apart from controversy over technical details of evolutionary theory, the discussion of organic evolution seemed to have died down, or even out. In America the Scopes trial of 1925 was little more than an entertaining circus, but it seemed to have had a quieting effect on the whole controversy. The nation forgot, however, that scientific education lost the verdict in that trial, and now the purveyors of ancient myth as science are again clamoring for victory in the courts and legislative halls. The Darwin centennial in 1959 produced some attention to evolution, but it was largely a scholarly matter dictated by academic duty or journalistic interest. The discussion, however, was brief and was all on one side. Serious argument on the basic fact of biological evolution is over, of course, because it has been decided. It is interesting that the fundamentalists, deceived by their success in converting a scientific problem into a social issue, often enjoy the illusion that it was won by them. Or they are at least quite sure that the evidence is not yet all in and that they are justified in their expectation of eventual victory. Nothing excites their intellectual interest more than the news that a competent scientist has come out with criticisms of Darwinism, even though in fact he may be a confirmed defender of evolution by natural selection and is merely critical of technical details within the general theory.

Now what can be said, if anything, for the biblical fundamentalist's opposition to evolution, whether Catholic, Protestant, Jew, or Muslim? If he is totally naïve, very little. But if he is not entirely naïve, this much can be said, that unlike some others, he is at least consistent with his orthodox commitments and he possesses that faculty of sure discernment peculiar to the orthodox that enables him to smell out heretics and heresy from a great distance. He sees clearly that capitulation to evolution would destroy some very fundamental and precious elements of the religion which is fully rooted in the biblical tradition, because that religion is grounded in a conception of man which is at variance with any theory that identifies man with the order of animal nature. If a Christian, he is sure that Christ came into the world to save souls who had fallen from godliness, not risen from a distant cousin of the ape or from some primeval slime. The liberals have often ridiculed this radical statement of the issue, but it cannot be ignored except by an intellectual gloss that intentionally avoids the basic problem.

It is a simple thing to point out that the orthodox opposition to evolution is, after all, consistent with the traditional fear of secular elements in the culture, and that it is all part of an exasperating historical and scientific illiteracy which from generation to generation supports a literal-minded, unimaginative, untutored, uncritical, naïve conservatism. Or, to put it bluntly, that today's fundamentalist is not genuinely interested in truth; that his concern, rather, is simply to minister to his emotional life or possibly to promote the tyranny of a sacred book, perpetuate an antique theological tradition, or encourage submission to ecclesiastical authority.

Now there is a large measure of truth in this. But it is also true that the primary concern of the fundamentalist may be the salvation of the human soul and that he realizes better than some that in the matter of the ultimate disposition of the soul the Western world has put most of its eggs in one basket: faith in a theistic religion and belief in a doctrine of redemption that is rooted in an ancient theosophy generated by pre-scientific intelligence. To say that since 1859 that basket has been tossed around with some abandon is to put it mildly. It is futile to say to the sophisticated fundamentalist, "You'll become accustomed to this sort of thing, just as your theological ancestors became accustomed to the Copernican astronomy." The orthodox know that the question of man's centricity in the astrophysical universe is a trivial matter compared with the question of whether man himself is what religion has always said he is, a being who by virtue of a supernatural endowment is different from and superior to the natural world, however or in whatever direction stretched out it may be. Nor has their attitude toward evolution been tempered by the fact that orthodoxy survived the determinism implied by the conjunction of Newtonian mechanics and nineteenth-century materialism which had seemed so obvious a contradiction to traditional theism, or that determinism has sometimes been put to good use by some of the best conservative theologians. They know that the survival of orthodoxy has been in part by the grace of the doctrine of the freedom of the soul, a doctrine that to a remarkable degree has successfully withstood the onslaught of mechanics and everything else that physical science could conjure up against it. But the coming of a scientifically acceptable theory of organic evolution was a different matter. Here the very idea of the reality of the soul seemed threatened by a scientific theory. Here was an affront to religion that went straight to the heart of the very meaning of traditional religion. Regardless of what was intended by circumspect or pious scientists, and notwithstanding the factitious attempt to accommodate to science by the separation of the history of the soul from the development of the body, the fact remained that the very existence of the human soul was under attack. By the time *The Descent of Man* was published, the fat was in the fire and every defender of orthodoxy worth his salt knew that the stakes were the highest that had ever been set and that there could be no compromise and no yielding. The issue was nothing less than the question whether there is a cosmic ground for human hope — not hope for some far-off achievement of the good society, or even for the survival of a disembodied abstraction called "humanity," or even for the preservation in a Platonic heaven of all human values — but a hope for the salvation and eternal life of particular, individual persons who live and breathe in this world and whose religion means to them the ultimate defeat of the powers that threaten their extinction. George Romanes, an old friend of Darwin's, laid it on the line: "Never in the history of man has so terrific a calamity befallen the race as that which all who look may now behold advancing as a deluge, black with destruction, resistless in might, uprooting our most cherished hopes, engulfing our most precious creed, and burying our highest life in mindless desolation." [8]

There is something admirable, of course, in the refusal of the old-fashioned liberal to accept this dilemma, in his determination to reconcile religion not only with science but with the whole of secular culture. There is always something admirable in an attempt to infuse faith with reason and protect reason from dogmatism. Admirable, but all too often futile. It was the tragedy of liberalism that it supposed that it was faithful to the justified demands of science while at the same time preserving in religion what had really counted all along. When biology abandoned the Aristotelian doctrine of fixed species, the liberal Protestant was confirmed in his conviction that religion not only did not depend for intellectual support on Aristotelian metaphysics but was in fact antithetical to it. He magnified his commitment to science, but as often as not it was a commitment with a reservation that allowed him a generous margin for interpretations which were often strained to support, or at least allow, metaphysical speculation that protected whatever seemed worth preserving in religion. The real value of religion, he found, was essentially experiential and not intellectual and, indeed, in the more recent sophisticated form of neo-orthodoxy, religion is more closely identified with myth than with science, and its ground in the nonrational and even irrational is fully exploited.

But try as they might, the liberals seem never to have made a genuinely convincing case for the truth of religion. Having repudiated biblical literalism and supernatural revelation, the liberal making a case for theism depended either on the possibility of a natural theology or on the criticism of reason itself. Natural theology, of course, is an old and honorable pursuit that in no way owes its exis-

---

[8] *A Candid Examination of Theism,* p. 51.

tence to the theory of evolution. It belongs rather to the philosophical tradition that habitually prefers reason to credulity and facts to myths and yet has a firm interest in the problem of the existence of God and the soul. After the initial impact of Darwinism, the English-speaking world was treated to a steady diet of natural theology, as can be seen especially in the Gifford Lectures. No one would deny that this was on the whole a rather well-balanced diet. Though occasionally over-rich, it was generally conducive to both philosophic and theologic health. But the trouble is that however brilliant, subtle, and persuasive the natural theologies may be, however clever their creators in smuggling God into everything from the primeval slime to the next step ahead, Hume's *Dialogues* cast a constant shadow over them, the skeptical shadow of reasonableness and critical inquiry. And this because natural theology, when it is genuinely sincere, is a commitment to reason, experience, and fact, even though it may be a commitment touched with piety. Even the best of the attempts at a natural theology, Frederick R. Tennant's *Philosophical Theology*, meticulously reasoned and constructed on a foundation of genuine sophistication in the nature of knowledge and uncommon erudition in the sciences and the philosophy of science, is not entirely convincing. It is not convincing unless by faith or sentiment we are already disposed to belief and find our intellectual consciences assuaged by this kind of argument.

It is unfortunate, of course, that the natural theologies have been unconvincing, because quite independently of the orthodox tradition they have offered us hope on a cosmic scale — sometimes on the impersonal side, but certainly cosmic. It is hope of a kind quite different from that provided by the classical religion, but in some ways even more attractive and more appealing. More appealing because it is free from entanglements with myth and miracle, but also because it is free from doctrinal and ecclesiastical alliances and is somewhat more pure on the moral side.

Most of the natural theologies have hardly hoped to do much for orthodoxy beyond establishing the reasonableness of belief in the existence of God and perhaps of the human soul, except that in recent years since the popularity of the new psychology they have sometimes attempted natural explanations of such matters as sin and guilt. Certainly they have scarcely tipped their hats in the direction of the Bible, and, if Christian at all, they have ignored even the rudiments of classical doctrine. Nevertheless, they have usually presumed religious respectability on the ground of their general compatibility with the great tradition and have claimed to be the preservers of whatever is fundamentally precious even in orthodoxy itself. Tennant, for instance, describes Christ as a revelation of God, naturalistically of course, and then asserts: "If acceptance of Christ's teaching concerning life in God's world, together with reverence for him and all for which he thus stood, may claim the name of Christianity with as much right as does the traditional interpretation of his personality, then Christianity may be said to be the climax of the historical development of natural religion, and the crown of natural theology." [9]

Now the trouble is that this may be good religion, but quite surely it is not Christian. At least it is not what Christianity has meant and continues to mean to the main body of Christian believers, the Christianity that has moved the world, the believers whose hope is drawn from the faith that Christ is divine and that through him we have eternal ilfe. Whatever hope the natural theologies offer, it is not an authentic Christian hope. Certainly it is not hope for personal redemption, for typically the natural theologies find nothing for the individual to be redeemed from. And at least since Hiroshima, it is no longer even a liberal faith in the redemptive processes of history.

It is somewhat ironical that the natural theologies seized with such regularity upon organic evolution as a major element of their theistic argument. Never before had anything offered such apparently limitless possibilities to the teleologist, and he worked it for all it was worth. In his famous essay on the influence of Darwinism, Dewey called it design on the installment plan. Thanks to evolution, outside the Catholic world at least, the argument from design surged ahead and soon outclassed the cosmological as a respected proof of the existence of God. Even some of the more sophisticated fundamentalists, especially among the Calvinists, found in evolution a confirmation of their doctrine of the evil character of the natural world.

[9] *Philosophical Theology*, vol. 2, p. 240.

All in all, the world was treated to the strange spectacle of one religious party condemning evolution because it destroyed belief in God — the other welcoming it with enthusiasm because it was the surest ground on which such belief could be made rational.

There was nothing new, of course, in joining evolution with religious philosophy. This had already been done by the Hegelians and Herbert Spencer on the grand scale. But Darwinism provided a scientific ground and support for evolutionary philosophy, bringing it down to earth, giving it a large measure of scientific respectability, reducing its element of speculation, and strengthening its plausibility through its theory of natural selection. Moreover, the obvious limits of scientific explanation seemed both to allow and encourage the use of religious categories by those who deal in final causes or ultimate purposes. There was nothing in Darwinism that changed this situation. Nor, by the same token, was materialism ruled out by Darwinism, though the fact that materialism as well as theism was the product of speculation was often disregarded. The field was open and both sides of the argument rushed in. But although the materialists were not idle, witness Ernst Haeckel (1834–1919) as a prime example, or Ludwig Büchner (1824–1899), those who saw in evolution some support for human personality, human values, and human hopes appear to have written the most words on the subject.[10]

While some theistic evolutionists naïvely supposed that evolution could be made compatible with the forms of orthodoxy, which required as much protection against pantheism as against atheism, others inclined in varying degrees toward immanentism. Whereas traditionally God had stood over against his creation, purposing in advance of the event and manipulating it from behind, so to speak, he was now described as within the process itself. And before the

---

[10] See Ernst Haeckel, *Die Welträthsel* ("The Riddle of the Universe"), 1899, and Ludwig Büchner, *Kraft und Stoff* ("Force and Matter"), 1855. Haeckel's metaphysics had more in common with twentieth-century naturalism than with extreme nineteenth-century materialism, but he has commonly been regarded as a materialist because of his determinism, his opposition to all supernaturalism, and his biological conception of thought and consciousness.

emergent rash was over, he would be, as Samuel Alexander's deity at least, way out ahead.[11]

Although a few heeded Huxley's warning that evolution reveals nature as demonic and inevitably sets man morally over against an indifferent cosmos, the evolutionists generally, joining hands with the industrialists, political democrats, and historical optimists, assured their followers that the world really looks good — everything moving onward and upward, for society, for the race, for human history. Presumably this was expected to bring satisfaction and joy to the individual soul — to be a part of the forward movement of the universe, to be an emergent from a lesser something in the distant past, to become, in a small way of course, an expression of the divine upsurge of the cosmic motion of the *élan*. Apparently it's a wonderful thing to be a little higher than you might have been if you had come along a little sooner. The old-time religion looked out for your soul, its promise an eternal joy in the presence of God in which you were still you. In the new style evolutionists' religion things were different; it isn't you that really counts. What matters is the fate of society, of the species, of the cosmos. Speaking of hope — there is an abundance of hope for the cosmos, and sometimes there is hope for human values; there may even be hope for the species; but those of us who are firmly attached to our individuality as persons must be satisfied with what we now are and have and with what will happen to us in our extinction. As Dewey put it in the *Andover Review* in 1887, "What, then in bold Anglo-Saxon, is the sense of talking about the goal of the process of evolution being a goal for man, except that it be something in which he is absorbed, swallowed up, forever lost?"

At least this was the prospect offered by most religious-style evolutionary philosophies even though it was not uncommon for them to claim compatibility with biblical religion. Fiske, for instance, the worst American offender, insisted in his *Cosmic Philosophy* that "The God of the scientific philosopher is still, and must ever be, the God of the Christian, though freed from the illegitimate formulas by the

[11] See *Space, Time and Deity*, Samuel Alexander's Gifford Lectures, published in 1920.

aid of which theology has sought to render Deity comprehensible." [12]
It is something of a mystery just how Fiske's Spencerian "Unknowable" is identifiable with the Christian God, or why the scientific philosopher's God "must ever be." As a matter of fact, the Christian's God is a divine Father about whom a great deal is known, such as, among other things, that he has a firm interest in redeeming human souls, or at least some human souls. This, indeed, accounts for the Christian's interest in him. In religious thought, the concept of God is a function of the concept of man and his predicament. The typical Christian's primary interest is not in God; he is interested in himself, in his own redemption and perpetuation as an immortal person. His morals on the one hand and his religious experience on the other are quite extraneous to the central fact of his Christianity. It is Jesus Christ as his savior that counts, not a de-anthropomorphized Kantian–Spencerian noumenon dressed up in a sentimentalized scientific garb and busily engaged in moving things along in the phenomenal world. Here is a sample of Fiske's description of his unknowable Christian God:

> What is this wondrous Dynamis which manifests itself to our consciousness in harmonious activity throughout the length and breadth and depth of the universe, which guides the stars for countless ages in paths that never err, and which animates the molecules of the dew-drop that gleams for a brief hour on the shaven lawn, — whose workings are so resistless that we have naught to do but reverently obey them, yet so infallible that we can place our unshaken trust in them, yesterday, today, and forever? When, summing up all activity in one most comprehensive epithet, we call it Force, we are but using a scientific symbol, expressing an affection of our consciousness, which is yet powerless to express the ineffable Reality. To us, therefore, as to the Israelite of old, the very name of Jehovah is that which is not to be spoken.[13]

Now Fiske, like most others of his species, is anxious to defend his doctrine from the charge of pantheism. Evolution philosophies

---

[12] *Outlines of Cosmic Philosophy*, vol. 2 (1874), pp. 421f.
[13] Ibid., p. 422.

have usually been frankly naturalistic or have been covered over with
something mighty like pantheism. He admits that his is not an ordinary brand of theism — it is the "higher theism," "cosmic theism."
Certainly it is not the anthropomorphic theism that has so long held
traditional religion in its bondage, which is a bondage to the categories of personality — intelligence, a volitional theory of causation,
and explanation by final causes. Not at all. This is a scientific and
genuinely Christian theism, whose God is unconcerned with such
mundane matters as the fate of persons. We can place our trust in
his workings, all right — yesterday, today, and forever. But we can't
place any trust in him — because he couldn't care less about us.

Not every philosopher who thrived on evolution was so far removed from the central meaning of traditional religion. Although
he gave it a somewhat religious and idealistic turn, Fiske was a slave
to Spencer's materialism. But Borden Parker Bowne was a personalistic Midas who changed everything he touched to personality.
Bowne, with far greater wisdom and subtlety in metaphysics, and
with less flamboyancy than Fiske, regarded Spencer as a combine of
"bad science, bad logic and bad metaphysics," a philosopher with an
"almost supernatural appetite for self-contradiction," in the last
analysis a "cadaver" fit for the "dissecting schools." Employing the
subtle mixtures of logic and metaphysics that were the common
weapons of the idealists, and taking his stand on Kantian subjectivism and Lotze's personalism, Bowne launched out against positivism, materialism, and impersonalistic idealism with a succession of
brilliant polemics that culminated in his celebrated essay "The Failure of Immaterialism," which William James once described as the
most important chapter in American philosophy.[14] Though far from
orthodox, Bowne did more than any other American philosopher of
the past century to establish philosophical foundations for Protestantism. As a good exponent of liberal Protestantism, Bowne was all
for evolution and progress, and in evolution and history he found
moral evidences of God and cosmic purpose: "Nature itself incul-
cates with the utmost strenuousness the virtues of industry, prudence,

---

[14] In Bowne's *Personalism* (1908).

foresight, self-control, honesty, truth, and helpfulness";[15] and "The slow moralization of life and society, the enlightenment of conscience and its growing empire, the deepening sense of responsibility for the good order of the world and the well-being of men, the gradual putting away of old wrongs and foul disease and blinding superstition — these are the great proofs of God in history." [16]

Bowne met evolution head on, took it over, and dominated it with his personalistic categories. Evolution would be impossible, he held in his *Metaphysics*, if there were not an intelligent World Ground, because the very notions of causation and continuity are impossible on a mechanistic basis. Unless reality is ultimately personal in character, every attempt at causal explanation must fail.

The unusual thing about Bowne, in contrast to Fiske, is that the prophetic moral quality of his philosophy won for him disciples, and his disciples had disciples, with the result that he not only exerted an important impact in liberalizing American Protestantism, especially Methodism, but produced a militantly aggressive philosophical school that has withstood the onslaughts of pragmatism, realism, and positivism and is today still in the running long after all forms of idealism were expected to fold their tents and depart.

It is obvious that no sophisticated philosophy has offered more support to religion and its traditional values than has personalism. It insists on some form of theism and is in principle compatible with the doctrine of personal immortality, although no respectable personalist holds that the doctrines of Christianity or of any other faith are deducible from its metaphysics. He claims simply that reason demands the reality of God and the human soul and justifies the belief that whatever is of ultimate worth is not lost to the universe. There appears to be some desertion of personalism in Bowne's own position that "only moral values are eternally significant," as it is difficult to see why moral values should be more significant to a Christian personalist than finite human personality. But all in all, here is a philosophy that offers human hope essentially of the kind that generated and was generated by the classical biblical religion.

[15] *Philosophy of Theism* (1887), p. 219.
[16] *The Immanence of God* (1905), p. 45.

There have been two main difficulties with personalism. The American mind has had difficulty digesting the Hegelianism that it inherited through Lotze. The problem arises not only from personalism's characteristic absolutism but as well from its insistence that science, evolution included, must be given the idealistic treatment. And, like idealism generally, in the early decades of this century personalism set itself up as the philosophic proprietor of religion and did not seriously consider the possibility that between idealism and naturalistic materialism there might be other philosophical positions compatible with the achievement and preservation of the ultimate values.

A refreshing revolt against this claim was that of William Pepperell Montague — refreshing twice. First, because Montague was a realist with naturalistic sympathies and even a materialistic metaphysics who yet refused to hand religion with its cosmic hope over to the idealists or to sacrifice it to the naturalistic humanists; and second, because both Montague and his religion were completely unchurched and were free from the tyranny of what he so aptly termed the "ancestral hypotheses." Perhaps it was this independence of traditional and institutionalized religion, together with his life-affirming and worldly piety, that enabled Montague to come up with his simple and profound definition of religion that so brilliantly expresses the hope of the human spirit — that religion is the faith that the things that matter most are not ultimately at the mercy of the things that matter least, and that what is highest in human hope and aspiration is deepest in the structure of reality.[17]

Montague had imbibed from his teacher William James a genuine feel for the temporality that evolution had encouraged in Chauncey Wright, Peirce, James, and the entire crowd of pragmatists and near-pragmatists. As with James, this pushed him toward an adventurous piece of theistic speculation — the finite God, cosmic moral struggle, gains genuinely to be made. It is somewhat strange that there was not a more favorable response to this temporal finitism of James and his disciples, especially since it offered the only plausible solution to the problem of evil. It was a noble heresy and deserved to be taken

[17] See *Belief Unbound* (1930).

more seriously. But the churches and the churchgoers turned their backs on finitism and temporality in their lust for the fleshpots of absolutism and eternity.

Montague had a higher regard for Herbert Spencer than most philosophers now have or have had, describing him as the "greatest British philosopher since David Hume with the possible exception of John Stuart Mill." [18] With others, however, he complained that Spencer's agnosticism was insincere, that he was essentially a materialist, and that he was so convinced of the adequacy of materialistic categories for the explanation of natural phenomena that he short-changed the telic and purposive facets of the world. Montague was an inveterate enemy of institutionalized Christianity, which he condemned as a destroyer of life and human happiness, but he was not therefore resigned to irreligion. Quite the contrary — he represents the temperate faith and cautious hope of those who find life worth the living and who therefore do not apologize for their interest in immortality; who are determined to be reasonable, but who recognize the limits of reason; who follow science all the way, but are not afraid to stretch their minds a little further, though never beyond the point of easy retreat; who are undogmatic enough to admit that religion may not be true and also to hope that possibly it is, to hope that the world ultimately may not be indifferent to the human soul and its most precious values. "When we raise the question of the truth of religion," says Montague in *Belief Unbound*,

> We have a great hope shadowed by a great fear. The fear is that the belief in a cosmic power for good may have no other grounds than the yearning of cowering human hearts, and that the voice of God which has so often been heard may be no more than man's own cry mockingly echoed back to him by the encompassing void. . . . If God is not, then the existence of all that is beautiful and in any sense good, is but the accidental and ineffective by-product of blindly swirling atoms. . . . A man may well believe that this dreadful thing is true. But only the fool will say in his heart that he is glad that it is true.

[18] *Great Visions of Philosophy* (1950), p. 405.

Is not Montague a prime example of liberalism, busily engaged in bringing science to religion and religion to science, assuring us that whatever retreats may be necessary, the great truths will nevertheless stand? He is not. Montague is not a typical liberal, just as he is not a typical humanist. For him, if there is no God in something like the old-fashioned sense, the cosmos is meaningless, human existence is utterly tragic, and ultimate hope is dead. And he admits that all of this may very well be the case. For him there is no sentimentalizing, no weasel reconciling. He does not on one hand deny the possibility of supernatural revelation and then on the other attempt to find supernatural objects revealed somewhere in the bosom of nature; he does not deny the divinity of Christ and then tell us that, of course, in Christ is revealed the surest expression of God; he does not commit himself to the natural evolution of morals and then demand for morality a religious sanction. In brief, Montague's statement of the issue is clean and honest. It is not a backhanded liberal compromise nor a subtle attempt to reconcile obvious irreconcilables out of fear of or sentimental attachment to a hoary and intellectually discredited tradition.

To return a moment to Spencer, the trouble with a mechanical theory of cosmic evolution as a ground for human hope is that on a mechanical basis what goes up must come down — or at least given enough time it's likely to come down. And in any discussion of the cosmos, there seems to be no shortage of time. Whatever the movement from simplicity to complexity, from "homogeneity to heterogeneity," from "incoherence to stability," and however much this movement may be a creation and extension of values, eventual decline and disintegration would appear inevitable. Now, of course, if the upward trend lasted another million years or more, this would no doubt be long enough to accommodate a fair measure of human hope. But most of us probably are not greatly concerned about what will happen a hundred thousand years from now since we will be long gone and forgotten anyway, as will be our children and our children's children. We hope that America will be a land of freedom and social justice in the year two thousand and eighty. And we hope that there will always be an England. But we aren't seriously worried about whether or not the species will grow to near-perfection physically, mentally, and morally by A.D. 100,000. We are too much under the threat of the final holocaust to think in such sanguine terms. The sentimentalized uses of evolution by writers like Henry Drummond, for instance, who guaranteed an endless Christian-flavored moral evolution, haven't made much impression since the collapse of optimism in 1914.

Nevertheless, the demand for irreversible progress was satisfied on the grand scale by the ingenuity of Henri Bergson (1859–1941), for whom such progress is not simply a contingent fact but is a fact necessitated by the very nature of reality in its basically temporal character. Neither mechanism nor the old-style teleology, insisted Bergson, explains adequately the evolutionary process. That process is genuinely creative with a cumulative effect, the present inevitably including the past. Devolution, therefore, is an impossibility and the world must move forward with increasing vitality, spontaneity, and novelty.

The Bergsonians have persisted in their efforts through speculative interpretations of evolution to establish a scientifically respectable case for an ultimate outcome of the cosmos compatible with the human values that have been achieved over millennia of biological, intellectual, and cultural advancement, and consonant as well with the Judaeo-Christian religious tradition. Lecomte du Noüy, convinced that the "scientific capital accumulated by man . . . [leads] inevitably to the idea of God," closes his *Human Destiny* (1947), a teleological treatment of organic evolution against a cosmic background, with this stirring passage:

> Let every man remember that the destiny of mankind is incomparable and that it depends greatly on his will to collaborate in the transcendent task. Let him remember that the Law is, and always has been, to struggle and that the fight has lost nothing of its violence by being transposed from the material onto the spiritual plane; let him remember that his own dignity, his nobility as a human being, must emerge from his efforts to liberate himself from his bondage and to obey his deepest aspirations. And let him above all never forget that the divine spark is in him, in him alone, and that he is free to disregard it, to kill it, or to come closer to God by showing his eagerness to work with Him, and for Him. [P. 273]

This is high rhetoric and expresses an admirable commitment to whatever it is in the upward moral and spiritual movement of the world that deserves our commitment. But the achievement of this superhumanity of du Noüy is in an unthinkable future, and although he calls his drama of evolution "Christian," it is difficult to find much of Christianity in it. Christianity from its inception has been a religion of the salvation and redemption of the individual person. For du Noüy the end of the individual is to lose himself, not lose himself for other persons, a loss in which by a divine alchemy he would find himself, but to "contribute to the advent of the superior conscience preparatory to the pure and spiritual race destined to appear one day" (p. 141).

Now to repeat a familiar objection, all of this must look very good to those whose cosmic hopes are hopes for the cosmos. If Bergson's intuitions are sound, the cosmos is going to do all right for itself. It can't miss. But what about Bergson himself, who had this idea, and the rest of us? Bergson died in the France of the Nazi occupation.

More concerned with the individual person in the evolutionary process and somewhat more scientifically and philosophically respectable was the work of Teilhard de Chardin set forth in *The Phenomenon of Man*, another religiously-inspired speculative treatment of evolution that purports to be "Christian." Like du Noüy, Father Teilhard held that evolution is an anti-entropic process which in contradiction to the second law of thermodynamics counters the degradation of energy and the movement toward uniformity by producing higher forms of organization — now the noosphere, which has risen to a psycho-social level. Although Father Teilhard professed that his *Phenomenon of Man* "must be read not as a work on metaphysics, still less as a sort of theological essay, but purely and simply as a scientific thesis. . . . [a treatise on] man *solely* as a phenomenon [but one which] deals with the *whole* phenomenon of man," his work is indeed both metaphysical and theological, a piece of highly speculative cosmology though supported impressively with scientific data.

A concern for man the person, Father Teilhard held, involves a concern for the cosmos. "Man is unable to see himself entirely unrelated to mankind, neither is he able to see mankind unrelated to life, nor life unrelated to the universe."[19] The evolutionary process

[19] *The Phenomenon of Man* (1959), p. 34.

eventuates at the Omega Point, the final synthesis, "God, the Centre of centres," the culmination of the Christian vision, where "God shall be all in all." It is, confesses Teilhard, a "superior form of 'pantheism'" but without annihilation, "the expectation of perfect unity, steeped in which each element will reach its consummation at the same time as the universe" (p. 294). "In such a vision man is seen not as a static centre of the world — as he for long believed himself to be — but as the axis and leading shoot of evolution . . ." (p. 36).

This much, at least, can be said for Teilhard's theory, which certainly is, as he says, a vision, an eschatological vision, that he seems determined to save the person rather than have it vanish in the evolutionary struggle of intelligence from what he calls "the encircling illusion of proximity" to the new dimension of universality. At the Omega Point, he says, "The Future–Universal could not be anything else but the Hyper-Personal" (p. 260). But Teilhard seems quite ambiguous in treating the question of the ultimate disposition of the individual self. On the one hand, "Thus it would be mistaken to represent Omega to ourselves simply as a centre born of the fusion of elements which it collects, or annihilating them in itself. By its structure Omega . . . can only be a *distinct Centre radiating at the core of a system of centres*; a grouping in which personalisation of the All and personalisations of the elements reach their maximum, simultaneously and without merging . . ." (pp. 262f). But this is followed by quite a frank expression of pantheism, or at least some kind of monism:

> Its [egoism's] only mistake, but a fatal one, is *to confuse individuality with personality*. In trying to separate itself as much as possible from others, the element individualises itself; but in doing so it becomes retrograde and seeks to drag the world backwards towards plurality and into matter. . . . The peak of ourselves . . . is not our individuality but our person; and according to the evolutionary structure of the world, we can only find our person by uniting together. There is no mind without syntheses.[20]

[20] Ibid., p. 263. In his introduction to *The Phenomenon of Man* (p. 19), Julian Huxley wrote:

> In any case the concept of a hyperpersonal mode of organisation sprang from Père Teilhard's conviction of the supreme importance of personality. A developed human being, as he rightly pointed out, is not

Teilhard de Chardin's cosmic evolution is an impressive attempt to reorient the hope of mankind to an evolutionary theory. It meets Darwinism head on, absorbs it, and goes far beyond it. Certainly he intends to gather up and save for the universe whatever is worth saving. But in occidental culture, at least, it is not likely that many except mystics and confirmed monists and universalists, a very small segment of the occidental religious population, will be persuaded by his so-far-distant pantheistic Omega Point, notwithstanding the emotive attractiveness of his poetic vision, his professed scientific competence, and the ingenuity of his attempt to tie evolutionary science to Christianity. His religion has a high moral tone and his metaphysics is an interesting heir to the tradition of Bruno and the German romantics, but it is only by a tour de force that he can relate it to the framework of Christianity. I do not say this as a criticism of his ideas, but rather as a commentary on the probable extent of his influence on religion. His impact on the philosophy of religion is another matter. It may well prove to be extensive.

Here it is difficult to avoid the complaint of the existentialists that at every turn in modern metaphysics the individual has been sacrificed — to abstract reason, to abstract science, to the universal, the species, society, history, the cosmos. For the liberal evolutionist everything seems to count except the individual. And yet, as the existentialists would say, the individual person alone exists — exists to hope in vain, to suffer in anguish, and to die to annihilation.

But the existentialists, whatever their strengths, have done nothing positive for human hope. In their more constructive moments they have formulated vague notions of transcendence—self-transcendence.

---

merely a more highly individualised individual. He has crossed the threshold of self-consciousness to a new mode of thought, and as a result has achieved some degree of conscious integration — integration of the self with the outer world of men and nature, integration of the separate elements of the self with each other. He is a person, an organism which has transcended individuality in personality. This attainment of personality was an essential element in man's past and present evolutionary success: accordingly its fuller achievement must be an essential aim for his evolutionary future.

Because the church had denied Father Teilhard, a Jesuit, permission to publish *The Phenomenon of Man,* it was withheld until after his death.

But to self-transcend appears to be simply to attempt to make the most of a bad situation by rising above it and above oneself. They have given man no place in the cosmos. They have been honest, however, and courageous, and even in philosophy and theology courage and honesty are virtues. At least this is the situation with secular existentialism, which has an eventually naturalistic base. With religious existentialism the matter is somewhat different, for here there is the now-familiar alignment with the new forms of orthodoxy and all that this represents for religious faith and for the life and hopes of the individual.

Emil Brunner is the most competent philosopher among the genuinely neo-orthodox. Here again we come face-to-face with the problem of evolution and fundamentalism, but this is a sophisticated fundamentalism that disposes of the difficulty with enviable ease. "The more deeply scientific knowledge probes into the obscurity of pre-history," admits Brunner in *Man in Revolt*, "the picture of man becomes still more 'primitive,' and the fewer are the traces of a higher form of existence corresponding to the distinctively 'higher' nature of man." [21] "Thus to-day we are confronted by the fact — and preachers of the Gospel would do well at last to confess that this is the fact, and to realize its meaning — that the average man of to-day knows or believes about the origin of man only that which remains in his memory from his instruction in natural history about the 'origin of man.' The ecclesiastical doctrine of Adam and Eve cannot compete with the impressive power of this scientific knowledge" (pp. 86f).

But whereas the liberal German theological tradition had abandoned the biblical account of origins and had, as with Schleiermacher, Pfleiderer, and Troeltsch, settled on an idealistic, Hegelian-type description of man conceived in evolutionary and historical terms, where man is described as what he is becoming rather than as what he is coming from, Brunner takes the bull by its orthodox horns, opposes the idealistic framework of liberalism, and insists on the traditional interpretation of the biblical concept of man while at the same time giving organic evolution a free field. "Abraham," says Brunner, "is

[21] *Man in Revolt* (1939), p. 86.

no nearer the good creation and the event of the Fall than I am, because he lived at an earlier time." The creation and the fall simply are not events. There is a better reason even than evolution, he says, for abandoning the historic Adam-and-Eve framework of Christian anthropology. That framework has obscured the "fundamental content of the Christian doctrine of the origin of man" and has "burdened it with dubious suggestions." The fundamental truth is the concept of man "in conflict between his divine origin in creation" and his sin (p. 88). The biblical account of man's historical beginning must be abandoned not for the sake of science but for the sake of purifying Christianity's most fundamental doctrine, a doctrine which is not about Adam but is about every person who comes into the world. Evolution cannot be used against biblical religion and should not be used for it.

Brunner's position is not entirely unlike that of Reinhold Niebuhr, who holds that Darwinism has not contradicted the Bible; it has simply contradicted the Aristotelian metaphysics and its conception of fixed species that had for so long prevailed as the foundation of the biological sciences. And the biblical religion is better off without Aristotle and his creation-denying metaphysics. Certainly Niebuhr is correct in a sense, as there can be no doubt of the conflict with Aristotelianism, and as for the biblical story, how can one say seriously that a scientific theory contradicts a culture myth. Clearly the neo-orthodox appear to have placed themselves in a safe position as far as evolution is concerned, and this has been possible because their interest is not in man's origin, but in his nature, and they have new non-biblical tools for getting at that nature — depth psychology and psychoanalytic theory. They have outdone the fundamentalists in their description of man as sinner. Darwinism, indeed, with its dog-eat-dog implications for the economy, was useful to them. Nor do the neo-orthodox have need of biblical stories to establish man's finiteness and contingency; their ontological analyses take care of that department. Finiteness and sin are all a neo-orthodox theologian needs to make his case, and in his hands it is a highly sophisticated case. It is not the naïve version of the creation of man and his fall in time that constitutes the material for the neo-orthodox theology. It is rather the fact of "man in contradiction," that man is by nature both the image of God and its destruction. Evolution has nothing to do with such matters. How man comes to be what he is is of no concern to religion. The genetic postulate and the whole problem of growth and development that accompanies it, however valuable for certain studies, have no meaning for theology. Says Brunner, "No Christian ought to deny to-day, on account of his Christian faith, the extreme probability of the Doctrine of Descent, and no theologian ought to deny it on account of his theology." [22]

If man is an animal, insists Brunner, he is for that not less human, for he is distinguished by spirit, culture, and morally responsible personality. He alone has ethical norms which are not facts of nature, concepts which are not associated sensations, and civilization which is not simply the satisfaction of biological impulse. He alone produces science and seeks truth for its own sake. He only is created in the image of God. He only can hear the word of God. As a creature of God, man is both within nature and above it, and the purposes of God are so concentrated upon man that not only human history but "the history of the whole Cosmos shall be consummated in God–humanity." Nothing that science can ever discover or ever do "can shake or even touch this truly Christian theanthropocentrism." [23] Obviously there is ground here for cosmic hope, for the cosmos itself is subordinated to man. Just what it is concretely that is to be hoped for is not at all clear, but the situation is guaranteed. How do we know? By the Word of God, says Brunner, revealed to us by faith.

Brunner and his species have their case sewed up very tight. So tight that not only is there no known contrary evidence, we can't even look for such evidence, because no one can describe it for us to enable us to identify it. There is no possibility of seriously engaging in this kind of argument. In the whole history of religious thought, there have been no defenders of the faith who have enjoyed more subtle ingenuity than today's neo-orthodox. If the liberals disarmed their enemies by going naked, the neo-orthodox have disposed of them by becoming invisible.

[22] *Man in Revolt*, p. 408.

[23] See *Christianity and Civilization* (1948), First Part, pp. 82–90.

Now to make a long story very short, it is fairly obvious that organic evolution struck the old orthodoxy a telling blow — though the orthodox have managed to stay on their feet — and in doing so it struck a mortal blow against the dominant hope of Western man, the hope of an immortal life. The liberal religion that attempted to save the day on rational grounds has failed, because in pretending to reconcile irreconcilables it was faithful to neither and compromised both. As a moral philosophy, it has been a courageous and not totally ineffective effort to ameliorate the condition of Western society. But its attempt to find salvation in human history has become a hollow irony. The new religion of science has engaged in both piety and poetry, but in its eloquence on the universe and the universal it has failed to nourish the hope of the living, existential, individual person. The new orthodoxy that has partially replaced liberalism has played it safe. It hasn't worried at all about science or history and has done very little about society. But it has paid the price of security by sinking into irrationalism and obscurantism, two qualities that recommend it highly to our generation.

By establishing the continuity of man with the animal world, evolution has undermined the traditional religion and much of what it has stood for. It isn't that evolution has done this alone, for obviously it has been aided by religion itself in its failure to extricate faith from its moorings in antiquated and indefensible foundations, and by, among other factors, recent psychology with its essentially biological conception of the mind. Rather, it is evolution together with the sciences as a whole, and not so much the physical sciences as the human sciences, where men examine themselves, their institutions, and their ideas, and especially where they examine these in terms of their evolutionary and historical development. Nothing brings more consternation to religion than an honest look at its own history. But nothing among the sciences when taken by itself has had quite the impact on religion that evolution has had.

Of the other substitutes for orthodoxy, none seems quite convincing. The idealistic evolutionary theses that furnished the foundation for much liberalism attempted to draw the sting from Darwinism when it appeared. When Hutchison Stirling published *The Secret of Hegel* in Britain in 1865 to combat evolution, positivism, utilitarianism, and other assorted evils, he wrote, "Enough of this talk about monkeys and species; let us get down to fundamentals, to things that really matter." But the idealistic theses were usually plagued with high speculation, an indifference to genuine empirical science, and an identification of metaphysics with logic that has long since discredited many of them. The romantic evolutionism of the Bergsonians, with its roots in Neoplatonism and Schelling, has failed to capture the mind of a world generally suspicious of intuition and mysticism and traditionally averse to every suggestion of pantheism. And both forms of evolutionism, idealistic and romantic, while usually vague and indefinite in the matter of what it is that is the proper object of human hope, have been discredited in their moral optimism by the tragic events of the past decades and the fear of the future. Nothing will dispose of an optimistic philosophy of history more readily than a good look at the mean facts of history. The world quite obviously is not the pleasant, forward-moving affair we once believed it to be.

Despite the genius of Bergson and Father Teilhard, nothing definitive on the subject of cosmic hope is likely to be said by evolution — or for that matter by any other branch of science. Regardless of whatever evidence is produced, there will always be some among the more intelligent who will continue to solace themselves with the "the facts are not all in and the last word has yet to be said, let's not capitulate to a mere theory that the best scientists are questioning" argument. Others will find God in evolution, regardless of any facts, just as they manage to find him in astrophysics, sticks, stones, and quantum mechanics. Still others will find, no matter what, that God is disproved by evolution, just as for them he is disproved by quantum mechanics, psychoanalysis, and biophysics. The matter of cosmic hope centered in belief in God is usually not a genuinely rational quest. Too often it is simply an instinctive, irrational drive that looks for vindication by reason.

When we come right down to it and insist on being honest with ourselves, for those of us whose passion for reason and reliable knowledge has robbed us of our enchantments it appears that about all that is left is some kind of reverent naturalism. Not the bad type of naturalism that was formerly called materialism and seemed to deny the reality of much that is of greatest value, but the good type that is usually called naturalistic humanism, or something like that; the type of naturalism that makes a place, and a large place, for mind and moral values and for spiritual aspiration and commitment and insists that these are as real a part of nature as are matter and physical events. This naturalism can generate an authentic piety and reverence for life. And it can enable an individual to invest life with purpose and meaning.

To reflect honestly on ourselves and our world must inevitably make us sad; because, with all its beauties and joys it obviously is not a very good world; for every beauty there is ugliness, and for every joy a plenitude of suffering and despair. We can do little more than face the tragedy of life courageously, intelligently, improving where possible the estate of man by enlarging his understanding and reducing his suffering, sustaining where possible the hope for the future which the past century has so nearly destroyed.[24] And perhaps the most precious hope for those of us who have failed to see that the cosmos is really on our side is the hope that our failure is a fault of our own finite knowledge and understanding and our lack of faith and that in some inscrutable way the world will ultimately vindicate the longings of the heart as well as justify the reasons of the mind.

---

[24] Bertrand Russell's essay *A Free Man's Worship* will probably survive as the classic, if somewhat overdramatic, statement on the human predicament, more rational and more morally responsible than the typical run of existentialist jeremiads.

Index

Because of the frequency of their occurrence in the text and footnotes, the terms Catholicism, Christianity, Islam, Judaism, Protestantism, and their cognates are not listed.

RELIGION, REASON, AND TRUTH
was composed in Intertype Garamond Foundry display type
by Donald M. Henriksen, Scholarly Typography, Salt Lake City.